DIVINATION AND HEALING

DIVINATION *and* HEALING

Potent Vision

EDITED BY MICHAEL WINKELMAN
AND PHILIP M. PEEK

The University of Arizona Press
Tucson

09   08   07   06   05   04   6   5   4   3   2   1

Library of Congress Cataloging-in-Publication Data

Divination and healing : potent vision / edited by Michael Winkelman and Philip
M. Peek.
    p.   cm.
  Includes bibliographical references and index.
  ISBN 0-8165-2377-0 (cloth : alk. paper)
  1. Divination. 2. Shamanism. 3. Healing. 4. Medical anthropology. I. Winkelman,
Michael. II. Peek, Philip M.
  GN475.7.D58 2004
  133.3—dc22   2004001864

Contents

I. Epistemologies and Cosmologies

II. Varieties of Divinatory Experiences

III. Divination and Healing

Preface

This volume examines phenomena of divination and their relations to healing from traditional, modern, and post-modern perspectives. The paradigm shift from a positivistic view to interpretivist frameworks requires a reconceptualization of divination from a false or mistaken epistemology to cultural systems for decision-making and therapeutic processes. The contributors here provide a range of perspectives on divination. While some of their findings reinforce traditional assumptions about the roles of social control, of spirit relations, and of community support as foundational to the divination process, they place these considerations within new epistemological frameworks that emphasize the use of alternative modes of knowing.

The classic emic perspectives on divination—information from the divine—persist as central features of divinatory systems. But these spirit concepts can be viewed from perspectives that recognize their role in a relational epistemology and as modalities of human knowing other than verbal discourse. And while the spirit concept can be "psychologized," it remains as a poignant reminder of a very different ontological system operating in these practices.

Divination is not merely an epistemological system reflecting a different set of assumptions regarding agency, knowledge, and communication. Divinatory practice is also a form of behavior and social interaction. The communal context has been long recognized as a central feature of divinatory practice. The chapters in this volume illustrate the roles of social context, including not only negotiating an acceptable interpretation and plan of action but also dynamically transacting therapeutic processes through the negotiations.

The authors of the chapters are commended for making this contribution toward specification of the processes and mechanisms of divinatory revelations and their therapeutic effects.

Michael Winkelman
Tempe, Arizona
June 2, 2003

DIVINATION AND HEALING

Introduction

Divination and Healing Processes

MICHAEL WINKELMAN
AND PHILIP M. PEEK

The relationship between divination and healing links the conceptual domains of diagnosis and therapeutics. Divinatory assessment of the causes of illness and misfortune in most cultures considers a range of contributory and distal factors beyond the narrower connotation of the immediate cause implied by diagnosis. Divination is a broader inquiry into life circumstances and meanings, of which diagnosis of the immediate causes of a malady is a part.

Divination's etymological roots in the concept of the "divine" suggest it is a survival of ancient paradigms of thought. The practice of divination is not, however, antiquated, as its vitality and centrality in contemporary life in cultures around the world continues to attract investigations (Abbink 1993; Desjarlais 1991; Eglash 1997; Gufler 1995; Kirby 1993; Langer and Lutz 1999; Nuckolls 1991; Peek 1991; Pelissero 1993; Pemberton 2000). Attention to divination has grown, perhaps more in African studies than elsewhere. But details of these esoteric practices are seldom revealed to outsiders, and the limited scholarship that existed until recently about divination systems tended to marginalize these practices or misrepresent them as fraudulent ways by which charlatans manipulated their communities.

Classic approaches to explaining divination tended to reflect the broader theoretical and ideological contexts of Western science and social inquiry (see

Peek [1991] for review of the history of divination; see also Caquot and Lei-bovici 1968; Devisch 1985; Loewe and Blacker 1981; Zeusse 1987). Conse-quently, inquiries into divination generally fail to take seriously the emic perspective. That is to say, while divination is putatively concerned with acquiring information used in decision making, scientific perspectives have typically rejected the legitimacy of such claims. Sidestepping the problemat-ic issue of what would appear to be a false epistemology—or, worse yet, outright subterfuge by diviners—anthropological perspectives traditionally sought explanation of divination's bases in latent social functions and psy-chosocial effects. This tradition of explaining divination in the context of ful-filling latent social functions rather than those functions stated by participants is exemplified in Park's (1963) perspective. Park characterizes divination as eliminating disorder in social relations through facilitating decision making and legitimizing the results. He considered the psychological release that comes from the divinatory assurance and reduction in anxiety as secondary to the social implications.

Social-control views of divination may be legitimate interpretations of some practices, but they do not accommodate paradigm shifts that have occurred in anthropology, and medical anthropology in particular. Tradition-al views of healing processes as social entertainment or dramatic enactments of social processes have shifted to the recognition that ethnomedical prac-tices produce therapeutic effects. Therapeutic effectiveness demands an empirical role for the divinatory or diagnostic practice. How do divination processes play a role in therapeutically effective healing responses?

Epistemological Perspectives on Divination

Peek (1991) characterizes divination systems as an "epistemology of a people," a system of assumptions about the nature of knowledge. Stroeken's chapter explicitly addresses the epistemological dimensions of divinatory practice, turning traditional thinking on its head. Rejecting traditional functional and social interpretations of divination, Stroeken in this volume proposes that div-ination among the Sukuma is designed to provide information about "the real." He distinguishes this notion of the real as "sheer being and matter, as opposed to the imaginary possibilities and appearances." This argument recalls

Douglas's (1979:129) observation: "Any culture which admits the use of oracles and divination is committed to a distinction between appearances and
reality. The oracle offers a way of reaching behind appearances to another
source of knowledge." Stroeken's analysis here rejects a postmodern perspective on divination as concerned with the symbolic order. Rather, a concern with ascertaining the real is reflected in the Sukuma practice of seeking
a divination from mediumistic diviners outside the local community to reduce
the possibility that the revelations reflect local rumors or common background knowledge. Concern with the real is reflected in a search for divinatory revelations that are repeatedly verifiable.

Academic perspectives on divination often ignore the highly skeptical
behavior of those who use divination. Skepticism is reflected in the right of the
client to take back the consultation fee and leave if flagrant errors occur during the initial phase of consultation. Diviners from distant places are often
preferred, and consultants may maintain their anonymity to avoid revealing
information to the diviner. Clients seeking divination may refuse to sit down
with the diviner until the diviner reveals significant information about the
case. The divinatory contingent often tests the diviner by trying to fool him or
her into offering incorrect diagnoses. The good diviner immediately spots
the ruse and informs the client. This further validates the diviner and provides
security in the process. Throughout Africa, diviners will also test the divinatory mechanisms by asking obvious questions ("Am I alive?"), or they will
test the waters—that is, they will determine whether or not spiritual forces
are in the right mood or alignment to permit cross-world communication to
occur. Lyon, in this volume, notes that Native American diviners will often
have to sort out false spirits and wrong answers, regularly testing and cross-
checking to validate these systems. Multiple divinatory verifications attest to
the petitioner's effort to ascertain an empirical and veridical characterization
of the situation they confront. A skeptical attitude and concern with verification of information is reflected in consulting several diviners and comparing
their revelations before taking steps to resolve illness or other problems.
Diviners will often use several divinatory mechanisms to cross-check the
quality of the information received. Divinatory outcomes may be subject to
further corroboration in the diviner's nighttime dreams.

Stroeken chastises the tendency to scientifically depreciate the divinatory processes and rejects the notion that divination involves seeking the wisdom

and advice of elders. Why not consult elders if that is what is desired instead of seeking out diviners? While divinatory discourse can be interpreted as symbolic and socially mediated communication between diviner and client, this fails to respect the indigenous perspective, which views the interaction as a means of obtaining access to the real. The willingness to submit important questions to the oracular processes reveals a disposition to accept information from sources beyond one's direct control and information other than that available to the conscious rational mind.

This brings us back to the basic implications of divination, relations with the divine, the spirit realm, the presumed primary causes of phenomena in the world, and the source of information provided in divinatory revelation. Spirit relations remain a ubiquitous explanatory model in divinatory and healing practices, providing information and energies manifested in visions, voices, and movements of objects in divinatory systems. If we discount this emic perspective on divination, rejecting the "spirit hypothesis," what are the alternatives? Classic explanations based in latent functions, social-control mechanisms, and psychosocial processes do not effectively engage the cultural realities of the divinatory subjects. With full respect for, if not belief in, other cultural systems, we seek to more completely understand divination's role in treating illness.

Generalizing about Divination

The chapters in this volume illustrate a variety of divination forms and processes. Divination engages many different cultural activities. Questions presented to diviners may deal with the past, present, or future; they may concern illness, social disharmony, and difficult decisions, virtually anything that troubles people. The following suggests some possible universal cross-cultural principles examined elsewhere (for example, see articles in Peek 1991 and Pemberton 2000) and addresses how divination processes provide information and also aid in healing.

Divination assumes answers to our questions are not always available by normal means. Diviners manage systems of knowledge to reveal otherwise inaccessible information through mechanisms such as readings of cast objects or esoteric texts, or directly as a spirit medium. Diviners often turn to ancestors, spiritual forces, and deities for information that must be translated and interpreted, made relevant to the contemporary reality that brought the client to the diviner. With this information, the divinatory contingent develops plans of action.

Divination is an enormously practical enterprise. It works for its practitioners and clients. The often-biased literature attacking the use of divination to guide human affairs has not aided us in comprehending the truly effective elements of the enterprise. Many studies of decision making and healing minimize divination's role, providing too little data or becoming mired in esoteric details. They seem to forget that, pure and simple, divination systems help people. Divination helps people negotiate their lives, make decisions, cure ailments, and reknit social fabrics. The question of how divination actually accomplishes these feats is not so clear.

The activities of divination provide seeds to understanding how these systems serve their clients. Central to divination's success is that people do it. The physicality of divination sessions, the experiential reality of visions and voices, and the divination speech, the social declarations, also have powers. While there is a strong sense that divination practices are successful because people want them to be, that doing "something" is better than doing nothing, more profound dynamics are involved than just positive thinking. Lyon references "spirit-power thinking" in revealing a cognitive shift necessary for diviner and client to effect healing.

A prominent feature of divination processes in most cultures is a consultation with the spirit ancestors or forces associated with them. Many chapters in this volume illustrate divination may be an inherently conservative process, linking the individual and present circumstances with an interpretative psychosocial framework of past social norms and traditions. Majumdar's chapter shows divination emphasizes traditional social roles, morals, and values, placing the causes of suffering in the context of ruptured social relations and the need to adopt appropriate social roles and traditional normative expectations for healing. Majumdar also shows that divination is not just a means to achieving a social consensus, but a way of asserting one's rights in the face of injustice. Functionalist perspectives emphasize the product of divination, not the process by which the information is obtained. Functionalist perspectives also risk a patronizing view that divination works simply because people believe it works. Examination of any divination system reveals that functionalist harmony is not always realized, for disharmony may be just as easily a result of the oracular message. Those in power can manipulate oracular messages, but this is another issue.

The complexities of the actual divination sessions argue against simple decision-making models. Divination is a context in which a socially acceptable outcome is negotiated, the development of consensus among many points of view. Rather than a blind acceptance of tradition, these processes involve skepticism and a selective interpretation of tradition. Although engaging social-control mechanisms, divination procedures provide a dynamic adjustment process for individuals and their circumstances. Divination can even facilitate culture change, negotiating between the past and present.

Divination does not automatically resolve doubts, provide answers, or settle disputes. Often divination responses offer more problems than solutions, releasing repressed tensions and conflicts into social discourse and requiring further consultation. Divination is a field of struggle among multiple interpretations and is potentially a venue of the powerless against the powerful through the constructive and adaptive roles of possession and the associated divinatory revelations. Divination reveals a process of making life subjectively meaningful while providing a social critique and a mechanism for revealing the implicit contradictions in society. Divination is part of a broader quest for meaning, focused on explaining the "why" of one's poor health and the actions necessary to reestablish well-being. Divination involves "multivocal" processes mediating between diverse domains of knowing, experience, and meaning, providing integrative psychocultural processes that heal.

The social dimensions of the lives of the people who seek divination, combined with the semiotic, constructive, and interpretative processes involved in divining make societal dynamics and divination processes necessarily related. Divination provides information of relevance and heals by situating people's personal experiences within broader social contexts. The social processes necessarily involved in divination offer little explanation as to the internal processes by which information is acquired and through which consensual outcomes are achieved.

These chapters add to the understanding of those *internal* processes of divination by showing their mediation through the bodily and visual, linguistic and social activities. In superseding the classic rejection of the empirical validity of divinatory outcomes, the chapters here provide expanded views of the efficacy of divination. The authors place divination in a broader evolutionary context assessing the adaptive consequences of divination and their contributions to individual, familial, and social well-being. In doing so, the chapters of this volume provide an analysis of the role of divinatory functions and their relationship to healing processes.

Information Channels in Divination

Divination presumes primary causes of phenomena in the world and the information source for diagnosis to derive from interactions with spirits. While we may be reluctant to embrace their "spirit hypothesis" of external autonomous entities, we should engage an understanding of what spirit experiences mean for those who engage them. In particular, we should ask questions about the nature of the information provided by these spirit encounters. This approach of "naturalizing" the spirit encounter attributes an empirical reality to the experiences but places ontological origins in social and brain processes.

As a problem-solving, question-answering process, divination is concerned with communication. Diviner and client need to be in concert; their queries need to be clear and directed to the proper source. The resultant communiqué must be carefully assessed, perhaps translated from cryptic symbolic forms or esoteric spirit speech. Then the divinatory contingent must resolve the message with the problem before them in order to generate a successful plan of action.

Divination practices provide a number of sources of information, conventional and creative, social and personal, ordinary and nonordinary. Divination practices engage in a number of communication channels, often simultaneously, that in general might be characterized as involving somatic, visual, metaphorical and prelinguistic levels (Winkelman 2000). These include

- experiences interpreted as spirit communication that involve fundamental structures of cognition (Peek 1991);
- altered states of consciousness and their visual experiences, a presentational symbolic system (Winkelman 2000);
- sensations, particularly bodily-based sensations derived from the hands (Lyon and Turner, this volume); and

↜ information derived from the study of material object systems with standardized interpretations (for example, divining baskets).

Nonrational and Nonordinary Cognition

Divinatory processes necessarily incorporate logical, rational, and analytical cognition but presume a primary source of information involving intuitive processes. In both the internally focused divinatory altered states of consciousness and the use of publicly observable mechanical divinatory apparatus, there is a presumptive reliance upon internal primary cognitive processes or modes of cognition not directly available to observers. These often-heralded intuitive processes and the esoteric systems used to interpret them have not been directly considered under previous paradigms as a source of empirically valid information. But if they play a role in directing empirically effective therapeutic action, there must be involved some cognitive processes of relevance (see Winkelman 1982, 1996, 1997, 2000).

Peek (1991) voices these perspectives on divination procedures, characterizing them as engaging nonrational processes and nonnormal modes of cognition. The willingness to submit important questions to divinatory procedures illustrates a willingness to take information from sources beyond the direct control of one's rational processes. Peek illustrates that divination systems combine this intuitive-synthetical mode of thinking with logical-analytical thought, making the diviner someone who is effective in communicating between modes of thought on behalf of the client. Divination procedures access nonverbal information channels of the limbic brain and lower brain centers, behavioral, nonverbal, and emotional communication processes that MacLean (1990) refers to as protomentation, paleomentation, and emotiomentation (see Winkelman 2000 for discussion). These processes are symbolic but are experienced in systems that can function without the mediation of language.

Spirits have generally been interpreted in anthropology as manifestations of social structures. Winkelman (2000) extends this perspective in proposing that spirits be understood as fundamental operations of the brain and mind and as manifestations of an "indigenous psychology" reflecting internalized psychosocial and cognitive structures. Theories of consciousness illustrate the inevitable use of models of human nature in our perceptions. The perception of the world as having spirits results from the inevitable consequence of the human tendency to perceive the unknown "other" as having qualities like our own self, as well as the qualities of the social "others" upon whom we depend for input and feedback in modeling the self. The inescapable human tendency to engage in an attributed cognitive similarity means that we perceive the world as being like ourself, animating the world with human qualities. These human qualities of identity and intentionality—disembodied from our physical self—produces animism, the primordial human perception of a spirit world. The use of spirits in divination processes can thus be seen as a mechanism for allowing the externalization of unconscious cognitive processes. The spirits experienced in shamanic visions and spirit possession are principal manifestations of nonnormal cognition associated with divination (see also Winkelman 1982, 1997, 2000). A number of elements of the divinatory enterprise involve harsh physical acts, deprivation, ingestion of substances, and other activities designed to produce altered states of consciousness in diviners and clients.

Altered States of Consciousness and Visionary Experiences

A central feature of divination cross-culturally is the engagement of an altered state of consciousness that establishes relations with the spirits. The altered state of consciousness is a natural response to many different conditions that result in the production of slow-wave brain discharges in the serotonergic connections between the limbic system and brain stem regions (Mandell 1980; Winkelman 2000). These synchronous brain waves are manifested in high-voltage slow-wave EEG activity, especially theta waves, of three to six cycles per second. These linkages between the attention mechanisms in the lower brain regions (reticular formation) and the limbic brain produce ascending discharge patterns that synchronize the different levels of the brain and the frontal lobes. Altered states of consciousness integrate information from the lower levels of the brain into the processing capacity of the frontal cortex, particularly integrating nonverbal emotional and behavioral information into the frontal brain. This integration of information from preverbal brain structures into the language-mediated activities of the frontal cortex provides intuition, understanding, enlightenment, a sense of unity, and personal integration.

The altered states of consciousness of shamanism are characterized by visual experiences (for example, a soul journey and vision quest) that share important commonalities with dreams and their information capacity. Many of the articles here show divination often involves a reliance upon some form of internal vision, imagery, or "seeing." A majority of the chapters in this volume present evidence of the visualization of ailments and their agents. The use of image as an interpretive mechanism for diagnoses reflects a reliance upon presentational (as opposed to representational or linguistic) symbolism (see Hunt 1995; Winkelman 2000). This presentational modality is characterized by the immediate nature of the meaning and reliance upon imagetic primary processes. This is in contrast to the possession and mediumistic traditions where the vocal/aural mode is the dominant mechanism for communication of information. The distinction between the presentational visual modality and the representational system of language appears directly related to differences in approaches to divination, one based upon intuitive images, the other upon internal voices. They are not, however, completely separate in divination practices. The spoken disclosures of the medium may derive from visionary experiences (as illustrated in Majumdar's chapter), and the shamanic visions may be prompted by the voices of the spirits (see Fridman's chapter). These two modalities of symbolic experience are often mediated in divination, with the diviner serving as the conduit and the mediator.

Visionary experiences activate brain structures and processes associated with perceptual information processing and dreaming. This visual information system provides a basis for communication and representation across domains of experience, linking unconscious, nonvolitional, affective, and psychophysiological information with somatic, psychological, and cognitive levels of the organism through images and analogical processes (Winkelman 2000). These visual symbol systems provide analysis and analogic synthesis and engage the self-representational capacity that is based in the same symbolic system that underlies dreaming (Hunt 1995). Dreaming is found throughout mammalian species, constituting an adaptation for producing memory associations during sleep. Dream visions provide the closest engagement of the ego with the operational structures of the unconsciousness and reflect an "unconscious personality" that can be managed through ritual (Laughlin et al. 1992). Dreams of clients and diviners are central to divination systems around the world, particularly Africa and the Americas.

The Body as Divinatory Medium

Divination systems around the world rely upon the senses of the diviner as well as the client/patient. Turner and Devisch (this volume) note the various senses employed in diagnosis as well as curing. Fridman (this volume) illustrates sensory stimulation in sonic driving (that is, drumming) and aromatic cleansing, contributing to healing and the induction of altered states of consciousness. The olfactory sense is critical—a topic about which we know all too little. Reliance upon the body for information is exemplified in the use of hands as diagnostic instruments that may "speak" or provide other sensations for the diagnostic process. These divinatory approaches illustrate the use of intuitive modalities of assessment based upon the body's somatosensory capacities. This presence of body-mediated systems in divination is inevitable since conceptualization is based in bodily experiences and templates (Newton 1996) and complex communication and meaning formation processes are mediated by body-based metaphors (Kirmayer 1993).

Shamanic divination of illness employs the shaman's hands in both physical and psychic modalities. The hands might be merely placed upon the body to gather sensations, or they might be systematically moved on the body. Massaging and kneading specific areas, and observing the patient's response, or extending the hands without touching the patient, are methods used to determine ailments (see Lyon, this volume). The renowned Navajo hand trembler exemplifies the diagnostic use of the shaman's own body in receiving information about the nature of a patient's condition. Peek (1991) points to the prevalent use of the otherwise tabooed left hand in African shamanistic divination, implicating the access to right-hemisphere intuitive, holistic, and analogic modes of cognition.

Turner's chapter focuses upon bodily-based modes of perception as "deautomization." This shift from habitual automatic motor behavior provides a heightening of physical perception that may be seen as the primary goal of divinatory ritual. Use of the patient's body as a source of direct responses is illustrated in chapters by Lyon and Turner, where the patients' somatic responses are an indication of their condition. While the community poses questions, the patient's body provides the medium of communication with the spirit, shaking or remaining calm to express agreement and disagreement. This interaction also reveals emotional relationships between patient and group, as portrayed in the patient's somatic responses to questions.

Visualization is very common in the divining and treatment of sickness and other problems. One's visual "field" is not recorded whole by the eyes but constructed in the back of the brain, in the occipital lobe. The technical means of recording brain functioning now permits one to document that the occipital lobe is active whether "really" seeing something or just imagining it; this is also true for the dream state. From sports psychology and contemporary healing therapies, it is known that the visualization of an action and its completion (or an ailment and its elimination) can lead to its realization. Much divinatory healing seems to employ such methods of the visualization of healing.

UNCONSCIOUS BEHAVIORAL PROCESSES. Ouija boards, tarot cards, and Samburu and Ndembu castings of objects exhibit a notable feature of divination systems: objects are physically manipulated by the practitioner or client and the configuration of their "fall" is interpreted with a system of standardized meanings and applied to the individual circumstance. The malleable nature of the material systems manipulated for divination suggests that they are designed to allow both conscious and deliberate manipulation, as well as unconscious behavioral dynamics to produce relevant information. The use of unconscious processes implicates a deeply embedded human information capacity shared with other animals. Humans have a variety of unconscious capacities for information processing exemplified in "blind sight" (Hookway and Peterson 1993), subliminal perception (Bornstein and Pittman 1992; Cohen and Schooler 1997), and "psi" (Winkelman 1982) that illustrate our ability to access information not directly available to consciousness. Divinatory use of these types of systems for circumstances where many possibilities are known but specific outcomes are not, indicates the use of unconscious capacities to help direct one toward an appropriate outcome. The mechanisms by which these behavioral capacities are used remain underexamined.

SUMMARY. Oracular systems obviously benefit from multisensorial processing. Too little is known about this phenomenon, but there is no doubt that divination systems employ several sensory modes, often simultaneously. Whether the operative factor is a sensory overload for the diviner and / or client or it is a process of synethesia that enhances cognition and curing is not known. Associations are established through taste and touch, through sound and sight, and in normal or (more often) altered states of consciousness. Regardless of the experiential source of divinatory information (for example, visual, auditory, or somatic), it is generally shared in verbal communication. This introduction of divinatory information into social discourse brings a variety of interpretive and negotiatory processes to the formulation of the revelation. Divination brings many different forms of knowing, sources of information, and perspectives to bear on the problem. These include perspectives elicited from clients, family, friends, associates, and others. How do these processes contribute to healing?

Divinatory Contributions to Healing

The principal healing processes of divination illustrated here include the following:

- ↬ diagnosis, including defining of the ailment, the effects of transference and catharsis, and anxiety management;
- ↬ the social contextualization of personal life, a narrativization process;
- ↬ the healing power of community relations; and
- ↬ dramaturgical elements found in ritual action and the power of speech.

Diagnosis as Healing: Explanation, Transference, and Anxiety Management

The healing of divination begins with the processes of diagnosis that reveal the unseen, articulate the unheard. A previously unknown condition is given a cause, a meaningful location. As the formless and ambiguous is structured and explained, curing has begun. Determination of causes places the dilemma within a larger framework of meaning that aids healing. Locating these issues in time and space in family history, for example, begins healing by placing the individual's suffering within a shared system of beliefs. Clients are assured that they have some recognizable ailment that is treatable and perhaps curable. Diagnosis can heal through evoking a number of emotional, psychodynamic, and psychosocial processes. Diagnosis provides relief from uncertainty and the unknown, making circumstances intelligible within one's worldview and eliciting beliefs and conviction that provide motivations toward healing.

FAITH, TRANSFERENCE, AND CATHARSIS. The chapters illustrate the healing of divination through client-diviner interactions that occur in interactions leading up to the divinatory activity. Healing is elicited by faith and placebo effects and other mechanisms derived from the patient placing their problems in the hands of charismatic others. Jackson (1978) discusses the transference between patient and diviner that promotes healing. Diviners frequently work in areas in which they themselves have been healed, adding credibility to the likelihood of their success in treating a problem. Their personal odyssey may permit contact with spiritual entities well equipped to aid that specific ailment. Frequently the diviner and client will form an elaborate and deep bond, sometimes due to professional contact over many years, while in other instances there are ritual activities that create and maintain a bonding, as Lyon illustrates among Native Americans. In various parts of Africa there is a formal "twinning" process that occurs between diviner and client (Peek 1991, 1998). The therapeutic effects of bonding and trust are facilitated by the nature of diagnosis procedures. In discovering the patient's condition and its antecedent causes, the diviner builds a relationship with client and family. A major dimension of this "diagnostic healing" derives from the dramatic performative enactment in a public context, where the patient's dilemma is transacted by all present, producing a therapeutic milieu for the social group. The interactions during the diagnostic process provide a number of cathartic opportunities and therapeutic effects, allowing the patient to unburden his or her grief as the diviner details the patient's travails in the diagnosis of causes. The diviner counsels and consoles in the revelation of causes and the potential remedies. The studies presented here demonstrate the ritual production of catharsis and abreaction, as is dramatically evident in Turner's essay on Ndembu divination. There is an "acting out" by the diviner, and often the client and/or community as well, which expresses and releases frustrated emotions.

ANXIETY MANAGEMENT. Colby's chapter illustrates a healing function of divination systems in a reevaluation of an old perspective that divination reduces anxiety and stress by mediating consciousness and cultural processes. Divination reduces individual and collective stress by addressing uncertainty. Diagnostic processes alleviate anxieties and concerns, removing doubts, fears, and indecision and providing explanations that have psychological and emotional effects and therapeutic consequences. Divination imposes stability on an uncertain world, shaping individual and collective emotions in transacting group interactions with the unknown to manage personal and social concerns. As Colby (this volume) points out, Ixil divination standardizes, emphasizes, and solidifies religious belief in a very effective way: people are exposed to this religious knowledge at a time when they are emotionally upset or stressed, adding an emotional charge to their learning about Ixil deities and what they sanction or punish.

Heinze's chapter places divinatory activities in this context of the need of all cultural systems to reduce anxiety and provide direction. Her research illustrates that in contrast to characterizations of traditional cultures as fatalistic and stable, divination implies an ability to change the future, preventing illness and misfortune and altering the course of events by modifying the forces that affect one for better or for worse. Divination enables one to modify one's future and one's karma through ritual. Fratkin's chapter shows divination enables clients to avert future problems. Divination portrays a field of actors, possibilities, and the forces arrayed against one, permitting a deliberate response rather than suffering as the victim of others and their potentially unknown plans.

This view of divination as a stress-reduction process places in new light the collective aspects of divination related to proclamations of traditional cultural expectations. Colby suggests divination procedures are particularly effective in resolving stress and producing social integration because they operate upon "emic cognitive units." These are embodied in the motifs, metaphors, and proverbs of a culture and are found within the interpretative frameworks of divination systems. These cognitive units provide stability by placing individuals and their life situations in the broader context of cultural beliefs and cosmology. Divinatory interpretive systems are part of a cultural logic and reasoning processes that people use to make sense of their lives.

Self-Contextualization and Personal Narratives

Divination systems place individual concerns in the context of normative social life by characterizing the individual's situation within the frameworks and interpretations provided by tradition, formalized systems, and esoteric texts. Colby illustrates this in emphasizing the fundamental "anchoring" role that the Mayan calendar provides. This is similar to the Odu verses that are linked to the configurations of Ifa divination among the Yoruba (see Olupona, this volume) and the numerology that underpins Samburu divination (Fratkin, this volume). Majumdar notes the use of the "Book of Fate" among some Indian diviners. Other examples of such divination systems are the I Ching of China and the sikidy system practiced in Madagascar. Such ancient bodies of fixed esoteric material, be they written or memorized, provide the vehicles for interpretation and diagnosis that situate the individual within social scripts, a form of narrativization.

Divination processes heal by creating and validating a narrative or history of affliction for the client that contributes to resolving the problems. As Pennebaker (1997) emphasizes, the process of giving expression to one's concerns and not repressing thoughts about some traumatic experience is beneficial; consequently, the kind of expression that goes on in a divinatory session must have some therapeutic value. Most of the contributors to this volume provide culture-specific evidence of the importance of these personal narratives. Majumdar expands on Good's (1994) concept of "narrativization," illustrating divination as a form of life counseling in which therapeutic effects are achieved by discussing the patient's life in reference to traditional beliefs, making the individual's suffering intelligible. Devisch discusses the histories that Yaka diviners develop, and Turner's extensive case study demonstrates the central role of personal narrative in healing. These narratives link personalized stories with general etiological accounts. Some accounts are localized, while others reveal "cosmic" histories, mythical accounts of culture heroes, or lives of great kings; but in either case, the object is to locate the afflicted individual within a larger framework of purpose and meaning. Causation might lie in past history, in forgotten actions, in ancestors, in accidental behavior, or even in conscious but not (yet) regretted actions or words. Establishing this "correct" history often serves to eliminate its consequences. It is as if by revealing the past causes of the present, one's path is made right.

Parkin (1991) observes that divination serves to "straighten the paths from wilderness," the inchoate is given form, the invisible is perceived, the inaudible has voice, the vaguely heard is clarified. The above-cited techniques of visualization, narration, and so on all serve to move the client from chaos to clarity. For many clients, this alone is healing enough; but for most it is but a start. To have life synchronized and made intelligible is essential for healing. It moves individuals from the specific to the general and back again, producing associations that place a person in a comprehensible situation that clarifies events and behaviors. This re-places the individual within the larger social fabric. The victim is reintegrated and harmony is reestablished. Locating the afflicted in the caring and supportive social network of kin and friends, these narratives place the previously isolated individual into the broader, perhaps even cosmic, order of things. One's individual life story is sorted out and "straightened" in order to fit the proper scenario. The labeling or naming process, along with the narrative storytelling component, both serve to reassure the individual that her or his ailment is recognizable and reintegration has begun. The ordering and reordering made possible through divination heals through "wholing." Divination reconnects the individual with the family, the social group, and his or her predestined life plan. A sense of place is absolutely critical to one's well-being. Divination functions to answer such fundamental questions as Where do I belong? What has displaced me? How can I regain or move to my proper location?

The oracular nature has otherworldly origins, but, more important, the message has interpreters. For example, Colby's chapter notes that Mayan diviners first seek all details of an individual's life, only later sorting out what is or is not relevant. The work of translation and interpretation of these special messages does not end with the diviner. Often the entire divinatory congregation becomes embroiled in debate. Whatever the revealed cause, it is socially contextualized. Most authors here attest to the role of the social group in mediating the diagnostic sessions. The client, family, kin, and neighbors provide an important source of diagnostic information, as well as an interpretation of the relevance of the information provided by the diagnostician. Interaction with the social group often plays a fundamental role in determining the diagnostic outcome. Interpretations unacceptable to the social group may be reworked by the diviner, producing an interpretation more suitable to the opinions of the parties involved. There is a dialogue not only between the healer and the "supernatural realm" but also between the healer and the clients and vice versa that integrates the patient's particular circumstances within the general symbolic worldview and the social universe. The Ngawbe practice of family therapy sessions perhaps most clearly demonstrates this (Bletzer, this volume).

A second type of re-placement occurs through these divination narratives—placement of blame and the clarification of causation, responding to the need to know why. Blame and causation is seldom with the individual, or at least not with the patient or a consequence of his or her conscious actions. The person may have violated a taboo, but unknowingly. Most intriguing are the instances of illnesses caused by "the sins of the fathers," which are, literally, being visited upon the children. Among some African peoples, for example, curses called out years in the past still remain active and harm the living long after their cause is forgotten. But divination does not allow us to forget. For the Yaka (see Devisch, this volume), it is through the process of divination that the memory of the group is revived, a forgotten matter is brought forth by the diviner, and a long unresolved issue is finally laid to rest.

Community Relations and Healing

The chapters here reveal that the individual, alone, is not necessarily responsible for his or her condition. This differs from the individualizing approach to disease causation found in Western medicine and psychiatry. Many non-Western societies operate in more communalistic fashion, absolving the individual of solitary guilt and often establishing that the individual is the innocent victim of others' actions. The individual is the way by which the problem is manifested and is part of the solution, though not the sole cause of the problem. Turner's chapter reveals the role of community in mediating the cure through their participation in the diagnostic process, which defines the nature of the malady and relieves its consequences. Divination often provides healing through the community's contributions to defining the conditions that have aggrieved the patient, a sharing that provides the patient with relief from the burden.

Devisch and others here present the healing functions of divination in terms of reinforcing traditional social expectations, acting as conservative devices demanding that circumstances be interpreted within traditional frameworks. The cause of illness may be ascribed to failure to live up to traditional kinship expectations and social norms; healing requires restoration of normative role expectations.

Devisch's analysis illustrates divination's cultural and ideological assumptions that the foundations of health maladies derive from ruptures in human relations, specifically those associated with close kin or ancestors. The cause of

illness is often viewed as a just punishment for transgression of kinship expectations or other social norms. Divination processes evoke models of the moral
and ethical order that situate the individual's circumstances within normative social expectations that impact others' behavior and relations. By stating
the ideal and obligatory social relations, divination indirectly demands that
social relations be restored, that social reality mirror the ideal. The absolutely critical reweaving of the social fabric is perhaps the most healing change of
all.

The therapeutic aspects are illustrated in Stroeken's characterization of
the healing effects of divination as ecodelic. By reestablishing the patient's
relationship within his or her social environment, diagnostic procedures
enable the patient to reassimilate "self" to the social other. Not only is the individual healed through reintegration into the group, but the healing of divination also reunifies and heals the group. Lyon illustrates the therapeutic role
of the social relations that not only mediate diagnoses but also provide interactions with the healer that build confidence, trust, and a sense of assurance
that the healer will meet the client's perceived needs. Bletzer's chapter illustrates the diviner's role may be primarily one of sanctioning communal and
therapeutic processes. The official presence of the diviner, the primary ritual
specialist in society, demands attention to the proper performance of family
rituals that facilitate therapeutic transformations. His case studies from Panama may reflect the dynamics of primordial human efforts to resolve emotional
conflicts by the intensified dynamic of intragroup (both household and homestead) interaction the ritual context provides. Bletzer notes the Ngawbe
household-centered ceremonies provide the prototype for multiple homestead ceremonials; these ceremonies are striking but not unique. Similar
dynamics operate among the Ndembu and Yaka in central Africa. Fratkin's
analysis of the Samburu *laibon* also illustrates the role of family-healer interaction in divining the source of health problems.

The group context also contributes to divination's role in ritualistic healing. Divination is a decision-making process regarding a pragmatic plan of
action that must be implemented by a group. Turner's chapter illustrates the
social dynamics of divinatory healing processes, a ritual adjustment of relationships strained by conflict and reintegration of people into disrupted social
networks. The social integration effect requires an effort on the part of the
community, illustrated in the healers pleading with them to sing. The words

they share are part disclosure, part divination, and part the flow of human relationships unburdening themselves of the emotional impediments to social harmony.

Dramaturgical Elements: Action, Speech, and the Senses

A major technique of healing through divination involves the dramaturgical elements embodied in speech, behavior, and sensory experiences. Clarifying symptoms, discovering causation, absolving guilt, and prescribing action are not just abstractions or words alone but frequently are acted out during the divinatory process. As Turner illustrates in describing Ndembu divination, diviners prepare special areas or stages for the performance of oracular communication, props are carefully prepared, and entrances and exits of spiritual entities and human participants are emphatically marked. One could speak of the healing arena, the "theater of divination." Divination must often take place at a certain place and time in order to be effective. Strikingly, for numerous African societies divination occurs between village and bush, between day and night. The diviner frequently wears special regalia that marks the occasion, along with special divinatory apparatus.

Although talking and visualization constitute key elements of most systems, direct actions and practical behaviors by the diviner and attending individuals are basic. Throughout the ethnographic literature on divination and healing there are accounts of ritual tying or untying, binding or loosening, blocking or unblocking to control or get rid of an ailment, an inappropriate feeling, and so on. The patient and diviner are untying and casting off, for example, a sickness, a family curse, or repercussions of a taboo violation. Whatever the culture-specific details, a therapeutic effect is derived from the physical ritual action. Devisch speaks of clearing blockages in Yaka divination and healing through spoken words and physical actions. Among the Maasai, "tying" is a positive means of controlling elements. The healing of divination depends not upon the logic of reasoned argument, the insight of the oracular message, nor the sanctity of the revealed word, but on its actuality, its enacted reality.

The role of divinatory language and oracular speech, "the power of words," especially in oral-aural cultures, has been too little studied (Peek 1981). Divination systems often involve esoteric languages, develop revealing life narratives, and employ special multiple sources of information. But, first and foremost, divination makes audible, in some form, the normally inaudible beings of the other world, whether the messages come through divinatory objects, chicken entrails, or spirit possession. All of these actions contribute to the healing and well-being of the patient/client. Bletzer's chapter demonstrates how important proper speech is for curing among the Ngawbe. When the family gathers for their household-centered therapy, they use a very specific speech code. Among the Ndembu, the power of words during the ceremonies is absolutely central (see Turner, this volume). Peek (1991) argues for the need to study how healing is produced by symbolic objects, anomalous helpful creatures, ambiguous speech, and a whole range of "betwixt and betweenness" that attends divination.

Winkelman (2000) analyzes the "psychophysiologically based integrative mode of consciousness" that shamanistic healers employ, a characterization that clearly applies to the state of consciousness of many diviners as well as patients described in the chapters here. There are instances of spirit possession aiding the oracular process and being frequently directly involved in the curing as well. Whether it is the diviners, attendants, or the clients themselves who become vehicles for cross-world communication, it is clear that there is more than a message. The spirit relations involve altered states of consciousness that have powerful healing potentials (Winkelman 2000).

Finally, it must be appreciated that all of these activities are taking place in a carefully orchestrated fashion. The diviner is many things: a mediator between worlds, a translator of messages, and a healer; but diviners also must organize and guide the proceedings—they are directors of these healing dramas. The divination sessions so well described by the contributors to this volume all involve complex and highly sensitive proceedings where all elements must be in proper order and alignment (witness the Ndembu session described in Turner's chapter). Often the client must be guided through various actions. Equally, the diviner goes through set rituals to obtain sufficient information from the client, to obtain proper information from the spiritual entities, to clarify those messages, and to prepare the medicines and responses. Great caution must be taken with procedures even if the diviner is not actually present. Effective healing through divination clearly involves simultaneity of sensing and reasoning by both diviner and client that engages both mind and body.

Conclusions: Old and New
Perspectives on Divination

Divination works. It is a human universal that persists. These facts alone seem enough to encourage the continued study of divination and the associated healing process. Much research on divination continues to seek typologies, but the variety of forms, techniques, meanings, and uses means endless problems for such an approach. Far better we seek clearer descriptions, more extensive fieldwork, and closer analysis, as the chapters here demonstrate. From a solid body of ethnographic data, researchers can approach comprehending the effectiveness of these systems of knowledge and healing.

There are a number of common elements among these systems, but there is an enormous range of different combinations that need to be better understood in relation to their related worldviews and theories of causation. Classic perspectives on divination as a mechanism of social control are expanded in contemporary considerations that take new perspectives on the social processes involved in this discourse. The rejection of positivist frameworks and development of medical anthropology and anthropology of consciousness perspectives on the efficacy of traditional healing have opened up new perspectives on divination's bases and processes. In addition to the psychobiological implications of the use of altered states of consciousness, there are new epistemological perspectives on the nature and role of the concept of spirit in divinatory processes. This acceptance of the epistemology of spirits provides better access to emic perspectives on these activities and their cultural roles. The influences from medical anthropology also allow an expanded view of the healing of divination, the generic processes by which divinatory processes have healing effects. Divinatory activities provide many healing processes as well as a broad range of mechanisms for affecting social life and decision-making processes.

As we see in Heinze's survey, cultures exhibit a number of divination systems. Comparative study, as attempted here, encounters even more variety. Divination engages both rational and emotional elements as it treats mind and body. Varying cognitive modes, multisensorial experiences, spiritual and familial aid, sacred texts, and spiritual possession are among the resources marshaled through the techniques of divination to restore harmony and health. While some may question divination's efficacy, none would deny that it presents medical prescriptions and leads to specific healing treatments.

It appears that divination itself produces healing. Diagnosis, in the form of naming and locating an ailment, places one's condition within a cultural context and starts the process of reassuring the client that there are answers for his or her questions and that healing can occur. The social dynamics of divination places individual circumstances in social context, contributing to a "wholing" of the individual that constitutes health. Throughout divination practices, dramaturgical elements are deeply embedded, contributing to healing.

Studying divination requires a participation that goes beyond the classic participant-observer role in studying these practices by observing them in others (for example, Young and Goulet's [1994] *Being Changed by Cross-Cultural Encounters: The Anthropology of Extraordinary Experience*). Turner's chapter illustrates her role in community divination, revealing some impacts of her presence upon the social lives of others in the community. With more solid ethnographic research that engages a participatory dimension of the social lives of the other, we are able to begin learning how divination systems not only reveal answers to our questions but also enact the healing necessary for people to resume productive and fulfilling lives.

I

EPISTEMOLOGIES AND COSMOLOGIES

1

In Search of the Real

The Healing Contingency of Sukuma Divination

KOEN STROEKEN

The Sukuma live in northwest Tanzania, with a population of about five million forming the largest cultural group in the country. They combine cattle herding with agriculture, including cash crops such as cotton. On the whole these fairly self-reliant, extended families make a strong peasant society that has to a large extent shaped Tanzania's economic history of the past decades. While modern trades and products are welcomed and processed by Sukuma culture, village life has as yet taken little interest in Islam or in Christian denominations, including Pentecostalism, and in that differs from the rest of Tanzania.

In central Sukumaland, where I spent two years of fieldwork from 1995 until 1997, two kinds of divination are commonly practiced: the mediumistic type *(ng'hambo)* and the chicken oracle *(buchemba wa ngoko)*. Both require some form of ancestral presence during consultation. In the first type the diviner enters an altered state of consciousness after receiving a twig (of the euphorbia bush) to which the subject's saliva has been transmitted. Diviners commence by shaking the gourd rattle or their winnowing basket containing old coins, with the twig lying on top. When addressing the subject, they have either reached their ancestral guide at that very moment or recollected a dream they had the night before. Even scientists are intrigued about inner reception of knowledge that cannot be accounted for, or what I would like to call "immission." The Sukuma believe the ancestral spirit to be its source.

Most highly valued are diviners who started their profession following an affliction caused by an ancestor who summoned them to carry on their tradition of divining. Other diviners, called "those of the fee," have been trained by an established healer. The most common example of trained divination is the chicken oracle, mostly practiced by men. Underlying this system of interpretation is more or less public knowledge shared by Sukuma elders. Because of its sound reputation, the chicken oracle is often used to cross-check mediumistic types of diagnosis (or to verify the ancestors' blessing before initiation rituals). Chicken diviners, however, are less solicited than acknowledged mediums, who are supposed to acquire the information in a more direct way from the ancestors. The suggestion is that such diviners have the advantage of being the medium itself of divination (instead of interpreting it) and thus in principle approximating the ancestor's immission better. In other words, the divinatory process hinges on the experience of something "real" preceding symbolic representation. That experience tends to be occluded when conceiving of the consultation as a series of social interactions or mental representations (compare Abbink 1993).

Using a case study, this chapter attempts to pinpoint the experiential meaning of divination and to demonstrate how the act of divination could have healing powers. As it permits intersubjective verification and appraisal, chicken divination has seemed to be particularly useful in illustrating how a culture's divinatory procedures operate on the participant's experience of crisis, how these offer cultural schemes to express tensions, and eventually go as far as to alter the patient's inhibited sense of the world.

Chance and Contingency

One day a healer, whom my collaborator and I visited regularly, showed us a trick called "quick pull," which he had obtained as a curiosity from a colleague of his. A small gourd decorated with resonant bells would move up and down a thread on a stick when he manipulated the two ends of the thread at the base. Some diviners, he said, would use this trick to impress their clients by hiding their manipulation—for instance, by asking questions to the gourd and steering it in reply. Now it struck me: Supposing that clients would indeed fall for this trick and that, in spite of its uncommonness, they would consider it to be divination, why would they be so readily impressed by it, enhancing the diviner's reputation? It occurred to me that the only plausible reason was that the gourd appeared to move and stop by itself, invoking something presymbolic, which the oracle offers amidst its rich symbolism and discourse. This is the real. Explicit reliance on it distinguishes divination from other forms of interaction.

Following a philosophical tradition of the early twentieth century (Bergson 1934:99; Meyerson 1925), Lacan (1977) adopted the term *le réel* (the real) to define the realm of sheer being and matter, as opposed to the imaginary (possibilities and appearances) and the symbolic order (language and culture). Lacan could not rid himself from the positivist definition of the real as pure chance. Whereas he conceives of the symbolic as "cuts in the real," the diviner addresses the real (ancestral spirits) for doing the cutting that makes the symbolic. The diviner can count on the client's belief that chance events *might as well be* animated—guided, so to speak. We may now understand why the interest for divination never boomed in anthropology (Peek 1991:91), despite the important cognitive as well as sociosymbolic place it occupies in most societies where anthropologists work. The diviner's epistemological stance leaves room for the role of ancestors in social life, in addition—rather than in opposition—to the role of coincidence commonly called "wind" *(luyaga)* or "eternity" *(liwelelo)*. The anthropologist's concern to study divination on its own terms is difficult to match with the scientific approach, which rests upon an axiom: the nonexistence of external, directive influences (Monod 1970:33).

And yet that axiom celebrating the rationalist ideal of self-creation is increasingly exposed as an unfalsifiable belief. Heidegger already doubted whether utter self-creation (for example, society as an autopoietic system [Luhmann 1986:174]) is not a contradiction in terms (Rorty 1989:109). Moreover, our notion of contingency etymologically signifies "that which reaches" (see its Latin root *contingere,* "to reach"). It shows how Western languages originally did not exclude a more animated meaning of chance and the real. Although speakers are probably not aware of it, in German *zu-fall* (chance) actually denotes events "falling to" the actor, and the French *arriver* (to happen) refers to the arrival of events. In that sense, the contingency of an event implies it is unpredictable to humans yet not necessarily escaping external determination. In divination the coincidence between the client's affliction and the oracular display may have reached from *elsewhere*. "To be reached" *(kushikilwa)* happens to be the term used by the Sukuma to denote the crux of mediumistic divination: the ancestor taking charge of the diviner's thoughts and speech. Some traces of this semantic association may also be recognized in the English word *lot(s)*, which can be used both to refer to oracular material and to a person's fate. In French *sort* can mean fate, spell *(jeter un sort)*, oracle, as well as chance *(tirage au sort)*, suggesting a similar, semantic cluster that defines divination in relation to contingency and the pre-symbolic (real) dimension of things happening. Sukuma also use one word, *ndagu*, to signify oracle, fortune or spell, and ancestor. This chapter argues divination is valued less as an intersubjective construction than as an event in which the ancestor or real speaks for itself. That is the point of consulting a diviner and the key as to how diagnosis can start the healing process.

The Ancestor as the Seat of the Real

In Sukuma divination three categories of precautionary measures could be distinguished. The first guarantees that the oracle is not merely a construct puzzled together by clever guesses; the second, that communication with the ancestral world is established; and the third, that this communication is not polluted by sorcerous interference. Sukuma divination means to favor in its purest possible form the "real" dimension of practice, which is recognized in contingency or animated chance.

The Sukuma want to assure that the advice they receive is not a product of local rumors, interspersed with background knowledge, life experience, and skillful conjectures of the consultant. Therefore, a common practice is to visit a mediumistic diviner outside the community, preferably living in another region. In contrast, the chicken oracle can be intersubjectively monitored and thus allows for a local diviner. Diviners accused of using spies to gain information on potential clients lose all credibility.

The client will give no clues as to the reason of consultation in order to prevent the diviner from speculating. It is up to the diviner to figure out from the oracle whether the subject's problem relates to affliction or to the search of fortune. Gradually the subject of the oracle has to be concretized. Who has transmitted his or her saliva to the mediatory object of divination (twig or chicken): the client or his or her relative, a man or a woman, a child or an adult? The symptoms and type of illness have to be specified by the diviner before venturing into its unknown causes. When an upset ancestor is involved, the oracle should prescribe the customary wear, such as color and type of bracelet or amulet demanded by that ancestor and corresponding to the latter's clan traditions. Any flagrant errors permit the client to leave and take back the money, usually a bill of 200 Tanzanian shillings ($0.30) placed on the ground between client and diviner. Such down-to-earthness probably prevented me from experiencing the kind of disturbing dreams Shaw got from the split between her objectivity in fieldwork and Temne beliefs (Shaw 1992:50).

The diviner's outsidership should also be achieved in relation to the diurnal world. Rumors rank popular mediumistic diviners according to their receptivity to ancestral guidance. It is not uncommon to find a diviner in his or her twenties at the top of the profession. For the Sukuma, it is not wisdom or life experience but mediumship that counts in the divinatory communication between living and dead. This primacy given to mediumship, as opposed to discursive communication, is obviously not limited to Sukuma culture, considering the foreign customers of Sukuma diviners.

Literature has amply stressed the liminality of the diviner, concretized in cross-gender roles or other ambivalent markers of therapists (Devisch 1993; Peek 1991; Turner 1975). In analogy, no animal other than the chicken seems better suited for an oracle, combining its nonhuman status with two-legged, domestic status. Sukuma say the chicken lives in the twilight of the homestead, perceiving what humans cannot. This privileged liminality reminds us of the pale fox in Dogon culture. At dusk on the Dogon village border the divinatory grid is drawn in the sand to express an individual's predicament. The symbolic settings are distorted at night by the fox and thus brought to life by this "creative power" coming from the bush (Peek 1991:140). Hence, the oracle exists by virtue of a contingent and external cause that precedes interpretation. This first cause is represented by the fox's footprints. What else could it signify but chance understood as animated? The fox's contingent movements on the grid correspond to a divinatory throw. No matter how many times one throws the lots, as long as there is no conscious manipulation, the exact position of the lots will be unpredictable, externally determined and decided for, just like the chicken oracle is. This contingent arrival (from elsewhere) captures well the perturbation of experiencing luck and misfortune in life. The throw enchants because it cannot be reduced to anything symbolic. In other words, it is not necessary that the participants consider invisible forces to guide the outcome of the throw, to infer that what makes their activity meaningful is the experience of exposing the real within the symbolic. *Whether in dream, spirit possession, chicken oracle, or cleromancy, divination is always mediumistic in the sense of an experience of the real.*

In the chicken oracle the ancestors manifest their presence by a little red dot (blood mark) called "canoe seat" *(nhebe)* detectable near the bird's spleen. It serves as a kind of meta-check on the value of the oracle. Another term for it is "eye" *(liso)*. Without the canoe seat, the diviner will throw the dissected bird away and say, "It has no eyes" *(Iti na miso)*. In other words, the real is lacking. What remains is a consultation with a wise man or woman giving opinions. The ancestor contains and supports the descendant, much like the traditional stool with the broad, encompassing seat. Understandably, this ultimate point of reference for an individual's state of being is expected to guide a practice like divination, which probes for the causes of affliction. Twice I proposed to my friend and collaborator, the son of a Sukuma healer, that we dissect a chicken together to do some review exercises on its entrails. According to my friend, such an exercise was meaningless because the canoe seat would be missing if no inner state had been aspersed into its beak. I checked, and he was right on those two occasions. I was, as he said, divining "nothing but a dead chicken."

The third category of precautions to guarantee that the client will divine the real and not a symbolic construct, has become particularly relevant. Sukuma discourse on illness and therapy mainly voices the alleged competition amongst healers to acquire ever stronger and new cures as well as protective screens that could outsmart the ongoing innovations by sorcerers. Especially since the resettlement programs of the seventies by the Tanzanian government and the AIDS tragedy starting in the eighties, sorcery is said to have boosted, importing expertise of regions ever further to the west. More than ever the authenticity or purity of oracles has become an important topic of concern. Sorcerers are claimed to insert unmatched methods of camouflage within their attack. "Cleanser" *(chogo)* magic erases any traces of identity in the oracle of their victim. To combat such disguise, the oracular object of transmission between patient and diviner, such as the chicken or euphorbia twig, should undergo a purification procedure called *nzubuka*—"cooling," or more literal-ly, "drawing from under water." This logic of purification permeates the third type of precautions against manipulations of the oracle. The chicken diviner usually performs the purification by dipping the oracle's feet, head, and wings in a bowl of water. After having inserted a reddish grain of sand, symbolizing the ancestor, or canoe seat, into the chick's beak, the diviner implores, "You, chicken, show the canoe seat. Travel and come back. You, decoy, collect it all, do not hide anything from us. Tie left hand to right hand. Go from the east, from the great mediumistic healers over there, down to the west."

The canoe seat symbolizes the ancestors and their guidance. The reference to the canoe, itself an object with marginal significance in Sukuma culture, has the effect of adding a dynamic quality to the oracle. It refers to the search for origin and truth that the Sukuma situate in the east and oppose to the trick-ery and novelty they locate on the western fringes of Sukumaland. More-over, the founding fathers of the great divinatory traditions lived in the east (Ntuzu Sukuma and neighboring peoples) and have designed the guiding prin-ciples that map the diviner's interpretation of the oracle. Starting with the basic codes of the social and ancestral world, such as relating the subject's left and right belonging, which signify patrilateral and matrilateral ascendants, the expert can symbolically articulate to others what the dream or chicken oracle has "collected" as a medium of the ancestral world. In mediumistic divination the possibility always exists that the malefactor used a disguise that outsmarted the diviner's repertoire of purifiers. Therefore, in serious matters, the Sukuma will consult several diviners and compare their oracles to decide which one comes closest to the truth—that is, to the "real" in its raw form.

Defining the Oracular Stance

The Sukuma mediumistic perspective on all forms of divination, illustrated by their concern to safeguard the raw purport of oracular immission, has large-ly been overlooked. The postmodern credo of human science stipulates that truth is "made rather than found" (Rorty 1989:3). Reality is believed to be a social construct, malleable, with symbols only referring to other symbols. Most divinatory systems display a different epistemology. Anthropologists

who take the scientific premises on chance and causality for granted (separating the symbolic and the real, equating the latter with pure chance) will try
to avoid epistemological clashes and accusations of superstition. They will
magnify instead the performative and rhetorical aspects of the divinatory
process. The diviner and consulter are characterized as constructing their reality: a "truth-on-balance" in which revelation and examination form two
moments (Werbner 1989:21, 25; 1999). Although an advance to Turner's distinction between ritual and divination as respectively revelatory versus analytical in nature (Turner 1975:15), the ancestor's immission is not given
primacy. Werbner's emphasis on "wisdom divination" underrates the basic
medium of divination, such as the casting of an oracular object. In shying away
from the seemingly arbitrary nature of the throw that could awaken scientific
depreciation and instead stressing the various symbolic readings of the throw,
he unreflectively reiterates that same scientific framework with all its hidden
assumptions.

By downplaying the flip of a coin for comprehending the divinatory
process, anthropology emphasizes an epistemology in which the flip equals
pure chance. The meaning attributed by the participants to the casting itself
(for example, as a home to ancestral will) is overlooked. As a consequence,
divination appears to the anthropologist as a negotiation with one person consulting a more "wise" other. But why would anyone consult a diviner, and not
an elder, if it were indeed wisdom he or she is after?

From actor-oriented approaches, such as Whyte's, one can deduce that
the experience of crisis has no agency in itself but corresponds to a logical
operator called "uncertainty" in relation to which pragmatic diviners and
clients take action (Whyte 1997:18, 67). Meticulous ethnography among
Sukuma will show that the meaning of divination, on the contrary, takes after
the particular context of crisis (and search for remedy) from which such practices originate. The Sukuma oracle does not re-create daily life but invokes
an altered perspective on the world, which the diviner has to empathize with:
illness or death have emerged, reaching us from elsewhere.

Whenever anthropologists divert attention from the real, they fail to cap-
ture the specificity of divination. For instance, we can conceive of divination
as a mode of cognition combining logical-analytical thinking and intuitive-synthetical thinking (Peek 1991:3, 5, 205); yet we know from the philosophical
work of Whitehead that the one always implies the other. So, too, do we con-

tribute to defining divination, without, however, differentiating it from other communication practices, when we note that a large part of the divinatory process does not follow a script but is autogenerative and open-ended—in the meaning of its metaphors as well as in the endless chain of negotiation between the parties involved (De Boeck and Devisch 1994:103, 108). The problem with these negotiations and interpretations after the oracle's immission is that the multivocality proper to the symbolic order rules and we thus witness the opposite of open-endedness as well: the search for diagnosis, for true motives, and for exact identity of the evil agent, typical of the client-centered character of Sukuma divination. The subject counts on the diviner offering some sense of completion, be it temporary, otherwise he will simply not be paid. Most of all, the relatively harsh and raw assertions of the diviner point to ancestral presence and will turn out to be necessary to accomplish the transformation of the client's condition.

The Case of Mayala

Now that we have acknowledged the role of the ancestor, or canoe seat, in Sukuma divination, the scene is set for a closer appreciation of the intricate interpretive system adopted by the chicken diviner. The following section examines one concrete case study of affliction and consultation.

A man in his late thirties, whom I will call Mayala, fell ill soon after he had held his mother's cousin responsible for the death of his child and had chased her away from his compound. As the fever grew, burning pains in his chest extended to the whole upper right part of his body. The diagnosis of a mediumistic diviner established that an evil agency had risen in the body from the feet up to the stomach in the direction of the chest. Mayala escaped death thanks to ancestral protection by his patrilineal grandfather's grandfather. He had helped to block the poison from its fatal course approaching the heart. The oracle revealed that the ancestor now expected his descendant to wear in his honor the accessories that used to characterize the old man in his time and which were now recited: "a copper bracelet and a twisted one, a walking stick, a white shell and a heart-shaped shell." Secondly, the oracle imputed Mayala's suffering to fate *(ndagu),* namely a bad spell from the "seeing" type *(ibona).* A sorcerer had retaliated for some reason "so that the victim would see." The sorcerer summoned the help of a corrupted ancestor, namely May-ala's patrilineal grandfather's father, known to have succumbed to an unexpected death far away from home. Another diviner claimed the evil spell was of the "knowing" type *(maana),* thus not the "seeing" one. After living alone for about two years at the healer's compound for intensive herbal therapy and eventually completing the ritual expulsion of the spell in the company of his household, Mayala regained his strength and felt cured, wanting to return home. To determine whether the danger was really over, he had a chicken divined.

The chicken oracle consists in carefully opening up the animal in order to detect any significant marks on the organs and on the flesh under the skin. The chicken diviner adopts an incantation, giving voice to the voyage his exploring fingers undertake in the bowels. As I was being trained in chicken divination at the time, I could note how the diviner, faced with a multitude of findings on the bird's feathers, organs, skin, flesh, and bone, chose to place certain relations into the limelight while leaving others, whether or not "corroborating" elements, in the background. At least as important as this inevitable procedure of selection is the gradual process of identification, which the diviner manages to establish between the oracle and the consulter. The identification is brought about by the diviner speaking for the patient and meticulously reproducing the latter's crisis via the medium of the chicken. The bird is placed with its back on dried grass, both legs spread out, invoking the imagery of a patient confined to his bed. The diviner clenches the left claw with his right foot and the other claw with his left foot, performing the manual operations of divination in "closed circuit"—his body a mirroring extension of the chicken. During the oracle, diviners also speak in the first person singular, identifying with the chicken, itself a substitute for the patient. In a monologue of successive questions and answers, the diviner expresses his relief or anger at what he perceives, as if he were himself the victim. Before the client replies, the diviner provides a provisional summary of his findings.

In Mayala's case the diviner's findings could be reproduced in three fragments, with the first establishing his general state of well-being:

> You chicken, your blessing is fine. But as I began to check your feet, I got angry. When I saw the right foot, I cursed the pains and the illness that began at your ankles. You chicken, have I eaten poison? At the mouth it denied so. My poison I have treaded upon on foot. It does not date from

yesterday; I got it some time ago. Then my body grew weak and cold. I shivered like a mad person *(mayabu)*. The coldness began when the sun arrived at that point. That is what the chick came to tell. However I am fine in the body, except for some muscle-aches. (Fragment 1)

Before engaging in more specified indications of afflicting agency, the diviner verified a series of general indicators of health that associate life with containment and tension. Three modes of well-being are distinguished. First of all, to measure the physical strength of the subject, the diviner held the bird's duodenal loop, which in oracular speech is called *lubango,* literally "blessing." Since it stands tensely erected, the diviner knows that Mayala is not bedridden. That is the meaning of the first sentence in the fragment above. Secondly, the gall bladder, or "gourd" *(kisabo),* was full, showing that the subject's body has the power to digest. The third modus of bodily vitality is the "home" *(kaya)* itself, symbolized by the bird's gizzard and called "stomach." It does not refer to the geographical circumscription of the compound, nor to the household as such, but to livelihood and status—that is, to the extended body of supportive social and ancestral affiliations this individual occupies in the world. This sociocosmic dimension of the homestead moreover refers to the extent to which the individual is safely enveloped by protective magic in the domestic realm and by the household and clan members. If the gizzard is not fat and swollen but emaciated or pierced, then the subject of divination has passed away. He or she no longer participates in the home's expansion or renown through cattle and children. More than the former two indications relating to the physical workings of the body, it is this "social death" that counts for the diviner as the deciding factor in checking the patient's well-being. To witness the sight of the "home" (the bird's gizzard) unpierced reassures the patient in his or her relation to the family, to the generalized whole of nearby others.

Next to the stomach's reference to the home there are three other dimensions of the homestead that structure the oracle. Besides the mentioned organ, they reflectively involve the flesh (compound), the bone (household), and the skin (ancestral space). A triangular area of flesh on the inside of the right knee depicts the compound in its spatiotemporal setting and is called *kaya* (homestead) as well. Here appear the traces of the attacks that have been inserted by the sorcerer "kicking the early-morning dew at the knee." The vagueness of its red determines the time span. As a third dimension, the hipbone joining back to leg denotes the household as a whole. If this bony ball is immaculately white and round, then it is said to reflect the shining teeth of a happy, laughing home. On the backside of the hipbone the lower back represents the head of the household. Any red spot there may considerably coarsen the tone of the oracle, as it reports of "the turning over of the headrest." The household head has been put in mortal danger by someone for whom he forms the headrest at night, namely by one of his wives.

Finally, as a fourth dimension of the home, the anal skin of the chicken, also symbolizing the black garment of the therapist, is turned inside out to reveal the demands of the ancestor (who, I should remind the reader, is the subject's "seat"). The interior side of this "sit-upon" skin vaguely maps out the compound with grayish or other color patches resembling the required altars and bracelets, which would honor the ancestors. The size of a swelling in the area of this chicken's "seat" renders the intensity of the ancestral role played in the patient's pains or misfortune. There, at the groin, are also rooted the bird's two long retractor muscles, which divinatory tradition has coined *luge,* signifying the tendon of the forearm. It verifies masculine power and potency, for these muscles between the hand and the elbow allow man to bend his bow, the symbol of fatherhood and patri-clan. This masculine power fades when the subject has engaged in extramarital affairs that were not accompanied by gifts. There the lover can be reminded of the sacrifice his mistress requires.

The diviner figured out soon that Mayala, who had inserted his saliva into the oracle, was the subject of divination. This he could make up from the position of the canoe seat. It lay to the male side (left) of the chicken's spleen. That no red marks were visible inside the chicken's throat or trachea meant that Mayala had not swallowed poison. However, several vague reddish marks could be found on the tip of the ribs, on the skinned shoulders, and on the lower back, suggesting muscle aches and weakness of the patient dating back some time. A split "tongue" (namely the pancreas) would signify that the patient is the victim of malicious gossip. The pitlike area, where the duodenum takes off from the "home" (gizzard) heading to the "tongue" (pancreas), is known as "in the cries of mourning" *(mu nyombe),* or "grave." A general principle in the divinatory method stipulates that significant events, otherwise left at the mercy of our hazy memories and reconstructions in discourse, are branded "for real" in the oracle, mostly in the form of red dots on the entrails, on the bones or on the flesh under the skin of the chicken. Retraceable in their spatiotemporal context, these "hot" moments of the subject's past (*nsebu,* hot or evil) are there for all to see: "they run bloody red." Another verb is frequently used: "to ripen" *(ku-hya);* these points have "ripened into" affliction (the heat of evil) as well as meaning (the mass of past events converged into this moment of crisis).

Both hands of the diviner further slide probingly over the intestines to check the color of their contents shining through. He has entered the realm of the "snake," which defines an array of potential illnesses located within the belly. Almost from the start of his exploration the diviner noticed that one of the bird's pair of ceca (appendices at the end of the small intestine), representing the subject's feet, was swollen and irregular in shape. Normally the ceca resemble two black feet, each ending in a white tip. Irregularity of the feet always makes a strong case for the most feared diagnosis: "snares." Mayala must have stepped on a sorcerer's trap that was prepared for him. This "stepping poison" enters the feet, rising upward heading for the chest, the traces of which can be seen in the clogging together of black spots in the intestines, starting from the "feet." A sorcerer's attack rising upward from the feet may also cause one of the most common afflictions treated by Sukuma healers, namely "twirls," whereby the victim is no longer able to control speech and behavior, becoming violent and uninhibited. It is contrasted with the more catatonic or epileptic attacks of *lusalo,* which leaves the victim stuck to the ground, with one arm pointing to the sky. In the latter case the evil agent has intruded the body from above—for instance, orally—to gradually descend. Next to strengthening the ancestral bonds, therapy aims at reversing the course of the poison. Accordingly, afflictions caused by snares are treated over a period of one to two years, causing the evil agency to retreat downwardly. In the first phase of therapy the notoriously aggressive "broom" medicine will induce acute diarrhea meant to expel the mass of black magic, after which the patients are occupied with concoctions aiming to get their intestines settled again.

Going over the long, coiled ileum of the small intestine, the diviner halts at the "sleeping," a tiny outgrowth that Western biology has coined Meckel's diverticulum. If it does not "sleep" but sticks out, then its tip shows the position of the sun when harm was contracted—namely, when the symptoms of snares, cold sweat, and shivers began. Mayala's oracle displayed a number of scattered black balls stuck in the small intestine (see fragment 3). These are digested residues pointing to old traces of the sorcerer's attack. The affliction thus must have occurred some time ago. This was corroborated by the three modes of the life principle (gourd, blessing, home) that showed no important flaws. From this the diviner deduces that the client has been divined and treated before and that the latter might have been prompted to consult the present oracle because of the danger that most patients are aware of, namely that the scattered remnants increasingly spread out in the intestines and eventually interconnect again into the feared elongated black mass of sorcery. The imagery derives its terrifying character from the often-employed analogy with fast-growing sweet potato plants. These are classified as *shilandi*: a category of plants and crops that are considered female because they creep or grow low, crisscrossing over the ground. Expansion or decrease of black remnants in the oracle's intestines show whether or not the witchcraft is reacting to the remedy. Here, "at the snake," confronted with the intruded poison threatening to renew its impetus, the continuous battle of the chronically ill takes place.

After establishing whether affliction is involved, and tracing its symptoms, the historical context should be recounted—the motives as well as the resolution. For that reason the diviner ventures onto the so-called cattle tracks, paths meandering through fields and forest, naturally flattened by the frequent passage of cattle. These refer to the subject's habitual pathways and favorite hangouts outside the compound. They are detected in the form of white lines on the flesh of the chicken's breast, where also traps lying in wait can be found. In Mayala's case, the diviner declared:

> I came to see those cattle tracks, they are all clear. When I followed the chicken, it came to block itself, standing in the shade. Just waiting, it had left the path. As it was hiding itself, I asked it, when checking the "tongue," if maybe we are insulting each other at home, or perhaps there is a quarrel at home? The chicken denied. The split in the tongue was only a very small, superficial cut. Then I came to hate the old widow. Those from the neighborhood are accompanying her. You see the bringer of the poison, who regularly passes by, at home, at our compound? She comes to check and to become acquainted. She has been given the poison. (Fragment 2)

A group of red dots was located at a distance from Mayala's path, meaning that the witch and his or her accomplices stand bashfully "in the shade" and not where the action or heat is. On the ribs the diviner discerned the accomplices, "carriers of the vessel," who are believed to "really know" the victim, like a family member or acquaintance who has easy access to the house. Since they were vague reddish marks and close to the tip of the ribs, the actual bewitchment took place long ago. Much emphasis is laid on locating the witch's accomplices in the oracle—for example, on the chicken's chest and wing bone. The oracle culminates in divulging the identity of the main evil actor by scrutinizing the feathers of the wings. In Mayala's case, the diviner concluded:

> The witch's canoe seat is hidden here at the doorway, so she is kin. Where lies the corresponding feather? The subject of the chicken calls her "small mother" (maternal aunt). The subject of the chicken has become self-conceited *(ndoshi)*. The bringer is not of my family, because that would have been very visible at the knee. . . . Poisonous remainders from long ago are stuck inside. If they join up they can grow again like a potato-plant. They do spread out, but to say I am in trouble again, no way. That has come to a standstill. If it had been a "seeing" curse, o man, you'd still be quite burdened. . . . Those who are waiting in the shade, their talks sound like if they are afraid. If they still had the need, they would be close to the path, checking constantly whether they could do their job. . . . So, just keep on using the ordinary medicine. (Fragment 3)

In diagnosing a problem, the system follows the direction of life transmission, situating the cause of the problem in the ascendant lines. The divinatory system does not follow the diurnal definition of self, namely as an accumulator of social and economic capital from where a social network of allies and dependants extends. The patient is not portrayed as a link in the succession of clan generations but as the end point of the chain that has resulted in his or her present fate. This dependent position of the divined individual reflects the altered worldview and self-image proper to affliction. The dependency of the descendant in relation to the whole of the clan also appears in the principle of mediumistic divination, which stipulates that only the outer twigs of the euphorbia tree can represent the patient. The euphorbia tree invokes the totality of ascendants. By the same token, the system of chicken divination depicts the subject as the culmination of influences from clan and community. It locates the subject on the joint of the wing, namely on the junction separating the two main categories of flight feathers, the so-called primaries and secondaries. These two series of feathers correspond respectively to clan and neighborhood—in other words, to "inside" and "outside." Their influences add up to the problem to be diagnosed. They converge at this threshold between home and environment, where the chicken's first primary is situated representing the patient. Each subsequent primary feather symbolizes the (classificatory) parent of the previous feather or clan member. The left (father's patri-clan) and right (mother's patri-clan) wings each number eight generations ranging from the patient's parent to the founder of the clan. In short, the divinatory system outlines a cosmology in which the subject comes across as an individual, occupying a pivotal and solitary position facing the worlds of ancestors, clan and community. This starting point forms the ideal breeding ground for the diviner to generate a diagnosis that heals.

Red marks on any of the feathers betray the identity of the inflicting ancestor or sorcerer. Mayala's chicken disclosed a tiny red point on the female side of the "doorway" (spleen), suggesting that the witch is on the maternal side. This means the right wing, in analogy with the patient's right arm denoting the mother's clan and wearing that clan's keepsakes. On a covert along the second primary of that wing a red dot could be discerned, thus inculpating a classificatory mother *(mayu ndo)*. His mother's cousin, whom he had chased from his compound, belongs to that category, so Mayala found his private speculations confirmed by an authority. One of the feathers of the neighborhood incriminates the third homestead away from the subject's. Two accomplices, detected at the "cattle tracks," carefully planned the execution. They are seen on the two cavities or "pounding vessels" in the wing bone, which portrays the passage that connects them to the victim. If the diviner has not touched upon sorcery in any other parts of the chicken, the two receptacles in the wing bone rather relate to the prosperity of the clan, which will interest a fortune-seeking client.

The Harvesting Power of Imaginary Claims

What can be the motive of someone causing you harm or even trying to kill you? The Sukuma believe that debts can make you "ripe" to be harvested. It means that debts can lay a claim on your life. This idea is essential in understanding sorcery in Sukumaland, because it demystifies the popularly ventilated opposition between community sanctions and acts of sorcery. The expression "to be ripe" *(ku-hya)* applies to someone who has been fined by the community. In the oracle each red point, referring to contracted evil such as sorcery, has "ripened." How then does illness or misfortune relate to fines? The traditional word for credit is *shi-li,* which could be translated literally as "eating thing" (from *ku-lya,* to eat). The creditor in a sense has the right to "eat" his debtor. So, too, do the witches voraciously consume their victims. In discourse, sorcery is connoted with an individual's criminal act, which can be combated by protective magic and by community action. Yet, in the perspective of debt and credit, a more threatening view lurks, which better explains the emotions and the crisis of bewitchment. I am hinting at the victim's unspoken fear that affliction corresponds to legitimate sanction—lawful consumption—enacted in name of society as a whole. Facing possible death, the victim feels insecure about the world and may secretly wonder if the infliction is not justified altogether and if he himself has not given reason for bewitchment or ancestral sanction. These doubts can be expressed in the patient's fantasy of the neighborhood gossiping about him in daytime and intruding into his home at night to hold sorcerous feasts. The imagery invokes what sorcery actually means for the patient: not a magic battle between equal members of the community but a feeling of isolation and impingement by the imaginary community or generalized Other. The diviner articulates this feeling accurately: "The subject of the chicken has become selfish *(ndoshi).*"

On a cross-cultural level, we may recognize the feeling that even our closest kin can remain nontransparent others. The uncertainty of "what other people may really think" or the imagination of an appraising gaze can cross our minds, but it hardly ever sticks enough to inhibit our projects of self-assertion. The community's law normally does not suppress desire but on the contrary constitutes the cultural standard that serves the individual in assessing success and in knowing what to strive for daily in order to acquire social recognition. These rules and norms of social exchange and reciprocity can be negotiated and sometimes broken without further harm. However, in crisis, suffering, or anxiety, a shift in experience and in perspective on the world occurs. In the eyes of the bereaved and afflicted, the social game and its law, extending from the family to the community at large, has contracted to a rigid Law (with capital letter), a term invoking the temporary split which the self experiences in relation to the surrounding world. In the case of the Sukuma, it leads the afflicted to imagine the possibility of lethal bewitchment by one's closest family. The witch then fulfills the role of executioner of that Law.

Latent debts, contracted either by birth or by accepting gifts, grant the creditors with the power of laying claims upon the receiver. A red dot on the chick's knee, associated with women who kneel when greeting, can refer to an outstanding debt called "the cows of others." For instance, in-laws may be suspected of using retaliatory magic because of an unaccomplished bride-price payment of the groom. Even if the subject has entirely paid the bride wealth and knows of no other dues, he can hardly exclude the possibility of being burdened by a "cow of the maternal uncle," which he would owe to one of his nephews. Nobody can be sure about the actual state of his or her social debts and credits, simply because that balance depends on the opaque gaze of the others. Normally this imaginary gaze dissolves in the social exchange and communication with others. But what about those with whom the patient is structurally unable to exchange? One of the common metaphors among the Sukuma to imagine the victim of bewitchment is *litunga,* meaning "tied," and referring to a zombielike figure unable to communicate or exchange. In a magnified way, it may very well express the patient's experience.

When Mayala suspected his aunt of bewitching him, he was not merely reproducing beliefs programmed by culture. Witchcraft beliefs form cultural models that express the particular experience of crisis. In the case of Mayala, the law of solidarity among kin, which expects him to keep his maternal aunt as a guest, had become endowed with an unconditional quality. The oracle articulated his thoughts when referring to the witch's feelings of neglect. The alleged selfishness hints at Mayala's disloyalty to his maternal ascendant. Diviners know that the consultation reaches its peak when it manages to articulate the subject's deeper fears. This happened when Mayala's diviner disclosed the "granary" *(ifuma),* a pocketlike zone hidden underneath the flesh of the chicken's breast. Detecting a red speck in there, the subject meets the eye of the witch fixed on his goods and unshared food. As containers are associated with fertility and success, they are also expected to form a source of jealousy, a gaze that can only be defused by the gift that transforms the relationship between self and other. Since gifts have no transformative power within the family, it is indeed there that the witch can be best embodied.

The diviner knows which doubts and anxieties affliction brings along: how night after night the client has been speculating, alone or in the company of close friends, on the "what," "why," and "who" of the ailment or bad luck persisting. But, most of all, the diviner identifies with the patient's belief that "the witch is in the home" *(Nogi ali mu kaya),* and he proves to know very well what it implies. This expression refutes any analysis that limits divination to a social event or a family matter. Such analysis suggesting that it would not be the individual but the group facing the problem ignores that it is precisely the social that the afflicted Sukuma experiences as problematic. In other words, if later in therapy family and community are ever involved as a whole (which rarely happens in present-day Sukumaland), there may very well be a reason for it: the healer's intuition regarding the patient's problematic relationship with these encompassing units. The above expression associating home and sorcery, instead of labeling a particular figure, points to an unspoken sense of generalized Other. This is also confirmed in the synonym for witch, namely "intrusive gaze" *(ngwiboneeji),* and in the divinatory system of the chicken oracle that I have outlined. To fear the witch "within" refers to the patient's feelings of isolation and exclusion in relation to the sociocosmic environment. Struck by illness or harsh misfortune, something seems to happen that prevents the victim from releasing the gaze of the generalized Other.

In an ingenious manner Sukuma divination attempts to reverse this process and thus produce a healing effect on the level of the patient's sense of the world. Before divination, causal agency remains unidentified. It lingers on in the shape of "the Others." The diviner's task is to specify the inflicting agent and thus break with the crisis perspective that assumes the evil to represent a sanctioning Law. Then the affliction is no longer imagined as an execution in name of the world at large but as the makings of a particular angry ancestor or a vicious neighbor. Naming the cause "witch" or "great provoked one" *(i-samb-wa,* ancestor) is part of the solution to crisis. Why do consulters feel relieved and invigorated at the end of the diviner's session? As much as diagnosing problems and advising on therapy, divination helps those affected by crisis to feel at ease again in the sociocosmic world. That constitutes what I would term the *ecodelic* power of divination: uplifting the split between self (or inside) and world (or outside) by letting the world manifest *(delos)* itself to the individual as his habitat *(ecos),* his home and source of well-being. This invigorating manifestation of the habitat happens by dissociating the evil agent from the sociocosmic whole of community, ancestors, and clan. Sukuma divination accomplishes the dissociation by letting the Law itself "speak" to the victim. As I will show below, this key role is reserved for the assembly of ancestors, who side with diviner and victim in their search for the truth. Not only do the ancestors guide the oracle, but the chicken diviner can actually perceive their relationship with the subject in the "collection-point" *(nghu-manilo)* of paternal (left) and maternal (right) ancestors situated at an intersection of arteries called the drum straps.

Both mediumistic and chicken divinations usually propose a threefold therapy worthy of the inclusive tenor proper to Sukuma culture: conserving some of the ancient hunter's sacrificial symbolism while adding agricultural logic to their pastoral traditions. The threefold therapy does not fundamentally differ from that in other Bantu cultures. It usually consists in ritual sacrifice to be performed on the ancestral altar within the compound, bracelets and amulets of ancestral tradition to be worn by the patient, and herbal medicine to be ingested daily. The result is a healing tradition affecting the total being, the body in its social and ancestral habitat. In therapy the momentary comfort that has been instigated in divination is more thoroughly pursued and brought onto another plane in order to activate a healing that ideally would last. However, the purpose of this chapter is to delimit the analysis to the divinatory act itself. This focus has permitted me to show that, once affliction is understood as a problem between self and environment, then the relation between divination and healing appears to be very intimate and to precede the role of group attendance and ritual therapy. It is indeed significant to note that the vast majority of divinations in Sukumaland do not lead to direct measures against the suspected witch and that the therapies or ritual requirements enunciated in the oracle are often postponed or just partly performed. In many cases diagnosis appears to offer a satisfaction in itself. Its ecodelic power accounts for that.

The "Doorway" in the Oracular Paradigm

Divination responds to crisis and therefore cuts through the societal model of harmony, unity, and complementarity of distinctions. The diviner explores the subject's intimate condition of health in the chicken's digestive tract from "home," over "gourd" and "tongue," to "snake" and "feet." These enchanting metaphors cover a reality of raw emotions and fears, of disunity and crisis. The murderous involvement of family and community members may appear on the oracle's flesh and bone: knee, hipbone, lower back, tendon, breast, and wings. Before touching upon these points of contraction, the seat of the individual's relationship to the world has been scrutinized, starting with the canoe seat, also known as "eye." Seeing through everyday life's sham and pretense is the goal of the oracular eye.

This red point near to the spleen represents the relationship between client and ancestors. As I have demonstrated, the eye or canoe seat fulfills the metafunction of validating the consultation: it shows whether the ancestor is present in the oracle. In appearance it tells about the quality of the relationship: a swollen speck suggests an angered or corrupted ancestor. In its relative position the canoe seat partly divulges the subject's identity. The women's canoe seat appears on the "inside," or right side, of the spleen, while the men's appears on its "outside," or left side. The spleen itself is termed "cooking stone," which carries a strong female connotation. Manipulating the cooking stone like a kind of shutter, the diviners call it the "doorway" *(lwigi)* of the oracle. Dividing outside and inside, the doorway represents the main hinge of the divinatory grid. In its gendered division, the doorway reproduces one of the main sources of crisis: on the one hand, women correspond to one term (the right side) in the code male/female; but on the other hand, given the female connotation of both doorway and cooking stone, women also embody the medium of the code. The "compound" (namely, the gizzard) and its public passageways, to the male side of the spleen, are separated at the doorway from the "womb of the home" *(ibyalilo lya mu kaya),* which is situated "behind" the spleen—namely, to the right. This domestic womb refers to the inside of the house, starting at the doorway, next to which the placenta used to be buried after birth. The divinatory paradigm accentuates that the women occupy that life-giving core inside the house, while they are known to come from the unfamiliar outside, according to the patrilineal, virilocal rule of exogamy. In that inner space of the home, they cook, give birth, and determine the household's well-being. The divinatory system makes a gender division by secluding the women from the encompassing compound, where men communicate and exchange with visitors. Yet, at the same time, it situates the women on the crucial "slash" of the distinction—namely, the "doorway" (chicken's spleen) that divides left and right, male and female. I contend that in this divinatory scheme, wife and husband are deliberately depicted as relating to each other in impregnable ways, like house to compound, private to public, medium to symbolic code (exogamy), absolute inner and outer side to social status.

Mostly women and often wives are suspected of sorcery. Therefore, divination has little interest in leaving room for the complementarity between male and female, inside and outside, which is otherwise celebrated during the rituals of initiation in the Sukuma society of elders. The ideology revering the domesticating powers of men, with their "bow" aiming at the "back" of wives, does not suit the Sukuma diviner. He knows that the consulter identifies more with a person in distress—for instance, a husband who fails to control and fathom the women of the compound. They occupy the undomesticatable interior or life-bearing core of the home, from which he remains excluded and yet depends upon for food and descendants. The diviner, speaking in the first person, aligns with the subject's feeling of powerlessness in concrete conflicts and antagonisms involving generation and gender. Therefore, Sukuma divination does not deal with the dreamy side of sorcery, such as the feasts of witches and the nightly sounds of hyenas and owls in popular discourse. Instead, it describes a world where one's source of well-being awakens the neighbor's envy, where partners and close kin seem unfathomable, and ancestors are quick-tempered. In short, it does not aim at rapidly expelling the patient's fears but rather at voicing these and picking up where the patient has left off.

Healing through Identification

The purpose of my contribution has been to show the proper "healing" qualities of divination, irrespective of therapy. In this section I will rephrase and link up the different steps of my argument. At this stage the key is "identification," in the double meaning of empathy between diviner and client and the singling out of the evil cause.

Can bewitchment, with symptoms ranging from anxiety to psychosis, best be treated by convincing the patient of its so-called fictitious basis ("There are no witches"), or is the opposite more effective? Lévi-Strauss has compared psychoanalysis to shamanism, where a transference between patient and shaman would set the scene for the "abreaction" in which trauma could be overcome by reliving its causes (Lévi-Strauss 1972:181, 198). The transference consists in the shaman's voicing the inexpressible psychic state of the patient. As the intricate chain of significant moments and social ties that had gravitated around Mayala were unfolded in the oracle, so too could he find his mood reconstructed from the hazy contraction of symptoms, pain, doubts, and memories. The story of the Zuni boy (172) offers another parallel with Sukuma divination. Once the Zuni boy accused of sorcery had admitted his guilt, he was surprisingly absolved by his community, invigorated as it was by this validation of their worldview, which had ended their state of uncertainty. In analogy with this community seeking "the satisfaction of truth, which is infinitely greater and richer than the satisfaction of justice that would have been achieved by his execution" (174), the distressed individual retrieves some of his poise after the social recognition of his experience and perspective on the world. So it appears that at the onset of the consultation the diviner does not shake up the participant's understanding of the situation nor offer "a more acceptable world for his client" (Fernandez 1991:219). His rare deviations from the client's expectations—for instance, regarding the identity of the witch—can be no more than variations on the same theme; otherwise, he would risk losing the client's confidence and the identification they have started up. If diviners may have given a "paranoid" (Turner) or "neurotic" (Lévi-Strauss) impression, it is only because it has served their profession to have learned to verge on the state of mind proper to affliction. A temporary loss of trust in the world could best describe the mood of bewitchment that questions the complementarity of men and women, the protection and loyalty of the ancestors, and the solidarity of one's kin and neighbors. Before realigning this mood, divination must invoke it.

Not only does corroboration produce soothing effects, but the consulter also derives satisfaction from having the suspicions pronounced by someone else. When these suspicions, which were contemplated by the patient in private, become externalized through the medium of an expert, understandably these may liberate the victim from the doubts and solitary moments proper to sickness. In the expanding (re)interpretations and secretive conversations about the oracle, the suspicions become gossip and indirect accusations, amounting to an act of invisible aggression comparable to witchcraft. The above three fragments of Mayala's consultation have shown how the diviner in empathy utters his indignation with regard to the witch. I have tried to demonstrate how essential the imaginary relation between individual and world becomes in crisis and divination. Thus the other side of divination appears. Much more than lending metaphoric expression to the patient's "inexpressible," the practice of divination actually restores the relationship between inside and outside, from the point of view of the patient. Divination is ecodelic, for in its very practice the outside—formerly the Other—can become perceptible again as a habitat for the self. It means a first step in leading the diagnosed to personally recapture the environment as the place where he or she belongs and can socially exchange, overcoming mental and physical seclusion. The mode of isolation is shifted from the victim to the evil agent. The patient's fears are of exclusion by the group ("pierced stomach"), of desertion or punishment by the ancestors, of neighbors' gossip or their sorcerous meetings in his compound, of not sharing in the medical secrets that all the others have, and of being reproached by the others for selfishness. As the diviner sides with the afflicted, the divide can start to wither away. The diviner goes along with the patient's worst fears and even specifies or intensifies them. He embodies the first being whom the patient can really trust and through whom he can take a first step toward restoring his relationship with the world.

The final purport of my argument is to emphasize that, far beyond the diagnosing diviner or the interpreter of the oracle, the primary role is reserved for the "real," namely the source of life itself, which via the oracle breaks the ominous silence experienced by the victim. (Therefore, oracles can be consulted by non-Sukuma clients who barely understand the diviner's words!) In Sukumaland the ancestors symbolize the real. The chicken oracle and the mediumistic diviner are its medium. The ancestors throw themselves in with their descendant's lot, helping him or her to scrutinize the sociocosmic world and to single out the evil in it. I have shown the importance that is granted by all participants to discerning the exact identity of this agency. As a consequence the cause of affliction appears to the patient no longer as a gaze embodying the Law but as a particular other, usually even a marginal figure. In Sukumaland the evil mostly takes the shape of an elderly widow corrupting an already deviant and ill-reputed ancestor. The diviner has accomplished his task when he or she has specified, particularized, and sometimes even marginalized the inflicting agents, who in no way (either as witch or ancestor) represent the world at large. Indeed, what better finding could crisis offer than the conviction that if evil exists in the world, it is not done by the group or oneself but by particular individuals? After the patient's recovery, conversations at night will sustain those ecodelic moods by imagining how extraordinary the witches are in their disposition: emotional, jealous, gluttonous, and fantastic to the extent of traveling on the backs of hyenas and sending out owls. For a while the evil seems so distant again from the here and now, where self, kin, and other villagers are believed to share, communicate, and exchange in one and the same world.

Conclusions

Divination cannot be differentiated from other social practices on the basis of its symbolic exchange, its rhetorical powers, the autogenerative nature of its communication, or the modes of cognition employed. The specificity of divination lies in the particular cosmological perspective. This cosmological stance emphasizes the unnegotiable given—in other words, the nonsymbolic or "real" dimension of events. Divination differs from other forms of consultation in that client and diviner use the oracle as a medium in order to be reached by the "real," by a contingency that is more than pure chance. Any act to which this "mediumistic" quality is attributed in relation to the real could become divination: altered states of consciousness, chicken oracle, or counting objects contingently encountered.

This chapter has illustrated how the chicken diviner establishes a process of identification with the patient by reproducing the latter's crisis. Hence, the diviner questions the complementarities of self and home, male and female, individual and community, the living and the dead. On this basis the client can confront the source of affliction. The oracle makes the crisis manageable by identifying and sometimes marginalizing the formerly overwhelming Other. In Sukuma culture the ancestors symbolize both the Other and the real, which, defined as chance (animated or not) and displayed in the chicken's unique blood marks, can hardly be called illusory. An oracle is valid if the ancestor (the real) rather than the diviner is directing it. By having the ancestors—the opaque and contingent source of life and death—speaking to and for the patient, the latter may experience the world again as his or her locus of belonging. Therein lies the "healing" quality of divination, prior to therapy.

Acknowledgment

This research has been sponsored by the Fund for Scientific Research in Flanders. I would like to thank René Devisch and Filip De Boeck for their comments and suggestions. I am also indebted to Richard Werbner for the inspiring discussion we had on his paper, read at the African Research Centre Seminar in Leuven, January 1999.

2

Drumming, Divination, and Healing

The Community at Work

EDITH TURNER

In this chapter I show how divination can take place, not in a private séance but as an integral part of a healing ritual, with participatory music to stimulate diagnosis/divination and the need for a united community. The performers, the Ndembu, are a people inhabiting the northwestern corner of Zambia. They are matrilineal subsistence agriculturalists, 40 percent Christianized in 1985 at the time of my account but still possessors of a wide knowledge of spirits and of collective healing rituals that are practiced for numerous cases of illness. In this hunting-oriented society, the *Ihamba* hunter spirit is of major importance for health and one's alignment with the ancestors. An Ihamba ancestor spirit might enter a living relative and make her sick because he has some grudge against her. It is then necessary to appeal to that spirit within her to come out and afterward be useful and give her people much meat. Ndembu do not regard spirits as metaphors but as real.

Tribal doctors possess their own benevolent tutelary spirits. The person learning to be a ritual curer may acquire such a helper when the spirit of a revered healer ancestor chooses to visit him or her. Thereafter the spirit instructs the curer in the course of the work. The curer now works in the spirit mode: the divinations performed are effected not through the doctor's own power but through that of the spirit.

55

The ritual I cite as an example of divination was necessitated because an Ihamba spirit in the form of a dead hunter's tooth, previously used as an amulet, had entered a middle-aged woman named Meru, with the result that her body was racked with a wandering pain. The ritual to cure her aimed to discover the name of the Ihamba spirit and locate it and remove it by sucking it out with cupping horns. To do so required an understanding of the three kinds of beings involved: the woman, the dead hunter in the aspect of his animate tooth, and the dead hunter in the aspect of a spirit, all of whom the ritual treated on different levels. The doctors knew that the tooth itself was a very difficult conscious entity, to be treated with respect. Meru, the patient, herself would need to "come out" with her grievances, her words *(mazu),* in order for the trouble to make itself known and for communication between the doctor and the spirit to be opened. No one knew at the outset which of her dead ancestors was afflicting her, so the doctors had to divine the name by gauging the actions and statements of the patient. The discernment and naming of the spirit were keys to the success of the healing.

As for the patient herself, her position in the small village was uneasy. I learned that her mother, her aunt Nyakanjata, and her uncle had been given as children to the previous headman as blood-indemnity slaves, so that her matrilineal rights had been superseded. Her own older male generation of relatives, hunters mainly, were now getting back at her from the grave, particularly through what should have been a lucky hunter's talisman, the tooth knocked out from the skull of a hunter at death. Meru was a nervous depressed woman.

Collecting the Medicines: How African Herbal Substances Achieve Their Efficacy

Early in the morning on the day of the ritual the doctors, Singleton and Fideli, along with my white assistant Bill Blodgett and myself as participant-observers, set out to the bush to collect herbal medicines. Bill Blodgett and an African helper taped the proceedings, so I eventually had the dialogue in writing. Here I use a narrative form and present the events as they fell out to allow the reader to gain a sense of being there.

We found fifteen kinds of medicine in all. Many of them were "coming out" medicines for bringing out the Ihamba; many indicated the spirit's existence as Ihamba, a conscious person. All the medicines pointed toward the cure, and as they came into use they were strongly focused on Meru and her trouble, along with the other objects used in the ritual.

Out in the bush in search of the first medicine, Singleton, the elder doctor, walked swiftly, weaving toward a bush he had spotted among the mounds. It was *mufungu,* the *ishikenu,* literally the "you-have-arrived" tree, the greeting tree, "the first." Singleton squatted down before the base of the tree trunk and took from his mongoose skin bag a lump of red clay; he rubbed the clay in a line down the west side of the trunk, then in a line from the foot of the tree to himself, and then on the east side of the tree. He drew the lines to call the spirit/tooth Ihamba to come soon, directing it along the lines. When this was performed, Ihamba knew "I am soon going to be out of the patient." Then Singleton took the cup of beer and poured it out at the foot of the tree on both sides. He barked out, *"Maheza!"* Instantly, I recognized the old chant we used to utter in the 1950s (Turner 1968:167).

"Maheza!" we shouted back.

"Ngambu!"

"Yafwa!" we returned—with special emphasis on the last word. It means, "Friends!" We answer, "Friends!" The hunter calls, "Sudden death?" And we answer, "It's dead!"

Singleton addressed the tree; his tone was urgent and harsh. "This medicine was brought to us by Kamawu; it came down from him to Koshita, and from him to Sambumba, and from him to Chisanji, and to my father Sangunja, and to Benwa. I have it now. I'm telling you how it is." He addressed the spirits and indicated the red lines. "See? We're putting this red clay of yours on the west side of the tree. I admit it's a pity we haven't done the tooth-removing ritual more often. Listen, you're getting honey beer, just give us your blessing; come on, give me the power to cure this woman well. Come quickly. You others, you guys who made it hard for us. You're the bad guys. I've given you your drink on the other side. You really screwed up, didn't you? [he used the pejorative word for having sex, *kusunja*]. Besides, you couldn't catch animals." In this address Singleton named each of his hunter-doctor ancestors who had handed down the ritual, finally reaching himself. The succession of names referred to a kind of tooth doctors' guild; he was speaking to those old healers, even including the bad lots, the *ayikodjikodji* (literally, those who gulped everything) as they used to be called in the old days (Turner 1967:138). When he was done, he rose to his feet and puffed out a breath, as a healer will after speaking with spirits. I was watching his actions and prayed in my own way, although I was not a member of the family, nor even of their culture.

Thus it was that Singleton was invested with his own father's spirit all through that day's ritual, and how it was through Sangunja that Singleton listened to the Ihamba in Meru, noticed how the spirit shook her, and eventually divined the name.

The herbal components that we collected in the medicine basket each had some affinity, some message or power effect vis-à-vis the spirit/tooth; one can see how a medicine component was a kind of person speaking to the spirit/tooth, who was also a kind of person. This is confirmed by the given uses of the medicines. Singleton marked with red clay the first tree from which he took parts, so that Ihamba would "know" it had to come out. Ihamba was capable of knowing. Another medicine was to make Ihamba "obey"— Ihamba was capable of obeying. Another was *musoli,* the "revealing" tree, to make Ihamba appear and stop hiding, which was one of Ihamba's habits. If the doctors were careful, said Fideli, "Ihamba would permit us to catch him without his running away." He had a will of his own. It seems the doctors would be able to tame his wildness. Another characteristic appeared when Singleton made a lid for the tin can that was to receive the tooth when it came out. The lid was cut from strong-smelling soap root bark "because Ihamba doesn't like a strong smell and won't escape." The doctor also used castor oil leaves as a lining under the bark because Ihamba "fears" the leaves. Then there is Ihamba's hearing. Many medicines "call" Ihamba out: the blood from a crowing rooster, medicine from a trumpeting elephant, the sound of clinking ax heads, a piercing whistle. Ihamba also "wants" to be fed on blood. Ihamba "recognizes" the power of the medicines. He is very touchy and is only willing to be served by qualified doctors. One has the sense that Ihamba is a conscious autonomous person, wily, intransigent, obstinate: "so difficult to control, so difficult," as Fideli, the junior doctor, said. This is the being whose identity the doctors were learning. Its character in general was well known, but its actual identity was not. Its identity and its effects on the body they were now going to divine.

Preparing the Ritual Site

By this time we were possessors of a collection of medicines of strong spirit power, mostly with one overmastering command, "Come out!" On our return we headed for the house of Meru, a classificatory sister of Singleton's. We found a spot behind her open-air kitchen to establish a shrine, and Fideli laid an antelope skin on the ground so that the apprentice could deposit the sacred basket. First, under the shade of a tree they planted a shrine pole, which was a forked pole made of bitter wood sharpened into horns to attract the hunter's spirit, along with a spirit house made from a section of termitary set on the ground in front of the pole. Then they spread the skin on which Meru was to sit in front of the shrine. They prepared the medicines, found a can to receive the tooth when it was taken out, and covered the can with the smelly castor oil leaf and on top of that the soap bark lid to keep the tooth in once it was taken out of her. The doctor lit the fire with matches, not by means of kitchen coals. All was separate and new. A mortar stood near and was filled with medicine leaves. The woman assistant Etina got busy and pounded them. Then she took a calabash of water and poured it first on the ground to the east of the mortar, then to the west, then into the mortar, filling it, to make leaf tea medicine. The libations were for the ancestors on one side and on the other for the *ayikodjikodji,* the useless spirits, those who must not be left out. Remembrance of spirits grew all around us in that ritual space.

Cupping horns lay ready in the medicine basket. We needed drums, so a boy was dispatched to find them. People were beginning to assemble.

Now Singleton medicated his doctors. He, Fideli, the first apprentice, the second apprentice, and I drank some of the leaf tea. For a moment it made my head swim, then after a minute my senses cleared. Singleton announced to the crowd, "If there are any pregnant women here, go away." The concentrated "coming-out" effect of medicines and objects was so strong that there was real danger of a woman having a miscarriage.

Singleton inspected the shrine, then said, "Look, we've made a mistake. We should have had Meru facing east, where the sun comes out from under the earth, not the west the way we've got it."

"We did that because of the shade," said Fideli. "But it won't matter, we'll leave it." However, it did matter in the end.

A small procession was approaching—the apprentice leading Meru, the woman with an Ihamba tooth in her body. The apprentice seated her on the antelope skin. She pulled faces at the sight of the medicines around her, at the razor blade lying in the basket. This was a miserable, proud, haughty, suffering woman. They washed her with spongy masses of the leaf medicine, squeezing all the pounded and focused "coming out" plants into her body until her whole body was drenched with the speaking and penetrating way-opening stuff. The medicines now began saying to the Ihamba, "Come out."

The doctors used red clay to draw a line down her brow and nose, temples and cheekbones—lines to protect her head. Then they gave her medicine to drink; the opening effect went into her stomach also.

Rousing the Spirit with Drumming; Divining Begins

The ritual power was accumulating. Now they started to perform. They took castor oil leaves, laid them over their fists, and with a concerted shout—"*Paya!*"—smacked the leaves with their palms—and the leaves fell on Meru, giving protection.

"Maheza!"

"Maheza!" they shouted.

"Ngambu!" said Singleton, and we shouted, "Yafwa!" The drums began with their rapid threefold beat. The doctors called for ax heads, and soon the deafening clink compelled our hands to clap, starting an effect like strobe lights in my brain. They sang in plangent woodland harmony:

Welcome, guest hunter, brother hunter.

The style of singing is what the Ndembu termed *kwimba na kwiteja,* literally, "song and agreement," or "call and response." The agreement meant "the community affirms it," expressed in a chorus that fell into place with great goodwill.

At this point Singleton came close to Meru and shouted, "*Twaya!* Come out!" directing his call into her body. He questioned the tooth that was wandering inside and troubling her, "Do you come from your grandfather Nkomba?" They were beginning to seek its name.

"Shake, shake, if it's you, Nkomba," he commanded her—and at the same time commanding the spirit inside her body. She twitched one shoulder, then the other; her body rocked in time to the music as she sat with her palms turned up.

"Maheza!"

"Maheza!" we all shouted in unison.

"Ngambu!" returned Singleton, and we replied, "Yafwa!"

"Are you Kadochi? Shake if you are. Quick now!" Singleton danced the antelope mating dance before her.

This was the first of the divinatory propositions, *makunyi,* translated by Fideli as "test," in this case divining by means of two opposite propositions: "If you want to come out, shake, but if you're refusing, die down, don't shake." In another sense it was an oracle, a subclass of the more general concept, divination. It is to be noted that Singleton often spoke directly to the spirit while at the same time looking for affirmation in the patient's body. It was she who would shake, but it would be the spirit shaking her. From time to time Singleton spoke to the patient herself about her troubles, going from spirit to patient to spirit again.

It was also the stage of *mazu,* the coming-out-with-grudges, literally "words." This expression, "words," connoted a certain action of prime importance to the success of Ihamba, the act of "coming-out-with" whatever was secretly bothering the patient about her fellows (called *chitela,* "grudge"). Other members of the community might also give "words." It was as if dark stuff ought to come out of the soul in this ritual. An almost perfect translation would be the literal etymology of the word *psychoanalysis,* which is "soul-un-loosen." In Jungian terms, the chitela is what erupts from the Shadow, and its eruption is therapeutic.

Already the group had increased to a crowd of about thirty persons, at least half of whom were children. A young woman with an armful of schoolbooks passed behind the crowd, saw what was going on, and gave a sniggering laugh. She went right on walking. Anger arose within me. "She thinks she's superior!" I thought.

The doctors were saying, "Maybe it's Kashinakaji's tooth. If you're Kashinakaji, shake. Come quick!" Singleton drove off the crowding children to make room for his dance; he sped back and forth bent forward with his arms stretched in front like forelegs, snorting like an antelope; then he danced all around the assembly in a clockwise direction, holding the people together and sacralizing them. Now Nyakanjata danced forward and put two pennies into the basket. Meru was shaking well, but Singleton ended the episode by pressing down on her head with his mongoose skin bag, which quieted her. As often as he beat down her tendency to shake, it came up again all the more strongly. This was a sign.

"If you want the cupping horns, shake," he told the spirit. Meru shook. Fideli got to work; he dipped the horn in hot medicine then unwrapped the razor blade. Meru looked at it: she was afraid of the pain.

Singleton assured her, "We'll only make one cut." Fideli gave one tiny stab at her back and as the blood ran down her black skin he set up the horn over it. He sucked hard and blocked up the end with solid beeswax.

"Twaya!" barked Singleton. "Come out!"

With two other horns, they sucked lower down on her back, pulling hard on the horns so that they stood up. Then the apprentice held out a leaf cup of medicine over the wounds on Meru's back and let the liquid drip down upon them, on the lower horns, and on her finger and toenails.

Coming Out with "Words"

Meru suddenly said her first "words." "I don't agree. I've got something on my liver [heart]. It's my children; all my children are dead." Then she uttered outright, "I just want to die because nobody's looking after me." The people heard her frankness and were pleased, and they sang: "The hunter doctor will come with a stranger."

But support for the song faded. Singleton was watching Meru. He said in a matter-of-fact, slightly argumentative voice, "There's a difficulty here. You said your 'words,' just a few of them, and now you seem to be aggrieved when you shake. You quiver as if you're not a gun hunter at all. What's worrying you when you quiver like that?" His voice rose. "What's up? I told you your brother Mulandu and I can help you with your worries. You spoke the truth when you said you might just as well have died because all your children are dead. You said, how can you stay the same and walk about when your children are dead? Sure you had worries, and we were happy when you came out with them. But I haven't seen you shake happily yet. You did when we began, but now you're stiff with worries. What's the matter? There must be something else."

They applied the horns again. There was something recalcitrant inside Meru's body that did not want to be dragged out. She was not helping at all.

The diviner's knowledge of the spirit condition of the patient made him concerned that there was a blockage. The doctor's way to deal with it was to clear the way. The doctors were tempting and tempting Ihamba to come out. In a sense it was equivalent to taking a fellow to a bar to let him talk, to let all his grievances come out—or somehow to induce tears. But it was still early in the ritual, and Meru could not yet bring herself to complete the mazu, to come out with the full "words."

"Beat the drum! Sing everyone." Irritation was growing, and uncertainty, and the weather was hot. Now they tried this song:

"Kambowa was my father's slave. Maheza!" It seemed in keeping with the mood.

Now Meru's own brother, Derek Mulandu, a man with an elderly face and concerned look, addressed his sister: "You're annoyed about money," he said. She listened, her head drooping to the left. Then he announced, "It was all because of her younger sister Liza: they had a bad quarrel about money. Meru brewed a calabash of millet beer and Liza took it away to sell it. Afterwards Meru—she's the older of the two—said, 'Where's the money?' The younger sister answered, 'Mika bought it and hasn't given me the money.' Actually Liza had the dollar in her pocket all the time. Liza was saying to herself, 'I'll see if my older sister will make a fuss.' Of course the older sister began to get annoyed, real angry. I was sitting there at the time. She and her younger sister started shouting at each other. Then the younger sister said, 'No, older sister, I've been fooling you. Here are your eighty cents,' and she handed her eighty cents, just eighty cents. The older sister refused the money. 'I'm not going to take it, because you're cheating me. I made the beer. Why do you cheat me? I say no, bring the full amount here. And quit being so quarrelsome, Liza.' Later Liza told me, 'That's right. I did it just to see what she'd do.' There you have it," concluded Mulandu.

Now Mulandu addressed Meru's body. "If you're aggrieved because your sister cheated you, shake, and if not keep still."

(Most of this sounded like a legal disposition. It was neither that nor psychoanalytic case material, but it was related to the inward tooth, stopped up by the stopping up of words or grudges. The flow of human relationship was the concern; we ourselves might envisage it as the traffic flow of human intercourse, either flowing smoothly the way the system intends or snarled and dangerous. To cope with the snarl the Ndembu do not use psychological terms like "psychosis," which are imponderables, explaining individuals' behavior, but they see something concrete amiss in the physical and social body—and they see that "something" as also spiritual.)

The weather was growing so hot that the people cut tree branches and set them up over Meru and the doctors for shade. Once again the doctors attached the horns to Meru and continued. Fideli turned Meru's hands palms upward, and they continued.

After eight weary episodes Fideli turned around and said, "It's so difficult to make Ihamba come out if the people don't sing."

Singleton stood in front of Meru with his eyes shut, quiet. He listened to something, then sang loud, above the other voices.

"It must be Kashinakaji," he said.

Kashinakaji (see also Turner 1968:133) was called *mandumi* (mother's brother) by Meru. Now, in his form as a dead hunter he had come back to afflict Meru. Kashinakaji's anger was caused by the desire for revenge felt by neglected males against women who head lineages, where the mother's brother did not have his usual power.

I was thinking for some reason of a Ouija board, then generally of the connection between the foreign body inside Meru, that ghostly entity the spirit, and one's emotional state in relation to the social group. The power and character of the Ihamba tooth—from which sprang the effort to get it out—spread to us all, while the Ihamba-extracting power of the medicines dominated the physical vicinity. Singleton was tracing the effect of ritual, tracing its delicate tuning in those sensitive psyches who, being kin, knew one another very well. The importance of tuning was seen in the simple statement, "It's difficult for Ihamba to come out if the people don't sing"—and the reverse, "It's easy when they do"—as we shall see at the climax. Choral harmonized singing was of major value in this ritual.

Singleton gave Meru more leaf medicine from a white cup containing orange root chips. "She'll be dizzy," I thought. He dripped medicine onto her head from a leaf cup. We all began to sing, and Meru shook. Singleton took the horn off her back, then picked up his mongoose skin pouch and held it in front of her face, afterward brushing her back with it. The mongoose, significantly, is a fierce, tiny hunting animal, beloved by human hunters.

The participants began a heated discussion on the subject of Meru's uncle Paulos, who was unaccountably absent. Mulandu was irritated because Paulos was not there. Meru looked grim and resigned. The drums sounded and she began to shake; at least a misunderstanding had been aired. They put a divinatory proposition to the Ihamba: if you want Paulos to come, shake. Meru's body did shake, so they sent the apprentice on the long trip to Paulos with a message asking him to come as soon as he could. Meru's face relaxed.

Bill also returned from a short break. To his horror he found that the boy assistant had flipped the tape cassette wrongly, turning it back to the already recorded side, thus erasing it. "Look what you've done," said Bill angrily. "You've ruined it." The crowd became silent. This moment of conflict was true Ihamba material.

"Tell Bill to say some 'words,'" said a woman.

Bill subsided and closed his mouth.

"How could he?" said Fideli. "He doesn't know the language."

"Perhaps those two foreigners are closing up Ihamba."

"They're doctors, why would they do that?" said Fideli.

"Both of them ought to add their grudges," she persisted. And her friend said, "Yes, Edie's the one who was here a long time ago."

Here Fideli announced, "Let me also give a few 'words.' This is the truth. Ihamba, I can see you shaking and shaking, as if you're genuinely grieving inside. You say, 'Although there are many people in this village, I haven't seen one of my relatives here. When they have a ceremony, I always attend theirs. How come they don't attend mine?' It's true, you're sulking; you say: 'Why are the doctors quitting nowadays? They complain it's a hard obligation, and leave off. These days our people don't tread the old ways.'"

Then Fideli invoked: "If the spirit's really annoying you, rise up quickly with healing skill from the ground. If not, be quiet, *nzo-o!*"

Meru, with her back stuck with two horns, said her "words" in a high oratorical tone. The words poured out: "I say as soon as someone brings me honey to make beer and I've just managed to get it brewed, a certain somebody takes the beer away from me. Then Ihamba comes. But I say no, no, no. If you don't sing for me, I'll die. I'm old, and all I have left is hardship, with my little children dying. And see what happens? I brew honey to make beer to sell, and then what happens? My younger sister sells it. It's my understanding that right up to today I'm still the elder and a certain someone's still the junior.

As for me, all I want to do is die, but I don't die. As you say, I've struggled in vain against my sister, and it's a sad thing. The way things are I'll die."

Singleton was still for a moment, attentive. He said, "I've seen him. It's Ihamba, so he's got to come out of her. Mr. Mulandu has put on his words and the things he said have also come out in words; he said things that revealed the bad spirit. It's come. We are now happy; we may say we're very happy. This is it, we're saying words. Ihamba, you'll soon find you've fallen down, and we've given money for you to come out. See, here's the money."

"Don't you realize your parents were sinners?" broke in a woman onlooker in a voice of reproach. "You're no Christian . . ."

Singleton continued to address the mingling of the spirit and the living Meru: "I'm now saying, forgive us, grandfather Ihamba. You're the father that produced me and the others. Don't let these people upset you. Just believe in the path your father followed. I'm yours, and I'll have to take you from the body of my sister so that I can keep you with me, grandfather. Believe in me alone, there's nobody else. Don't imagine you have to take notice of these women. No. Who are these women? They haven't got anything, they can't do anything. What can they give you? Just you pay attention to us. The man who's turning up any minute is your brother, your brother you wanted. He meant to come on Thursday. Now at last he's arrived. He's coming here right now and will find us."

He ended, "Maheza!" "Maheza!" we answered. "Ngambu!" "Yafwa!" we replied. Paulos, the revered headman, indeed arrived, wearing a hat and creating quite a stir; he was welcomed by many. He went to the medicine basket and put down the biggest village contribution yet, twenty cents. He had his own complaints about being ill-informed about the date.

Singleton patiently sorted out the misunderstanding. Having heard him out, Paulos went to stand to the west of the crowd amid a little knot of clients, including Morie, my local assistant.

Then, as the drums began again, Singleton savagely addressed the horns on Meru's back, "Twaya! Fuma! Get out!" as if he were shouting at a thieving dog.

Meru raised her voice again in a chant of complaint: "Etina never helped with the medicine collection. Why was that? My relatives don't love me." Etina was Meru's classificatory granddaughter.

Singleton indicated Etina busy playing on the percussion. "Don't worry about that," he said. "She's here now."

Meru was mollified. Singleton chanted the slogan, "Maheza!" and they responded.

Etina put on her own "words," they chanted the slogan, and everyone was pleased. But now Ihamba was refusing to come out because Meru was not annoyed. Maybe she was pleased because Paulos had arrived. Later it turned out that there were still further matters hidden inside her.

Meanwhile Fideli sang: "I haven't any father, can you sing for me?" He was referring to Benwa, his father, who had never put in an appearance all day. The breakdown of the unity of the neighborhood was all too apparent and was itself a large part of the trouble that Ihamba was bringing into consciousness.

The assistants bent over Meru to suck on the cupping horns. "Don't touch her so much," snapped Singleton. Now the heat was drawing up black clouds above us; Meru fell shaking in the midst of the singing, in the dim light under the shade branches, just as Singleton was saying, "What trouble it's giving us!" Voices broke in, "Look at that. She's down! She's in trance. That's just what you want. Look at that! Witchcraft is dancing in her. Finally you see it." There was a gabble of voices around me and I leaned over, too. The doctors indeed wanted this thing to show itself so that they could bring it out. Singleton worked on the horn, but when he took it off it was empty—another disappointment.

Meru sat up and the horns were reset. Singleton said, "She wanted all her relatives to come around, but they're away. How many men are here? How many women?" He looked around disgustedly.

Meru spoke from her ritual position: "I feel resentment."

Singleton poked a tiny horn the size of a finger up into her hair above her brow. The drums began anew. He danced savagely backward, hopping on one foot. "Keep singing," he gasped. The sweat was running down his face.

Now a woman pushed forward through the crowd with some bitter words to say. It was Snodia, "sister" (in our terms, cousin) to Meru. "A certain woman was too busy brewing beer to come when her mother-aunt was having her Ihamba taken out." It was true, Meru only put in the briefest appearance at Nyakanjata's Ihamba the month before.

Meru burst out, "I'm supposed to die, then, and maggots will crawl on my body. I'm supposed to go to the village law court and confess, 'Yes, a certain woman was brewing beer.' It's never been good in this village. Remember all the children I produced; they went someplace and don't know I'm their mother." She indicated Nyakanjata. "*She's* the mother who brought me up. My daughter tried to help when she grew up. She brought me to this village, but there was fighting when they saw me come, and they chased her away. Nobody helped me with my illness. All the time I've been suffering from an Ihamba, my relatives and grandfather could see quite well how it was with me, but they just kept themselves to themselves, among the men. I've been out of it. Not even my brother came to my help. You say you're Christians and that God will do his work. You're doing nothing."

"We've seen Ihamba," said Fideli. "And you have put on your words."

Meru's pain got to us all; we stood with bitter expressions, gazing at her. Fideli took a leaf poke and dripped medicine on Meru's head. Singleton held his skin bag in front of her face, then brushed her face with it. But Meru would not shake.

Singleton again addressed the horns. By now his voice was harsh toward Ihamba. "If you're annoyed because Benwa isn't around, shake; if not stay quiet."

Other village members arrived. While the percussion thundered they sang keeningly: "Where does Wuyanga come from? Where does the elephant come from?" In the midst of the heady rhythm Meru keeled over in trance, her body twitching in the dust.

"She's fallen!"

"Twaya, come out!" shouted Singleton as he bent over her body and worked on her back with his mongoose bag and finger horn, stroking the trouble under the skin toward the cupping horn that oozed blood. "We'll show them *chiyanga!*" (from *Wuyanga,* huntsmanship), and the song took up the refrain: "Wuyanga, Wuyanga, Wuyanga, Wuyanga, Wuyanga, Wuyanga," hypnotically, endlessly. I also joined, "Wuyanga, Wuyanga," shaking my head with pleasure as I sang, ending with them in the "Maheza!" "Maheza!" "Ngambu!" "Yafwa!"

Singleton exclaimed, "This is the cause of it all. You're here in the village of your mother. You left your father's place a long time ago. This is what I'm saying. If it's on the side of your mother, something bad on that side, then it must come out. Maheza!"

The status of Meru's mother Nyamaleji was questioned. By the rules of slavery it was now clear that Nyamaleji was indeed a slave, given as blood-indemnity to be wife of her family's creditor, and now without matrilineal rights. Meru suffered from her low unsupported status, particularly that of being deprived of her grandchildren. Her own shadowy maternal uncle, Kashinakaji, who would have needed the support of her lineage, was angry.

Singleton called on the spirit: "Kashinakaji, if you really are in there trying to eat this person, come out!" Then he begged and bludgeoned the spirit: "I'm following exactly what Paulos said, I've said all my words. You need only listen to what I've been saying. Haven't I shouted loud enough? We want this thing to come out; let's beat the drums, let the drums touch the earth— you've been refusing, I tell you. Now! We want this thing to come out! Just that. If there's somebody there, come out! Kashinakaji, you're dead, you must keep quiet. But if you're alive come out! We're not happy. Maheza!"

"Maheza!"

"Ngambu!"

"Yafwa! He's dead!"

"We'll sing the Wuyanga song":

"I am chiyanga, I am a hunter."

"Maheza!" Singleton was straddling in his dance beside Meru, bending over her and shouting into her body. Her long face looked straight ahead with an inner fury. She was shaking sporadically, sometimes with jerks, sometimes falling over, dropping bloody but useless horns; the sun burned hot and frustration was high. Something was wrong, yet at this point many things began to change and jell, and now came a matter that hurt me, too.

The Turning Point

It so happened that as midday approached our ritual site became very hot, so I sought shade on the opposite side of the circle. This brought me near Paulos, where Morie, my African assistant—a man whom I discovered was an alcoholic—was standing saying something to Bill. Now, while I watched Meru's shaking, I became conscious of Morie's harsh voice in my ear.

"Paulos complains that you never came to his house last Saturday when you said you would. He waited all day for nothing." I sat rigid, feeling guilty as I often did with Morie. Why did he have to interrupt the fascinating process before my eyes?

I muttered, "Our calendar must have got mixed up." Morie turned to Pau-

los and translated this as "She forgot! Wunajimbiri." I was furious with Morie
for making me out to be rude, but it was true. I had forgotten.

I started around, now remembering that on Saturday we had had to go
to the funeral of Line, the old Mukanza carpenter. How could I have gone to
Paulos's village that day? But would it be auspicious to mention death and burial at an Ihamba ritual? Everyone around me quieted and I felt they were reading my mind. The silence grew total: why, they were waiting for me to say
my "words"! The matter of Morie's lifestyle was involved, and, what made it
difficult, it would mean shame for his father Kasonda if I "came out with it."
Deeply embarrassed, I looked down and gestured that it didn't matter, then
rose to get away from Morie and went off around the men to where Bill stood.
They had wanted me to come out with my "words": it was part of Ihamba.
My heart was full of rage against Morie. What could I do? He was my old
friend Kasonda's son and, what was even trickier, my landlady's son. I sat
trying to resolve my mind about Morie and Paulos. After a second I again
rose and went back around to Paulos, and there I grasped him by the hand and
told him about the Saturday burial; he seemed to understand. I arranged to
visit him on Monday instead—but where did he live, I asked?

"Morie will bring you," said Paulos.

Morie was still standing nearby. I shrugged and said, "Possibly"—then
returned to Bill and stood clapping to the drums that were playing the next
round. I felt miserable.

In front of me I heard Nyakanjata breaking in, "Her children don't look
after her, that's the trouble." Her feelings were laid together with Meru's in
sympathy. Snodia immediately put on the "words": "It's from the mother's
side." On top of these "words," Singleton repeated, "The mother's side."

This sent Meru right back to the primary cause, Liza's deception over
the beer. "Liza cheated me. She's not even here at the Ihamba. I'm annoyed:
Liza, my younger sister."

It was a stalemate.

What followed happened quicker than I could write it. Into Singleton's
mind came the memory of the mistake he and Fideli had made in orienting the
ritual scene at the beginning: Meru had been put facing west, and she still was.
His intention became clear to me as I was pushed back to make room for the
drums. We all moved back, and a lot of shifting took place. Meru was raised to
her feet, and the antelope skin moved, then they seated her on the other side

of the shrine pole. Spirit house, basket, pans, mortar, and receiving can were moved, and Singleton took up his new station also, so that at last Meru was relocated in the right position, east of the shrine pole, facing the dawning direction of the sun, where it first comes out. She was now headed into the epitome of emergence, into the epiphany of the sun. The scene was exactly the same, only in reverse.

"*E-eyo!*" said Mulandu with great satisfaction. "That's right." Meru looked outward, her face very serious; this was the position of frankness and revelation. I was gazing northwest across the shrine at Morie sitting south of it. The sky had grown dark and a wind came up. "This is about Morie and me," I realized, "at least as much as some of the other complaints." My thoughts pained me again, while beyond, the drums thundered and Singleton hopped rapidly, foot after foot, in front of Meru. My thoughts continued.

"They *wanted* my 'words.' They're to do with me and Morie. I'm 'annoyed' about Morie and must bring it out. But I can't confess publicly as it involves his father, who's Christian, and jealous, yet a friend—and then there's his drunken son. But how I want to participate, right here, and can't because of loyalty!—And these great people, waiting for my 'words.'" So I had to accept the impossibility, and accepting it, tears came to my eyes. The tears came out, out with stabbing pain.

"Okay, okay, okay, so there it is—and its woe. That's it!"

The Cure

And just then, through my tears, I saw the central figure sway deeply; all leaned forward, this was going to be it. I realized along with them that the barriers were breaking—just as I let go in tears. Something that wanted to be born was now going to be born. Then a certain palpable social integument broke and something calved along with me. I felt the spiritual motion, a tangible feeling of breakthrough going through the whole group. Then it was that Meru fell—the spirit event first and the action afterward. Singleton was very agile amid the bellow of the drums, swooping rhythmically over Meru with finger horn and skin bag ready to catch the tooth, Bill beating the side of the mortar with a stick in time with the drum, and as for me, I had just found out how to clap. You simply clap along with the pounding pole, and clap hard. All the rest falls into place. Your own body becomes deeply involved in the rhythm, and everyone reaches a unity.

Clap, clap, clap—Mulandu was leaning forward and all the others were on their feet—this was it. Quite an interval of struggle elapsed while I clapped like one possessed, crouching beside Bill amid the singing and a lot of urgent talk, while Singleton pressed Meru's back, guiding and leading out the tooth—Meru's face in a grin of tranced passion, her back quivering rapidly. Suddenly Meru raised her arm, stretched it in liberation, and I saw with my own eyes a giant thing emerging out of the flesh of her back. This thing was a large gray blob about six inches across—a gray, opaque thing, a kind of plasma in the shape of a sphere. I was amazed—delighted. I still laugh with glee at the realization of having seen it, the Ihamba, and so big! We were all just one in triumph. The gray thing was actually out there, visible, and you could see Singleton's hands working and scrabbling on the back—and then the thing was there no more. Singleton had it in his pouch, pressing it in with his other hand as well. The receiving can was ready; he transferred whatever it was into the can and capped the castor oil leaf and bark lid over it. It was done.

I sat back breathless. But there was one more task. Everybody knew the necessary divining for the afterbirth of Ihamba and for any of Ihamba's children left in there. Singleton addressed the body: "If Ihamba hasn't come out, shake, if he's come out, don't shake but be quiet, *nzo-o.*" Meru was quiet. At once there was a huge flash of lightning—the light of a clap of thunder that exploded simultaneously overhead. Meru sat up panting. The longed-for rain poured down, and we all rushed into the kitchen shelter.

"Go to the house, you two," said Fideli, and Bill and I rushed on through the curtain of rain to the house door. Bill stumbled before he entered, fell into the mud, and then came in out of breath. Singleton entered with his blue shirt dark with water, carrying the receiving can that he set down on the floor. I wore a big smile.

He held up his hands to us. "See, I have nothing in them," then he squatted down and dredged a long time in the bloody mixture. At length he drew out an old tooth, a molar, natural size, ordinary and concrete, with a dark root and one side sheared off as if by an ax. It was the Ihamba.

Later, Singleton and Fideli visited our hut to explain what was coming next in Ihamba and discuss Meru's ritual. Bill and I were extremely pleased to see them. The first thing that Singleton said was, literally, "The thing we saw, we were five." This was his statement that the doctors, too, had seen a "thing." Singleton was counting the five doctors, of which I was one.

We settled down to talk, and I respectfully described what I saw, but Singleton made no comment. He did not give any details about what he actually saw. I was in no mood to become analytical, so I did not push the matter further. When the keystone of the bridge is put into position and everything holds, you tend to just look on with your mouth hanging open. This is what happened to me. If I had become analytical at that moment, I would have been a different person from the one who saw the spirit form. The climax as I have recorded it gives every indication that all the doctors saw something and that their reaction was not notably different from mine—that is, great satisfaction at having seen it. I was there, and it was obvious.

Feeding the Ihamba

On December 6, nine days after Meru's Ihamba, the hunters had been successful and Singleton obtained the duiker antelope needed to finish the ritual. He cut out an internal organ; it was the gall bladder. Singleton removed it carefully and emptied a dark fluid from it, then he filled it with blood from the body cavity—"to feed Ihamba." He knotted the end of the tube, then turned to the liver and cut out a half-inch piece, which he trimmed into a disk, then into a small torus with a hole in the center. He took this disc and the bag of blood into Meru's house, and we followed him.

The winnowing basket lay ready on the dirt floor with Singleton's mongoose skin pouch on it, along with a clean Vaseline jar with a metal lid, now half full of maize meal made from the grain that is hard like a tooth. Singleton added his liver disk and the sac of blood to the things on the basket. Now he took out of the pouch some red clay that he crushed with the end of his tiny horn and smeared over his fingers, for protection; he then took up the liver ring and carefully removed from his pouch the Ihamba tooth and chose a tiny piece of red clay. Holding the tooth and clay together he inserted them into the hole in the liver ring. He put the ring containing the Ihamba into the Vaseline jar on top of the corn meal, stuffing it in and positioning it with his thumb at the center of the surface of the meal. Then he poured over it the blood from the sac and screwed on the lid. The bottle was now colored brilliant red above and white below, a union of blood and meal. At this point I could feel a kind of resolution had occurred. Singleton said that when the Ihamba was fed with blood, it was satisfied, and so it appeared to be. The tooth would stay there, rendered peaceful by the red clay and cool maize, happy to be settled in the liver and blood, in the permanent safety of the Vaseline jar.

Now that the feeding was done, Singleton called Meru into the house. She came running, radiant and smiling all over. Singleton took the blood sac and marked her on her shoulders and beside her eyes. She was obviously in good fettle, and the blood would keep her that way.

"Seeing" and Divining

When I consider the Ihamba tooth, which was the resultant, the trophy, the material prize gained from the long morning of ritual, and wonder about its appearance when dredged from the can—after I had seen its spirit, after its journeys in the body—what then? Somehow a tooth was present and was brought into ritual focus. Singleton used the same word, *Ihamba*, about the thing that was inside—that is, the sphere I saw coming out and the tooth. The doctors could "dissolve" from one to the other. The little hard tooth, transmuted from a big shadowy spirit form invading the veins and arteries that was visible, audible, and palpable, reminds me of a similar report made by Essie Parrish, a Native American Pomo shaman who spoke English:

> When that sick man is lying there, I usually see the power. These things seem unbelievable but I, myself, I know, because it is in me. . . . Way inside of the sick person lying there, there is something. It is just like seeing through something—if you put tissue over something, you could see through it. That is just the way I see it inside. I see what happens there and can feel it with my hand—my middle finger is the one with the power . . . The pain sitting somewhere inside the person feels like it is pulling your hand towards itself—you can't miss it. (Quoted in Harner 1980:127–28)

The skill of Singleton appears to correspond to that of Essie Parrish from an entirely different culture area. There are many references in Singleton's ritual to seeing and sensing Ihamba: Singleton said, "I've seen that it is Ihamba, so

he must come out of her.""We have seen Ihamba," said Fideli. I myself saw how
Singleton put his small horn on his finger and drew many lines around the
cupping horn on Meru's back. This is the diviner's skill of aligning himself,
literally pointing, to what cannot ordinarily be seen, by a process of "tuning
in." His power of aligning the senses, letting his hands and medicine horn point
to the site of the trouble, is his gift.

About this palpable sense of the Ihamba, Fideli said, "When an Ihamba
goes into a horn you feel it vibrating." All of this was vindicated for me by the
actual sight of the spirit form, gray, quite definitely there, like a thick cloud
of gunk. It is this object that was central to my memory, not the concrete
tooth. The tooth was vital to the ritual because afterward in the hard form it
could be pampered and fed. The cloud spirit had a name, and the acquisition
of the name, Kashinakaji, enabled the extraction, enabled Singleton to get a
grip on him—because he knew what Kashinakaji was after. In psychic matters, a name is a big clue. The name has much of the sense of actually being the
person. Many African peoples equate the soul with the name. When a person
inherits the name, that person inherits the soul.

So at the moment when Singleton clutched the "thing" in his skin pouch,
he knew it as Kashinakaji, the Ihamba who had been within, now seen as a
spirit form outside the body. Singleton then put him/it into the receiving can,
and later in the house its form was visible to everyday sight as a tooth somehow deriving from the spirit form. Then it must have meat, then it is the
hard concrete tooth that is numinous, and its feeding with blood produces that
palpable experience of satisfaction that I sensed in Meru's house.

Elements of the Cure: Deautomization, Focusing, and Release

The frustrations and hindrances in the process that seemed to appear naturally in Ihamba—a process perhaps comparable to the on-and-off periodicity
of childbirth contractions—gave time for the extremes of resentment and
tension and their opposite, relaxation, to develop to maturity in the patient;
time for the powers of the participants to focus more and more accurately, in
an intimate involvement with the cause of the trouble, with the patient's feel-

ings and with other aspects of the ritual; time in fact for all the hidden alley-
ways of the body and mind of the patient to be explored. The frustration
involved, the disappointment as time after time no tooth emerged, built this
involvement and created a potential for the appearance of the tooth and for
good health by default, so that the tooth and health sprang into existence by
a slingshot effect, by sheer necessity. In Ihamba the call and response pattern
developed into an almost desperate need-and-fulfillment pattern through the
shaking and the "words," and finally into what one may describe as an extreme
of tension and a bursting of the tension, like having a baby or an orgasm.

In such circumstances a situation comes into being in which nothing can
be taken for granted any longer. The participants have to look deeper inside
themselves than ever before. What happens is a process of "deautomization."
Deikman (1975:204), the expert on consciousness, says that when deautomization takes place, "the psychological structures that organize, limit,
select, and interpret perceptual stimuli" are undone by a process of "rein-
vesting actions and percepts with attention" (205). In Ihamba every tremor
counted, every word was significant. Even the expected path of this Ihamba
ritual was interrupted by the discovery that Meru was facing the wrong way,
a mistake that brought about the repositioning of the psyches of many of the
participants at a different level, including mine, and jogged us into a sharper
state of attunement. Deautomization, according to Deikman, results in a
shift from automatic motor behavior, learned through habit, to a mode that
is "(a) relatively more vivid and sensuous, (b) syncretic, (c) physiognomic
and animated, (d) dedifferentiated with respect to the distinctions between
self and object and between objects, and (e) characterized by a dedifferentia-
tion and fusion of sense" (206). It is marked by clarity of vision, a heightening of physical perception, and a "cleansing of the doors of perception," as in
Blake's phrase. It is the mystical experience itself as Deikman describes it
(207–8).

Thus, the Ihamba ritual gave the assembled people the experience of a different level of perception, even as an end in itself. The idea of higher perception in ritual as an end in itself was not considered an issue in anthropology
until the explorations of Wagner (1983, 1986) and others in the field of perception. In my essay on neurobiology (Turner 1986:225) I suggested that
there are levels of human action that go beyond the functional toward action

at a level that becomes an end in itself. Is Ihamba one of these? The switching between levels and facets and modes of behavior, the pleasure in the complex music, the more than psychological causes of the ritual, and the excitement of the climax transcend the function of healing for the body or even for society. They are most economically explained by the desire of the spirit to manifest itself, brought about by a combination of frustrations and the increasing focus on coming-out effects, a combination that in the end could not be resisted.

Let us scan the account to produce a version that highlights these two processes. First, we note the focusing power condensed in the contents of the medicine basket. It is the herbal trip in the bush that provides the potent collection. At the greeting tree Singleton rubs red clay onto the bark, and at this, Ihamba knows, "I'm soon going to be out of the patient." Singleton's medicines encompass the universe. As he said, "Medicines for the below and the above, for the inside; every medicine to make Ihamba come out." These, all fresh and pounded together, provide the liquid medium for washing the patient, for drawing out and carrying away the Ihamba. A whole mortar full of the medicine stands ready, and it gives continuity throughout the broken episodes of the ritual. The patient's body is sprinkled continually with the cool tealike liquid; eventually there will be few places where Ihamba can hide. The drums for calling begin, along with the ax heads' deafening command. Now the divinatory propositions begin, with the alternative commands, "Ihamba! If you're annoyed because of your sister, come out! If you're not, don't shake." A process of divination thus guides the doctors into the heart of the resentments of Meru and indeed of the family. The doctors say quite explicitly that the Ihamba will only come out when the bad "words" are out. The spirit does not come easily, resulting in failure after failure to extract the tooth, to the point of great despair. Singleton is feeling his way into the condition and the whereabouts of the Ihamba, listening for it. The patient is weary, which makes her dissociate and quit her superficial efforts—whatever her upper mind feels those are—and lets the deep effect, impelled by the accumulative power of the medicines, the compelling music, and the communication with the spirit take place. The tooth-spirit slips out and is safely held by Singleton.

Conclusion: The Work of Divination within a Collective Healing Ritual

I have shown how a collective healing works in the hands of a skilled diviner, with the background support of spirits and of living people conscious of the presence of spirits. In this ritual the healing community collectively came to the point. The people's music and participation in the spirit-aware milieu finally enabled the moment to reach its climax. Spirit awareness first came into being in the bush when Singleton invited his diviner ancestor to help him, and it climaxed at the end when I vividly felt the unison effect go through the group. We reached the intended goal when the community was one. That moment was not under conditions of ordinary social consciousness. It came at the end of the efforts of the doctor/diviners to engage the community in exactly the ways in which they knew Ihamba would work—when all were focused, with all their "words" out in the open.

We see how important music was here. In Ihamba, the drumming itself was at no ordinary level of human experience. In Ihamba the social nature of the ritual and the music was clear in the first place, even in the call-and-agreement pattern of song, as the very word *agreement* implies. The people's presence was indispensable for the fluid connections of power and for the very fabric of connection that could lift the occasion into miracle.

The ritual reaffirmed the importance of the social itself—just as anthropologists have maintained. At Ihamba it was the *community* of souls that experienced a collective nonordinary consciousness. They knew that that consciousness was going through a change. This is not a matter of an *individual* undergoing change or cure, as with most Western psychiatry.

The phrase "the social" will inevitably bring to mind the study of kinship and social organization. But that "social" is what Victor Turner saw as social structure, the laws constructed and taught to the members of society by itself, as opposed to *communitas,* the generic sense of fellow feeling, a basic union with others, which was a large part of this ritual and is the major method and tool for the work of religion—a different kind of social. I am tempted to call this "social II," as opposed to "social I." I saw and felt in Ihamba the moment when the consciousness of the social group was changed as well as that of the individual—producing the social in its most intense form.

One may trace in the course of the Ihamba ritual I have described the development of the support principle that characterizes "social II." One sees at first the laggardness of the singers; the appeal of the diviners to the spirit to indicate his name; the slow work of backup, eventually provided with fervor by the community, all combining at the climax as a great effector. Maslow (1964) talks of peak experiences. They are often social II occasions. In this Ihamba, the material demonstrates, stage by stage, that the success of the divination and healing rested with the group.

3

Calendrical Divination by the Ixil Maya of Guatemala

BENJAMIN N. COLBY

Ixil (pronounced *ishil*) Maya calendrical divination is based on a cultural logic organized by key metaphors covering religious beliefs, ethics, morality, and general prescriptions for locally defined success. Findings in new areas of interdisciplinary research concerning mind-body interactions affecting stress levels, sickness, and health facilitate a functional theory of divination consonant with forces both of natural and cultural selection. Ixil divination is shown to draw upon schemas that match culture patterns (for example, folktales and myths) from different cultural systems used by the Ixil. The divinatory model combines a narrative grammar with a decision module based on a list of twenty day gods, each with a particular set of attributes used to construct the reading. These, along with perceived attributes of the client and a mechanism for determining relative salience, go into the reading construction. The study was greatly helped by filming the ritual in the field, the collection of case histories in the field, and the visit of a daykeeper to the University of California, Irvine, campus to do hypothetical divinatory castings and interpretations to facilitate the working out of a narrative grammar and decision model for the process. A comparison of Ixil calendrical divination with Ndembu basket divination reveals interesting similarities and differences. One of them suggests the hypothesis that all complex divinatory systems will have a particular range in number both of divinatory objects and of speaking elements. This pattern/schema approach relates to a theory of adaptive potential (tested elsewhere) that argues for a universal set of optimal conditions that affect the health and well-being of individuals in any interacting social group.

Introduction: Ixil Calendrical Divination

Calendrical divination as practiced by daykeepers *(ʔaaq'ii)* among the Ixil Maya of Guatemala is complex and comprehensive, emerging, as it has, from what is probably the most sophisticated of the ancient astronomical sciences according to our knowledge of the archeological past. Out of that has come a 260-day calendar consisting of thirteen numbers and 20 days. Why the number thirteen is due most probably to an earlier lunar calendar since there are thirteen full moons in a year. However the 260-day calendar is based on the period between two solstices at a particular latitude in the state of Chiapas, Mexico, where the Mesoamerican calendar is thought to have originated (Malmström 1997). If one starts with a solar zenith moving southward along a particular swath of Mesoamerica, it is exactly 260 days before the sun comes back to that zenith. The astronomical precision of the early Maya is corroborated by the location and positioning of ceremonial centers to make solar and other astronomical sightings to provide a precise astronomical basis for an agricultural society with a more precise calendar than any of the Western civilizations at the time. This 260-day calendar was foundation for a highly complex social and religious system. Religious beliefs, ethics, morality, and general prescriptions for locally defined success all constitute a cultural logic that today has been handed down through calendrical divination and an associated body of folktales, myths, life histories, and dreams. In this chapter I will describe how divinatory variables among the Ixil inheritors of the classic Mayan society (with intrusions from the Spanish conquest) can relate both to a society's cultural logic and to a functional theory of culture that focuses on adaptive potential and well-being.

An ethnographic model such as the one presented here for Ixil calendrical divination represents a cultural code that I have worked out through successive approximations to a theoretical model derived from distributional studies of the patterns found in divinatory processes and the readings that came out of them. The culture patterns—the actual words expressed by such

*Shas Koʔw, the daykeeper, in front of his house near Nebaj, Guatemala
(photograph by Benjamin Colby)*

informants as Shas Koʔw, an Ixil daykeeper, are produced through mental representations or, as I shall refer to them, a network of cognitive schemas.

Divination is a cultural decision mechanism that mediates consciousness and cultural processes as they respond to such stressor situations as sickness and social conflict. The first step in divination is a cognitive process involving creative symbolic mechanisms that match up with a physical layout of seeds on which the calendar is verbally superimposed. The second and third steps, occurring simultaneously, are the expression of the divinatory reading and its reception by the client observer.

Cultural Logic and Its Functions

The functional motivation of individuals in this process centers on stress and success—how to avoid the first and attain the second. *Cultural logic* is used here to mean the way in which an individual's general knowledge and interpretation of the world and of human nature explains how and why people act the way they do and how their behavior is monitored and sanctioned by the gods and sometimes by fellow humans.

Forged through time over many generations and through changing situations, an explicitly codified divination is guided by an implicit narrative grammar and decision model that encapsulates life situations in that society. If analyzed to its fullest extent, a codified divinatory system can be likened to a cultural Rosetta stone that translates the behavioral, biological, and physical conditions in which individuals of a society typically find themselves and how the local culture-specific logic common to a social group relates to universal human phenomena that relate both to the biology of Homo sapiens everywhere and to aspects of the human condition that are universal.

The key Ixil metaphor in divination, and indeed in all religious thought in Mesoamerica, is the equation of sickness with the captivity of one's soul by supernatural beings angered by some perceived misbehavior. Ixil folktales show numerous occasions where this theme of captivity is played out. In one story, for example, the protagonist is transported to the world of the earth god inside a mountain where the protagonist talks to the captive soul of his godmother. Following her instructions, he escapes back to the world of the living. He then visits his material godmother, who is deathly sick and bears the marks of injury sustained by an inadvertent act of the protagonist when their souls were conversing inside the mountain underworld (Colby and Colby 1981). Captive souls inside mountains are a familiar theme throughout Mesoamerica. The Zinacantec Maya Indians I worked with in Mexico are among those groups having this belief (Vogt 1969).

Organizing metaphors such as this one ensure that the same cultural logic holds in different types of cultural productions, thus providing an overall coherence to explanations of life circumstances for members of a social group. This integrative coherence-maintaining function operates both within and between individuals. Within individuals they provide a cognitive coherence that is essential for well-being and the maintenance of traditional beliefs. Between individuals these metaphors promote social integration. The greater the coherence and cognitive concordance of metaphors and the cultural logic in which they are embedded, the easier the communication and commerce within a society. In human evolution, as human settlements grew and tribal units expanded to the point where not all members of a society knew each other, divination and other cultural productions provided this integrative coherence. Though divination is ubiquitous even today, I suspect that its major development through specialized priests marked a particular stage through which all the major civilizations passed early in their development.

Cultural logic works at all levels through language. Like language, divination is a system of systems. Like language it involves syntactic and semantic components along with the presuppositions underlying human communication, commonly referred to as pragmatics. It is in these underlying presuppositions and their organization that one can seek the prevailing cultural logic commonly used among a speech community.

There are, however, different levels on which communication occurs. In Mesoamerica the basic idea of the calendar and deities associated with it was widespread, stretching geographically across different language families. All of the 260-day calendars in use had thirteen numbers and 20 day names. There was also a larger, solar calendar of eighteen months of 20 days, with an extra five-day period at the end of the year. These calendars, even though the numbers, days, and months themselves were represented by different morphemes in each language, appear to have all diffused from non-Maya speakers in the Pacific coastal plane of Chiapas, Mexico (Malmström 1997). Since the days were deified, and each community had its local set of deities and sacred mountains, local variations on the Mesoamerican theme were numerous. Over all, however, the mechanics of the calendar, and the number of days and months, are invariant. Further, the underlying presuppositions, such as the idea of captivity and punishment for misbehavior, were in most particulars the same. They mesh well with the higher level syntactics and semantics of the narrative systems in all the Mesoamerican groups. These higher level components are based on syntagmatically longer chunks of information than the lower level morphemic or lexical units, and they presumably call upon different neural subarchitectures and pathways than the lower level units, as I shall explain in the sections ahead.

Determining Patterns of Cultural Logic

Patterns of cultural logic can be discerned through the analysis of myths, folktales, and rituals with respect to patterned strings of repeated elements. The strings are more readily analyzed into their constituent parts through distributional analysis, the usual kind of analysis utilized by linguists at all levels of language. Constituents of patterns of narrative and ritual are preserved through time through their embeddedness in the overall production.

Among the most easily spotted patterns are narrative motifs that appear over and over again throughout large regions of the world. In length these story units are intermediate between words, clauses, and sentences at the lowest level of narrative organization and full-length story plots at the highest level. Proverbs, metaphors, and basic narrative actions are also in this intermediate range and are intermingled with motifs. The worldwide occurrence of motifs suggests both an ancient origin and a high cognitive salience. Mesoamerican motifs include the aforementioned captivity of souls inside mountains by angered gods, the attachment of animal souls to the person, and the use of animal souls in witchcraft.

Ixil Maya Divination Today

Calendrical divinations have persisted over centuries through the upheavals of the Spanish conquest and subsequently over long periods of very slowly changing traditions. Like other cultural patterns, Ixil calendrical beliefs and practices have evolved through a process of cultural selection shaped over more than a thousand years of divinatory readings. In the twentieth century, calendrical divination was frequently practiced in the Ixil area prior to the upheavals of government massacres in the 1980s. They continue today; however, I suspect that the attenuation of calendrical divination has been extensive due to recent Protestant missionary work following on the heels of heavy government repression where travel outside villages and agricultural fields to sacred places was treated with suspicion and discouraged.

Knowledge of the calendar is imperfectly retained among the general populace, who depend upon the daykeeper to track the days. All daykeepers follow the days in their heads. As our chief informant, Shas Koʔw, said, when he first wakes up in the morning he thinks what day it is and the day is always there.

Ixil divination is used to determine why the client has had some misfortune or sickness. It is also used to determine the meaning of a dream or to tell the client what kind of destiny may lie ahead. By laying out special red bean-shaped seeds from the coral tree *(palo pito* or *bʼaqʼ mič)* and using the pre-Colombian calendar to count them, the daykeeper (ʔaaqʼii) makes his determinations.

Shas usually performed his divinations at his household shrine, though

Shas Koʔw's household shrine, before which household rituals, including divination, are held; Nebaj, Guatemala (photograph by Benjamin Colby)

on occasion he would take part of his divining bundle to the house of a client. When the ritual was not of immediate urgency, a client would wait for a good day as determined by the number and day god of that day.

Shas would begin his divination by lighting a censer and intoning a lengthy prayer invoking the aid of the gods and departed ancestors. While praying, he would pick up a handful of seeds and lay them out in pairs, forming a series of columns and rows. Once the layout was finished, he would start counting the days, each seed pair representing one day, just as we might read across a modern printed calendar, calling out the days of the week and numbers of the month. Shas would go through his layout, counting in sequence from left to right and down. In this way each seed stimulus in the layout gets linked up with one of the twenty day gods and thirteen numbers of the Ixil 260-day calendar. The last seed or seed pair and the far right-hand column of the other rows are the days that "speak" (for example, "talking days").

I had this process filmed in the field for a session in which the client and her family consented to having it recorded. I also observed other sessions. There was clearly a method to the process, but it was difficult to do the kind

of distributional analysis needed to get at the underlying logic without having a record of many more divinations, which was challenging in the field.
Observing a Mayan divinatory session is akin to observing a therapy session
in modern Western society or listening in at a confessional. Not many people
in the West would be willing to let an anthropologist observe such an intimate
proceeding. There was yet another obstacle in making observations. In
Guatemala an Ixil daykeeper's divinations are held in a land with overgrown
pyramids, four world crosses (each representing one of the four day god year
bearers—that is, one of the four days a new calendar round starts with), the
cemetery and its "comun" (where praying is done to long-departed ancestors),
and many other shrines and sacred spots. When I asked Shas Koʔw to try some
hypothetical divinations so I could better see how he did it, he was reluctant
to do so because of the concern of local gods and the spirituality of the area.
To get around these problems I invited Shas to make two visits to the University of California, Irvine, campus. By coming up to California, in a totally
different land with none of the Ixil sacred places around us, Shas was willing
to perform hypothetical divinations, laying out the seeds and deriving readings
without real clients and without the full ritual process. In this way I was able
to get a sample of more than fifty hypothetical divinatory readings to add to
the smaller sample of actual divinations. These, along with a filmed recording
of a divination and some records gathered by graduate student John Clement,
made up the database for the analysis. Through a trial-and-error procedure
of successive approximations, I developed a cognitive model that usually produces results similar to those of a daykeeper's for a particular casting. This
model utilizes the attributes associated with the day gods and day numbers
elicited from Shas and which were often cited during explanations of a particular reading.

The building blocks of divinatory readings, similar to the building blocks
of Ixil folktales, are what Vladimir Prop would call "functions" (Propp 1988).
I have referred to them as *eidons* (among other reasons, to avoid confusing
Propp's term with functional theory in anthropology [Colby and Colby
1981]). These cultural patterns are generated by cognitive, or emic, units
whose longevity attests to their vivid, cognitively salient character. Through
standardized divinatory interpretations, these units appear to have the same
distributional characteristics that eidons in folktales and myths do, except that
they are elements of short divinatory readings rather than longer stories.

Day God Attributes

A god with a particular set of attributes used to construct the reading represents each of the twenty days. Any daykeeper can reel the list off to an inquiring ethnographer. Each of the twenty day gods alone have special attributes used in divination. The attributes fall into three categories: kernel meaning, participant class, and event or state. The kernel meaning is the primary symbolic association assigned to the day god. The most salient and most frequently used, the kernel meaning's attributes derive from a rich body of folklore—folktales, myths, and beliefs—as well as background knowledge of numerous prior readings or precedents either from the diviner's own rituals or those of others he witnessed as an apprentice or heard about from other diviners. Though there are minor variations from one daykeeper to another, the general characteristics are rather consistent. When all twenty days are listed, they are always given in the order of the calendar, and this order never varies from one daykeeper to the next. There is also a high concordance for the kernel meaning. Variations are more frequent with the secondary attributes.

Stories or readings are determined by stringing together various attributes that can fit the narrative grammar. If, for example, the day god, ʔImuš, should appear in one of the talking positions of the layout, then the diviner has to construct a story that contains at least one attribute for this day. Each reading is usually a newly created combination of standard elements and unique embellishments that may apply to the client's situation. Thus, with ʔImuš occupying one of the talking positions, the daykeeper will choose among the following attributes to weave into his story: House god, house, females, clothes, or penance. What he chooses will depend on what other days have fallen into the remaining speaking positions, which of the thirteen numbers are associated with them, and what the diviner already knows about the client's situation either from prior acquaintance or from the initial conversation prior to the ritual.

Client Attributes

In the absence of specific information needed about the client there are generic or default presuppositions that go with what the diviner observes about the client, most notably attributes of age and gender. Determining what these presuppositions are would in itself be an illuminating ethnographic task. One can start with a rudimentary and rather obvious list for a client: has spouse; has children; has other relatives (living and dead); is about average in wealth; is a maize farmer (if man), works in the house (if woman); house contains an altar for ritual.

This list is then expanded with more specific details in the pre-ritual discussion between the daykeeper and the client. The problem that brings the client to the daykeeper, usually an illness, is assumed to be caused by supernatural intervention as a form of punishment for some transgression, mistake, or neglect on the part of the client. It is this misdeed and which of the gods is punishing that the diviner has to discover. Thus, when the client appears, the daykeeper inquires about details not simply of the sickness (which is not entirely irrelevant because it can sometimes, by its nature, yield a clue to the identity of the punishing god) but also about details of the client's past. The default list is thus revised and more information added to flesh out the picture of the client and his situation.

In analyzing the divinatory cases salience appears to be a determining factor for client attributes. Some attributes of the client are more salient than others, being more likely to be the cause of some kind of behavior or event that would anger one of the gods. By classifying the various attributes and circumstances into three progressively more salient groupings, based on the cases at hand, I arrived at the following attribute categories that can attach to the client:

Class 1: Ascriptive attributes such as age or generation, gender, and various physical attributes.

Class 2: Specific events that are likely to have consequences such as marriages, failed courtships, divorces, and having bought or sold land or other substantial properties.

Class 3: Circumstantial or acquired attributes such as wealth and ownership, social prestige and religious positions, being an alcoholic or having a quarrelsome nature or being neglectful of house, household shrine, or maize fields.

The three classes represent three levels of salience that come out in the readings, the first class being the lowest, the second an intermediate level of salience, and the third the highest level of salience.

These attributes can point to more than a single type of god-angering misdeed or transgression. By assigning weights to attributes and transferring those weights to the appropriate transgression, the aggregated weights will give salience to one or a small number of transgressions. Then when the seed layout is counted, some of the numbers and gods in the speaking days will resonate with these salient possibilities. This resonance acts as a confirmation that establishes the key elements of the reading (for more details on how the model works see Colby and Colby [1981]).

Layout Determinations

To get a predicate for a reading, one can derive a transgression from the particular deity that appears in a speaking day according to that deity's attributes (for example, if it is the maize god, the problem may be associated with maize growing activities; if the house god, it is perhaps a domestic difficulty). There are also classes of deities, such as those associated with the earth god, those associated with departed ancestors, or one of the four year bearers. Once a transgression has been chosen it has to be configured with the client, and with other objects or beings (in the participant class) as possible ingredients for a story or reading.

Presumably the daykeeper holds all this provisionally while working through the process. The ethnographic model I've worked out for this process requires a match in the transgression salience list that is represented by adding values according to the day gods and their numerical prefixes in the "talking days" of the layout. The ethnographer then combines all values for the various transgression candidates that match in the two lists and selects the one with the highest value as the predicate for the reading.

Obviously the diviner does not consciously look things up in a table or add up numbers and make a choice. Nor does the use of quantitative indices of salience mean that daykeepers consciously use numbers in their heads in attending to salience. The numerical values represent a hypothesized marking system or a neural excitation level of salience. They are simply ad hoc values that work optimally for the model, given the data available. Salience is the key element in divination. It is derived, presumably, from some unconscious calculation of frequency and importance in the diviner's head, to which my ethnographic model with its three-valued salience system is only an approximation. That something like an unconscious calculation must go on in the head of the diviner is not remarkable. Recently, studies by Elissa Newport and her students show that even small children must be guided in their language development by an unconscious ability to deal with salience through estimation of probabilities of sound and word occurrences (Gleitman and Newport 1995). It is likely that unconscious neurological processes do involve the selection of elements based on the degree of neural excitation and probability estimates, which is why I needed numbers for part of the model.

The speaking positions not used for the wrongdoing predicate can provide qualifiers and descriptors for the participants involved with other predicates. They, too, must match the possibilities of the client situation. Thus, in addition to the actual layout of the palo pito seeds representing the days in the count, the diviner utilizes information he has about the client and also about the general cultural expectations concerning the situation in which the client finds him- or herself. This information includes different weightings or saliences assigned to different aspects of the client's situation and attributes. All this goes into the decision process, where the diviner must identify the event that has offended one of the gods and whether that god or some other supernatural being is involved. All this information is then put together in a reading that is pronounced to the client. The basic process of matching has this rationale: the god is communicating to the diviner, but the diviner may be imperfect in his ability to correctly interpret what the god is saying, so that alternative readings might suggest themselves. The diviner's task is to find which of these several possible readings is the "true" reading that one or more of the day gods are communicating.

Thus a divinatory reading requires the combination of a decision model consisting of several modules and a narrative grammar that determines the order or case relation of the elements chosen for the reading. The key elements in this process involve (1) the transgression of the client and what the offending event and its consequence has been; (2) the notification of one or more gods by a notifier who can be an offended mortal or a god; and (3) the punishment and the god doing the punishing that has caused the client's misfortune and has brought him to the diviner.

In all this there is no active input from the client beyond what he reveals about the situation in the discussion that precedes the divination ritual, unless it be an occasional interjection or nod as the daykeeper gives his reading. Afterward there may be further discussion between the daykeeper and client.

In summary, both the default system and the salience rules are keyed to client attributes: age, sex, marital status, wealth, and other attributes. These, in turn, are linked to a knowledge system carried in the daykeeper's head that deals with the kinds of problems and concerns that clients with these attributes typically take with them to the divinatory consultation. The day-keeper proceeds from general assumptions to revisions among elements of those assumptions, and from the default set to some revision of it. This list of likely problems involves transitivity relations that place restraints on how they are matched with salience values derived from the reading. By transitivity rela-tion I mean types of case relations that in divination are represented in terms both of prescribed norms and high frequency transgressions of those norms.

Divinatory Functions

There are undoubtedly innumerable psychophysiological, social, and cultural functions of different types of divination around the world. Among those exemplified by Ixil calendrical divination are (1) the providing of a sense of cultural coherence, (2) the instruction of the members of a society in impor-tant religious beliefs, and (3) the opportunity to give expression to the sense of disequilibria and stress that may have brought the individual to the diviner.

Coherence

Within any particular culture-using society, stories, conversations, and reason-ing generally draw upon cognitive procedures and knowledge structures that have been generalized to apply to more than a single genre. This underlying cul-tural logic would have to have some degree of system coherence and, with the integration that coherence brings, provide for the maintenance of tradition.

The divinatory readings constitute part of a meta-level story in the sense that the sickness or problem is its motivating element causing the client to consult a daykeeper. When the client is given a divinatory explanation and afterward holds a curative ritual in which the appropriate supernatural beings are addressed, this is the engagement or main action of the story. Whether or not the client is cured is the story's final outcome. This sequence is mirrored in actual folktales of the Ixil where a person becomes sick and finds himself transported to either the skyworld or the underworld. The story ends back at the protagonist's house, where he is either cured or dies (Colby and Colby

1981). Meta-level stories like these have a powerful influence when they are conceptualized as a template for one's own life experience where a segment of that experience is processed through divination and curative rituals.

Instruction

Calendrical readings express various aspects of the cultural logic that shapes Ixil interpretations of their world and the behavior of people in that world. This is a particularly powerful form of instruction because of the high emotional affect involved. Learning is more effective under conditions of emotional arousal. All rituals are characterized by emotional mobilization, particularly those that relate to stressor situations like social conflict, crop failure, illness, and other misfortunes. Since sick individuals are obviously stressed by whatever sickness has caused them to seek a cure, curing rituals tap into these emotional aspects. Nor is sickness the only occasion for a divinatory consultation. Situations other than sickness cover a broad range of human concerns: keeping a full granary, having access to currency or barter goods, avoiding enmities, protecting one's family, making crucial decisions, and dealing with troubling events. In short, any matters that deal with success as individually or locally conceptualized can be areas of concern that would lead to a calendrical divination. They all are potential sources of anxiety and stress mobilization. Because of this a divination is instructional in the strongest sense, inasmuch as learning under emotional mobilization, while not an optimal mode of learning or education, apparently effects strong neural activation (D'Aquili et al. 1979; D'Aquili and Laughlin 1975; Laughlin 1997; Laughlin et al. 1992). While Ixil calendrical divination is more intellectual and less emotional than those forms of divination in which possession figures so dramatically, as with Ndembu basket divination, calendrical divination nevertheless involves a special mind state, as do the subsequently prescribed curing rituals.

Expressive Unburdening
and Some Comparative Notes

Recent findings point to a beneficial physiological effect that the expression or narrating of anxiety-producing experiences can have for an individual. Those who tell or write about negative experiences, especially traumatic ones, have fewer bodily symptoms and illnesses than those who keep them suppressed without expression (Pennebaker 1997; Pennebaker et al. 1989). This dimension of the healing process is undoubtedly tapped by divinatory practices.

Giving expression need not be confined to the patient, as Edith Turner (this volume) illustrates in her description of a Ndembu divining and healing rite, Ihamba. In that ritual other members of the patient's community give expression as well. During the ritual the members of a patient's family and the community suggest possible causes for her resentment based on their personal knowledge of the patient's history. After a long and arduous process of questioning by eliciting yes-no answers (indicated by the presence or absence of the client's responsive bodily shaking), the pain disappears. The pain is believed to be caused by the intrusion of the tooth of a deceased person, a tooth that, like the spirit of the deceased, has its own agency. Once the spirit owner of the tooth is identified and named, it is persuaded to come out of the body.

This Ndembu participatory ritual is not simply an expression of the patient's own internal view but an expression of the community that seeks an empathic matching with the patient's inchoate understandings of her own pain. Thus a socially derived conflict is transduced into a physical pain that is alleviated only when transduced back into a social expression. This process, incidentally, has an advantage over the therapy common in the West since Freud's time. The members of the community who participate in the ritual have lived and interacted with the patient on a daily basis. They thus have intimate knowledge of the patient's past behavior. That contrasts markedly with the Western therapist, who has to go on just how and what the patient remembers or chooses to reveal to the therapist. Further, by consulting a group, one can learn something from the degree of unanimity of answer to the questions put to the group by the diviner.

In contrast, while Ixil divinatory consultations provide an expressive interchange that is assuaging to a stressed individual, the interaction involved is principally between the diviner and the patient, rather than with members of the wider community. Very often the Ixil diviner may not have had any previous association with the patient, so that the burden is on the skill of the diviner and the information provided by the patient. A heavier burden is also placed upon the divinatory system itself, which, rather than a simple yes-no narrowing of the condition's cause, points to numerous possible explanations made up from standardized elements. Even there, the cure does not take place in the initial divination itself but only after subsequent rites of propitiation and atonement have taken place.

The Quintessential Character of Divination

Divination should have a central place in ethnographies of societies that practice it because so much that is important in that society is encapsulated in a divinatory system. It is a quintessential representation of life in the society.

This is certainly true of Ixil divination. The four year bearers, or ʔalkaaltes on which a new year can start are mirrored by the alcalde, or mayor, of an Ixil town. There is also a scribe day god, just as in the town hall. There are gods representing the household, maize growing, money and wealth, women's concerns, ancestral spirits, heaven, and the underworld. There is an entire cosmology and worldview represented by these gods; indeed, the most essential aspects of Ixil cultural systems are all there. No other cultural production covers so many essential characteristics of Ixil belief and behavior and in such an encapsulated manner.

In Ndembu basket divination, just as in Ixil calendrical divination, there are attributions and explanations of antisocial motives like jealousy, selfishness, and revenge. Explanations for these motives include circumstances of inheritance, social organization, economics, and personal relations. In short, an extensive folk theory of behavior and motivation with its ethics, folk psychology, and the rest can be derived from a large collection of divinatory readings.

MAGIC NUMBERS THREE TO FOUR AND TWENTY TO SIXTY-FOUR. Ndembu basket diviners construct readings on the basis of the same range of key symbolic objects as that of the Ixil. Basket divination uses twenty to thirty objects that are shaken and thrown (as one winnows wheat with a shallow, almost flat, round basket). The corresponding "objects" represented in the seed layout of Ixil divination are the day gods, and these, too, at an exact number of twenty, are coincident with the lower limit of the Ndembu range. The day gods have a rich set of symbolic attributes, as do the Ndembu basket objects. The thirteen numbers in the Ixil calendar do not figure in readings in the same way as the day gods; the numbers add only two or possibly three more attributes to any reading, that of good, bad, and possibly neutral, though these could actually multiply the number of attributes associated with each day god. The day numbers also figure in determining salience and hence affect the selection for what is thought to be the gods' true reading.[1]

In Ndembu basket divination, the top three or four objects are the ones used for interpretation. In Ixil calendrical divination the speaking days in the far right column of the layout are used for the interpretation, and these too are typically three or four in number. Interestingly, in Bathonga divination, objects like domestic and wild animal bones, tortoise shells, and stones, once cast upon the ground cloth, have four "speaking" clues: the side on which the bones fall; the direction in which they point; their disposition with regard to each other; and the relation of male objects to female objects.

The total number of Bathonga objects is the highest of the three, at sixty-four, two to three times larger than Ixil or Ndembu divinatory systems (Junod 1927, 2:552). I suspect that these numbers, like the magic number seven (Miller 1956), reflect a set of cognitive restraints and combinatorial requirements that are universal to all complex divination systems, a hypothesis that would be not too difficult to test or revise. The chief challenge lies in accounting for the number of alternate meanings (the degree of multiple vocalities) for a single divinatory object, a number that should diminish as the number of objects increases and vice versa.

That is, the configuration or combined divinatory sentence is determined from the divinatory stimuli, each of which is multivocal in its symbolic references. Multivocality for a set of three or four speaking positions is necessary in order to meaningfully match a link to known characteristics of the client's situation.

AUTHORITY. In a cross-cultural study, Michael and Cindy Winkelman found that as societies become more complex and authority relations extend beyond a local community to a large one with numerous hierarchical relations, there is a shift from voluntary soul flight mind states to possession mind states and other neurophysiological conditions (Winkelman and Winkelman 1991). This reflects a need to legitimize authority. In a local community the shaman is the ultimate authority in spiritual matters, but in larger societies local experts are seen to be comparatively less powerful. As in most other rituals in a more complex society, there is the need for supernatural authority beyond that represented simply by the diviner. In Ndembu divination the diviner is possessed by the spirit of a diviner-ancestor who may cause the diviner to tremble and shake the basket. Ixil daykeepers vest their authority in the day gods, who communicate with daykeepers in dreams and through the divining process.

Religious authority need not always be personalized in terms of direct spiritual possession or messages from specific gods. Authority might also come from a more depersonalized cosmic force, which I suspect is more characteristic among segments within large-scale advanced civilizations as with the Tao Te Ching and the I Ching of China.

Ethnographic Differences

In contrasting Ndembu basket divination with Ixil calendrical divination there are some ethnographically revealing differences:

POWER RELATIONS. Aside from the difference concerning the social nature of the divinatory consultation, there is a difference in power relations. Ixil calendrical divination appears to be a more authoritarian system than that of Ndembu divination, which has more fluidity and social participation. Also, though embedded in a rich context of lore and history, there is no invariant, explicit set of symbolic objects among the Ndembu that takes the listlike form of gods that the Ixil daykeepers recite. Ndembu participatory orientation versus Ixil individualistic orientation may be due to the greater emphasis on the control of life by kin groups among the Ndembu in contrast to the (relatively) low level of kinship interest and influence among the Ixil.

CHANNELING OF AFFECT. With the Ndembu system there is a social advantage in separating malevolent forces from benevolent ones within the same spirit. Extracting the tooth from a patient gets rid of the bad without demonizing the spirit owner of the tooth. Indeed, because the divination and curing can occur simultaneously and with serious and empathic community effort, the experience must have a highly significant positive value to be treasured by the cured patient. The Ixil, in contrast, do not work directly in the same manner. Indeed, calendrical divination is not the actual healing ceremony, which is prescribed in the divination. The healing ceremony itself is carried out by a different specialist, the *b'aalwactiiš* (literally, "father before god"), who is less familiar with the calendar. There is among these, however, a high priest *(b'oʔq'ol b'aalwactiiš)* who keeps the day count and determines the dates of communitywide ceremonies, particularly relating to the religious brotherhoods, or *cofradías,* which were established by the Spanish priests after the conquest.

Linkage of Adaptive Potential to Neural Models

For anyone to successfully negotiate a changing environment, as humans so often must do, it is necessary to maintain neural maps or models of that environment in its material, social, and symbolically interpreted aspects. It is also necessary to have a model of the self that is a multisystemic process dealing with all three realms at different levels. The biological/material self starts at the cellular immunological level, where self is distinguished from foreign elements posing a danger to the self. It projects on through to higher levels and eventually to a general bodily awareness. The social self involves one's sense of identity through family and other people of the same reference group and, if under threat from outside, may give rise to such defenses as an ethnic closing of the ranks. The symbolic self involves sense of identity in terms of language spoken, religious association, ideologies, and other symbolically mediated relationships that, in a defensive stance, have special emotional power. These different selves are cognitively modeled and are clearly scanned during divination. Indeed, a consultation must be motivated by a state of anxiety or disharmony in the neural model.

Adaptive Potential and Ixil Divination

How are the desired conditions of adaptive potential spoken to in Ixil divination? I have not developed any quantitative measures for divinatory effects, so this question is answered here only on an intuitive basis. In the material realm a sense of control is established in the daykeeper's ritual through the identification of a cause and the prescription of corrective rituals to enhance this sense of control.

However, the second condition in the material realm, diversity and openness to diversity, does not seem to be especially high in Ixil divinatory situations, which, through a tradition built on standardized interpretations, enforces uniformity of belief patterns for the patient, his family, and Ixil society in general.

In the social realm the cultural logic involving prescribed social behavior is very much a part of the divinatory process, and social harmony is often a stated goal. Further, the social support of the client's family at the divination may be beneficial. However, different societies show a divergence in degree of affection shown toward children (Rohner 1975, 1986), and this colors all social relations in a society. My intuitive judgment is that Ixil beliefs and cultural logic are somewhere in a mid- to low-range of affection, as reflected in its focus on punitive gods. Spiro and D'Andrade (1958) have shown an important relationship between supernatural beliefs and socialization practices in societies. Among the Maya, Vogt has documented a close relationship between social organization and the organization of supernaturals (Vogt 1969).

In the symbolic realm, coherence and creativity varies with the diviner's own personal predilections as well as those of the client. While the divinatory process involves the creation of specific interpretations, this creative activity is constrained by the system and by the repertoire of stock phrases the daykeeper may use in these interpretations. The divinatory mechanisms are a force for preserving tradition, not for encouraging creativity.

These various conditions of adaptive potential work best in their appropriate realms and sometimes work against adaptive potential when carried over to a different realm. For example, a major part of efficacy in the material realm has to do with control. Control in the social realm, however, has a different meaning and outcome. In the social realm, if people are regarded simply as objects or possessions to be controlled by others without regard for their own concerns, it would have negative effects for those who are being controlled and are consequently denied their autonomy. Regarding individuals as possessions or objects is dehumanizing. Control, then, can have opposite consequences depending on whether it is conceptualized in the biophysical system operating in the material realm—that is, control over objects—or is in the social realm. One of the things that divination does is to place control into the hands of the day gods and hence remove some of the onus from actions of fellow humans.

There are universal human characteristics that underlie all cultural systems. Just as all languages have noun and verb concepts, root elements of thought apply to other aspects of culture as well. Thus there is some degree of similarity among societies when it comes to folk beliefs of success. A casual inspection of readings by Ixil Mayan daykeepers, the Chinese I Ching, and others does not contradict this. In the broadest theoretical sense, then, if divination focuses on notions of folk success, it also should contribute, over the very long run, either to some degree of comparative (within the society) biocultural success of its practitioners and clients or at least to some mitigation of stressor situations endemic to a particular society. Thus divination has relevance to processes both of natural and cultural selection.

Concluding Observations: Ixil Divination as Decision Models

The Ixil divinatory model combines a grammar with decision modules that link to identity and success goals. These all connect with other cultural systems and representations of the perceived environmental field. A divinatory grammar alone does not predict a particular output but rather a range of possible or acceptable output sequences. Like a language grammar, it does not predict the content of any spoken or written communication. It only predicts its form and the function of its constituent parts. The decision component, in contrast, predicts content, the nature of the conclusions communicated by the diviner in a divinatory session. The process is information specific, paradigmatically organized, and usually has a variety of inputs but focuses on one or a few ultimate predictions or decisions as the output.

In descriptive practice the grammar component operates with emic categories, while the decision model component has to include etic data. The emic-etic distinction for divination is not as clear-cut a distinction as it is at the phonemic level in language, where the great variety of phonetic sounds actually made, or that possibly could be made, by a human speaker when spoken are categorized in the brain in terms of a system of distinctive features that define normally anywhere from around fifteen to forty-five phonemes, depending on the language (Jakobson et al. 1952).

Divination is an imperfect way to maximize biocultural success inasmuch as it follows local notions of folk success rather than a theoretical co-evolutionary focus of biocultural success. However, it provides strong mechanisms of defense that, even if illusory, nevertheless can have real effects on neurotransmitters, immunological functioning, and other information substance of the body, which all figure in the healing process.

The production of stress substances like cortisol and the catecholamines depends upon how a person perceives his situation and what his response to this perception is likely to be. Expansive responses are made possible by high adaptive potential, which is shaped very largely by cultural systems. Defensive responses on the other hand are more primitive and would be influenced by predilections that are more strongly encoded in genetic expression, with cultural shaping less pronounced. Divination provides a perception and interpretation of troubling situations that sets up a chain of responses provided by a cultural system that has survived across generations and through environmental perturbations in ways that seek ever closer approximations to optimal functioning. This openness to change varies with the divinatory system, however, and the cross-genre, cross-domain organization of cultural logic acts as a strong guardian of the status quo in cultural traditions. When events move beyond the capacity of a complex divinatory system to adjust, other forms of religious action may fill the breach, as appears to be happening with the rapid economic and religious changes in much of Guatemala today, some of it reaching to the more remote areas in Ixil country.

Note

1. Generally, the high salience numbers six and eight have positive significance; nine and thirteen, negative. However, unlike the day god names, numbers did not have special attributes, as they do for the Maasai—for instance, as described in this volume by Fratkin.

4

Owner of the Day and Regulator of the Universe

Ifa Divination and Healing among the Yoruba of Southwestern Nigeria

JACOB K. OLUPONA

Examination of the complex nature of divination and healing among the Yoruba people of southwestern Nigeria reveals the Ifa divinatory process as a performance in which the diviner, the client, and the social and cosmological order of the Yoruba people interact to bring about meaningful desired results of healing to individuals, groups, or the entire community. Ifa refers to both the divination process and the god of divination (Orunmila). A successful divination process arranged for healing occurs through the combined agencies of extra human beings and spirits, such as Ifa, the spirit of divination; Ori, the spiritual (inner) head; Osanyin, the god of medicine; and Esu, the messenger of the 201 gods in the Yoruba universe.

Since all these agencies are intricately interconnected in Yoruba cosmology, and their roles in divination and healing rituals are defined in the context of the Yoruba moral and social universe, it is important to lay bare this religion and worldview. The place of these agencies in the larger picture of Yoruba society and culture—and their relevance to divination processes and, ultimately, to healing—is also examined. Through the agency of Ifa, healing takes place when the diviner successfully diagnoses the source of a client's illness and presents and carries out the necessary sacrifice. Most sacrifices are offerings rendered to supernatural forces, whether the *orisa* or the malevolent agents, witches, and wizards. It is assumed by the diviner and the client that these offerings *(ebo)* are "substitutes" that Ifa spiritual forces are persuaded to take in return for the release of a person they otherwise vow to destroy. Thus, sacrifice is the ultimate control mechanism in divination. The healing process also consists of prayer and magical incantations that compel the spirit world to hearken to the voice and message of Ifa.

Yoruba Cosmology and Moral Order

Yoruba cosmology and moral order constitute an important intellectual and interpretive tradition for understanding divination processes and healing practices. An important entry point to the knowledge and resources of this tradition is the cosmogonic myth, which states that the world began in the sacred city of Ile-Ife, located in the center of the southwestern region of Nigeria.

The Yoruba universe, the created world, consists of three tiered places: the sky or celestial space *(orun),* the world or earthly level *(aye),* and the underworld or the earth *(ile).* Each of the three levels has a host of spiritual beings that communicate and circulate among the three spheres. However, each level is the permanent abode of specific beings: the sky is the permanent home of the Supreme Being, Olodumare. The earth is inhabited by 201 gods (the orisa) and is the world where humans live temporarily for the span of their individual lives. The underworld is the place of the dead. It is also the domain of the earth deity, whose cult is very significant in the regulation of the moral order. The sky, the abode of the supreme god, is the powerhouse where the control of and knowledge about human destiny is maintained. Creation of humans born into this world takes place here, and it is here that individuals select their destiny *(Ori)* before they set out on their journey to the world.

The world realm occupies a peculiar place in the Yoruba cosmology in that it is the most visibly active realm of the three spheres. Not only does it harbor the gods and spirits, for humans, but it is also regarded as a marketplace where humans enter for the purpose of trading and as a desert at the completion of their trading activities. The earth is also a free space where humans and gods interact through the medium of special hierophanies such as shrines, road junctions, sacred hills, rivers, and water regarded as manifestations of these deities. Some better known gods in the Yoruba pantheon assisted in populating the world at the time of creation. There was Ogun, god of war and owner of the cutlass who cleared the path for other deities to pass. There was Ifa, god of divination and the wisest of the gods; Ori, the divinity of destiny; Osun, the goddess of the River Osun and the only female deity in the first batch of orisa; and finally Esu, the trickster, messenger of the gods and the divine police officer.

The orisa, or the spirits, are seen as capable of performing both benevolent and malevolent acts, depending on the nature and circumstances of their encounter with humans. In addition to the gods, there are also the ancestors in the Yoruba moral universe. They are usually referred to as the "living dead" because they are regarded as still active in spirit, although they are dead physically. These ancestors exist in the underworld. Ancestral beings are linked to the lineage and family structure and ritual lives of the group. Ancestral belief is connected to the Yoruba idea of life on earth and the consequences of human activities in life and the implicit quest for immortality. A necessary part of any cosmology and moral order is the explanation of evil and misfortune in the world. Inevitably, humans suffer tragic misfortunes such as loss and sickness. In addition to the deities and spirits, malevolent spirit entities *(ajogun)* are present. They personify forms of misfortunes such as loss, paralysis, debt, or curse. Some scholars postulate that the ajogun are in constant struggle with good spiritual forces (Abimbola 1997). I doubt if there is any hard evidence of opposition and conflict between the ajogun and the orisa.

Prayer and curse are intricately linked, and the orisa are capable of executing both. The same principle applies to the use of herbs by diviners and medicine men and women. As Pierre Verger points out, the medicinal and magical action expected "of specific leaves will depend on what function they are meant to perform for the client. For example, a herbal leaf used in a medicine that produces a bad effect against witches may also be classified as a beneficent leaf because it offers protection for the same client against evil activities of the witches" (Verger 1976:246).

Yoruba tradition espouses the reality of a special innate force belonging only to women. This has been erroneously labeled a negative energy called *aje,* but the innate power, controlled and exercised by women, may not always espouse a negative principle. To ensure some form of control in the world, in the unyielding moral order and in the everyday reality in the Yoruba world, priests, diviners, and medicine men and women are available on earth to stand between the affairs of humans on earth, the spirit world, and the Supreme Being in heaven. Through their initiation, years of apprenticeship, and regular consultation, they acquire wisdom, knowledge, and other supernatural powers to enable them to intervene on behalf of humans. They can be consulted to guide humans onto the right path.

In this complex religious worldview, Yoruba diviners *(babalawo)* are responsible for mediating between humans and the supernatural world. The babalawo is the locus of supernatural power in the community, the arbiter of social tension, who maintains daily negotiation of life and misfortune of humans with the gods, spirits, and the ancestors. The prestige and authority of the babalawo are enhanced not because they possesses special mystic power, as does the shaman, but because they possess a significant body of esoteric knowledge acquired in the process of training as a diviner.

Method and Essence of Divination

The Yoruba consult Ifa divination for a wide range of personal, social, and religious matters—for example, before undertaking important obligations such as marriage or travel to a distant place, or on occasions of uncertainty. One of the more significant times the Yoruba consult divination is during difficult illnesses, especially when they desperately need an explanation of the cause and cure of prolonged illness. My explanation of the Ifa divinatory process relates to its role in uncovering the cause of a client's illness and restoring the client to a good state of health by first laying out the divination consultation. The essential divination process is a logical one, illustrated by interpreting symbolic and metaphysical meanings implicit in consulting Ifa. A client visits a babalawo to determine the cause of his or her illness and to find the best cure. The client sits on a mat in front of the babalawo, who lays out the divination paraphernalia, consisting of a divinatory chain (a string on which is tied eight halves of nuts) and a tray spread with a yellowish wood dust. Each nut on the chain has a concave and a convex side. The nuts may be decorated with small beads or a chain. The client takes a coin or currency, touches her forehead with it, and whispers into it her prayer or request, asking Ifa to reveal the secret behind her ailment and to find an appropriate solution to the problem. The client places the coin in front of the diviner, touching the chain with the coin, as if conveying her request to the instruments of divination.

The diviner begins the divination session by the invocation of Ifa. Ifa is showered with presents as an emphatic appeasement to assist in the process, and the diviner requests Ifa not to mislead his client. The invocation consists of the diviner's homage to the spirit world, the ancestors, the great diviners before him, and the four directions of the Yoruba universe as he moves the chain to the front, back, left, right, and center of the tray. He acknowledges all the relevant spiritual forces connected to the process. To cast the divination, the diviner holds the chain in the middle and throws it on the mat, making a "U" shape on the floor, so that the four halves of the nuts fall on each side. The nut halves will expose either convex or concave sides, thus displaying sixteen possible forms of the signature of Ifa. Each signature stands for an *odu* (divinatory symbol), which contains several verses of oral poems. The diviner then recites the appropriate odu that appears in the divination castings, and the client listens carefully. After the recitation, the client will say if any of the poems is relevant to his illness. It is at this stage that the client may reveal to the diviner the nature of his illness. The diviner will interpret the text and, through further questioning, arrive at a definite cause of his client's ailment. The diviner will prescribe the appropriate remedy, usually a sacrificial ritual, and the medicinal herbs that may cure the illness.

While the *opele* chain is the most frequently used in divination performances, sometimes the diviner may use a more prestigious and elaborate form, the *ikin,* a divination with sixteen palm nuts. The same result is obtained in using the opele divination chain. Each divination session produces an odu divination sign from 256 possible signs.

What is the essence of the divinatory process? Two forms of the divination process often cited in African societies are the mechanical and the mystical. The former involves the manipulation of divining instruments or objects to arrive at an appropriate answer and treatment for the client. The latter centers on possession by, and appeal to, a deity. Marshall has argued in the case of the !Kung San's divination system that mechanical forms of divination fall into the category of magic and "secular" rather than religion because they do not involve communication with mystical powers (Marshall 1962; Child and Child 1993:82).

Although Ifa divination is primarily mechanical, the preamble to the Ifa divination session indicates that mystical powers in control of the cosmos are invoked. Ifa divination is also premised on the communication process between the diviner and the spiritual agencies responsible for proper divination performances. Bascom remarked that the result is influenced by divine guidance (Bascom 1969:70). Like in the Ainu divination process in Japan (Coon 1971:732), an invocation and prayer to the mystical forces precede the actual mechanical manipulation of divinatory instrument. The invocation of Ifa provides an important clue to the rationality of its divination mechanism. What are the meanings and rationale of Ifa divination performance for healing? Our exploration of the three-stage process of Ifa divination—consultation, diagnosis, and sacrificial offerings—begins with the ritual invocation. It is a poetic ritual prayer addressed to the relevant cosmic powers (the gods, ancestors, etc.) that the diviner knows could influence the outcome of his client's diagnosis.

The diviner is convinced that the proper invocation to Ifa guides his consultation to the right path, so that an unequivocal truth may emerge. By his invocations, the diviner symbolically dramatizes the creation of the cosmos, the three-tiered layers of the Yoruba world. At the core of divination is the idea that the universe and the events therein are guarded by the spiritual and temporal ontology of Ifa. The regulator of events in the universe, Agbayegun, and his divination activities, brings order to a potentially chaotic universe. The spiritual dimension refers to four cardinal points of the universe plus the center, the fifth and most central point.

The five important axes of powers are replicated in the Ifa divination tray. The divination tray, usually a carved wooden structure, represents the universe. The circular tray is a "replica or reproduction, on the human scale, of the cosmos [and] of creation itself. It is an *imago mundi,* an image of the original world order" (Livingston 1993:62). At times in the course of divination, the babalawo may draw these axes in the yellow powder on the Ifa tray, indicating the connection between the four cardinal points and the center. The center of the divining tray, like the center of the world, is the link to the center of heaven, the abode of the Supreme God, Olodumare, and the storehouse of sacred knowledge required to unravel the "secrecy" surrounding the client's ailment and to disclose hidden forces and the cause of the client's ailment. This is analogous to Turner's (1973) notion of the center "out there," a place outside the immediate domain of the client, which nevertheless can be accessed through divination.

The visual signs of placing the divining chain opele on the four corners and the center of the tray captures an intricate religious symbolism. By this visual act, the tray becomes the earthly sacred center from which the diviner makes present the heavenly center and the ultimate storehouse of Ifa's knowledge (Pedaya 1998:85). Ifa divination also connects the diviner's probing act with the source of the client's being, the *Ori* (personal destiny). By this process, divination exposes the client's destiny, the realities that condition his formation, and the configuration of sacred powers governing ceaseless transformations (Sullivan 1988:346). The essence of the divination ritual process, then, is to access the truth about the client's situation. As Peek remarked, "As a ritualized means of acquiring normally inaccessible information, divination utilizes a culture-specific, non-normal mode of cognition" recognized and believed to be true by both diviner and client (Peek 2000:26).

Spiritual Agencies in Divination and Healing

In the divination process, diagnosis and cure of illness directly involve three spiritual deities: Ori/Ori Inu (divinity of destiny); Osanyin, god of herbal medicine; and Esu, the messenger of the gods. These agencies have a role in the divination process and consequently in healing. At the core of divination performances for individuals is Ori, the ontological self. For individuals, Ori plays a very significant role in the diagnostic process and healing. Ori is variously called the second self or duplicate self and is regarded as a deity in his own right. Like the Chi in Igbo tradition, Ori is the ego's ontological self who directs movement and behavior. It is also akin to the Fon notion of Se, which Montilus describes as "the invisible force that directs life" (Blier 1995:176). Several Ifa verses describe the relationship of Ori to the destiny of the individual as a sacred pact that happens at the time individuals are molded in heaven by Obatala, the god of the creation of physical bodies. The Ori represents one's destiny, and personal self is the seat of wisdom.

When a child is born with the visible physical features resembling the child's relative, the inner head (Ori Inu), concealed under the outer Ori (Ori Ode), is regarded as the most important spiritual feature of an individual. In any personal ritual performance, the visible head, regarded as the center of one's being, is the most important ritual spot because it is the passage to a person's inner destiny. Ifa is intricately connected with an individual's Ori because Ifa was privy to the choice of the individual's Ori in heaven. His presence at the juncture of the making of a human being enables Ifa to "access" an individual's destiny through the divination performance and to provide prescribed ritual and herb remedies for turning around bad situations in the individual's life. Ifa in this context is described as "the powerful one that turns a bad Ori (destiny) into a good one."

Moreover, Osanyin, deity of herbal medicine, plays an important role in curing illness. Babalawo healers train rigorously in the art of herbs and sacrifice. The diviner's medicinal knowledge of native plant species is vital to the divination process. Osanyin guides the use of herbal leaves *(ewe Osanyin)*. For example, if the *odu ogunda-okanran* appears on the divination tray in the consultation of a gravely ill client, the babalawo suspects that the forces of witches or wizards are responsible. A leaf referred to as *ido,* or Indian shot *(Canna bidenada bertoloni),* is used as an ingredient in preparing a medicine to counter the forces of witches. The following Ifa incantations are recited in the process of preparing the medicine:

> May the wizard be unable to kill me,
> May the witch be unable to kill me,
> The wizard, no matter how wicked, does not eat ido,
> The witch, no matter how wicked, does not eat ido,
> The wizard is wicked and eats ido,
> May his mouth be heavy. (Verger 1977:45)

If the Odu Ose Meji appears in the similar case of illness, the babalawo may indicate that Osanyin's leaf of *aje ko bale (Croton amatilis),* literally, "witches dare not perch on it," will be used to make a medicine. The following Ifa verses are recited for the medicine:

> You must change to perch on my body,
> Old witch (woman) owner of bird,
> As you have no chance to perch on *aje ko bale.*

A third spiritual figure in divination and healing is Esu—the trickster god, messenger of the gods, gatekeeper, and carrier of sacrifices to the spiritual world. Esu's shrine sits at the gates of a city and in the homes of diviners. Whenever a sacrifice is made to a supernatural being—whether deity, ancestor, or spirit—a morsel from the sacrificial food is offered first to Esu. This offering secures Esu's cooperation to deliver the goods to the appropriate places. Esu does not hesitate to spoil a client's sacrifice if Esu is displeased with the offering. Esu may even infect individuals with pathogens. Esu plays a major role in divination ritual. As a sign of the close relationship with Orunmila, the divination tray carries an icon of Esu's face carved in front. As a babalawo performs divination, Esu watches to ensure a proper ritual. An Ifa invocation alludes to the joint role of Esu and Ifa thus:

> A strong wind is the name we call Ifa.
> A typhoon wind is the name we give to Esu.
> We belong to the lineage of the honored one.
> Oh, Great Strong Wind, turn evil into good for us.
> Oh, Great Whirlwind, turn evil into good for us.

In preserving life and bestowing honor to humans, Ifa and Esu remain close allies. The invocation implores the "superheroes," as whirlwind and typhoon traveling at light speed to turn evil into good. As Blier (1990:43) remarked of Dahomean (Fon) religion, the god of the "whirlwind" and "motion" is associated with "potentiality, great abundance, creativity, and wealth."

The Theory of Disease

As in most African groups, Yoruba theories of sickness and disease are connected to the construction of the world and social and cultural life. *Aye* (the world) is a complex place. Aye here refers to "the surrounding world," the "world of life," and the hidden mystical world as experienced by humans (Jacobsen 1998:79). Essentially, it is thought of as a pleasant place; however, when a Yoruba suddenly utters the word *aye*, it automatically invokes a place full of evil machinations of humans and the gods. The world requires that humans must tread carefully and courteously to survive in it. The world is potentially dangerous because it is inhabited by a variety of human and spiritual beings, gods, ancestors, animals, plants, witches, and sorcerers. On the other hand, life is to be lived to the fullest. The essence of religious life is the quest for the four manifold blessings: life, wealth, children, and longevity *(ire alafia, ire owo, ire omo,* and *ire aiku).* Yoruba peoples seek explanation of sickness and illness in natural and supernatural causes, though the distinction between the two may be quite difficult to make. Because traditional Yoruba theories of sickness tend to relate more to nonnatural causes, the Yoruba seek diagnosis, explanation, meaning, and treatment of disease through the lens of divination practices.

In non-Western traditions, the source of illness often follows a category of natural and unnatural causes (Ortiz De Montellano 1990; Jacobsen 1998). Following the anthropological discipline, Ohnuki-Tierney proposes two broad categories of illness (1981:37). One refers to illness that conforms to the "standard diagnostic culture" and requires standard treatments using "Matura medicine" (37–39). The other is illness caused by supernatural agency, whose cure is religious ritual. The Yoruba disdain such distinctions between natural and personal causes of illness by using a holistic approach to illness and cure for illness.

Traditional Yoruba society can classify any form of prolonged illness as supernatural. Such illnesses are taken to diviners for diagnosis and cure. Even in modern Yoruba society, Western medicine may be considered first, but if the illness persists, divination is a credible option. The primary cause of sickness is located in the sociocultural fabric and the immediate environment of the patient. Sickness is not caused by something "out there," unknown and unimaginable to the afflicted person. As the Yoruba say, "The enemy may reside outside one's house; the instigator of one's misfortune lives within one's household."

This worldview of healing makes diagnosis of diseases much more immediate and locates it within the cultural matrix of the client. During divination, the diviner may interpret an odu that appears to a client to mean that a witch in the client's father's lineage is responsible for the illness or that a neighbor caused a client's constant stomach trouble. The diviner will then ask the client whether he has offended someone in his father's lineage or in the neighborhood. However, through more probing, the diviner will come to a more precise diagnosis.

Illness may result from a number of supernatural forces, gods, spirits, ancestors, witches, and sorcerers. These forces have unlimited influence and control in the affairs of humans in the world. Of all the principle deities in Yoruba cosmology, Esu, the trickster god and messenger of gods, is particularly responsible for causing human misery, especially when any of the gods is offended by humans. Devotees of the orisa who neglect to make regular sacrifices to the deities or neglect to keep their taboos and prohibitions invite sickness and illness. As the messenger of the gods and the one who keeps the records of those who offer and do not offer sacrifice to the gods, Esu is quite equipped to cause affliction and disease among humans. Although all the gods are essentially beneficent, they can cause human sickness. Because of the belief in the underworld agencies of ajogun, Yoruba explanations for evil ultimately lie in the traditional context of witchcraft beliefs. In addition, there is the notion that certain individuals, usually women, possess innate mystical forces. These individuals have access to the spirit realm and are able to use their knowledge of the spirit world to inflict disease on others. Illness is generally interpreted as a state of disequilibria with the spirit world. Witches and wizards manipulate the spirit world, which normally is prone to bestow blessings on individuals in order to cause illness. Bringing this disrupted state of being into wholeness is the task of the diviner and the divination process.

Diagnosis and Interpretation of Odu Divination Texts

The Odu Ifa, the divinatory oral narratives, are central to the healing process. These are composed of myths, proverbs, and legends that make up the mythical worldview of the Yoruba people. The Odu in Yoruba imaginations are also personified as supernatural beings transformed into the spoken words of Ifa. They are verbal manifestations of divine power. These spoken words convey power and imagery of the mythic past. This is similar to the shaman, who in order to obtain a cure for a client must disclose manifest forces by embodying them, acting out, through music, dance, and songs, the symbolic gestures and the supernatural state that conditions his own body and soul (Sullivan 1988:459). Similarly, the diviner recites the appropriate verses that embody the primordial power and events, recalling plausible events that are similar to the client's own situation. By so doing, he convinces the client that in all likelihood his or her situation will be taken care of by Ifa.

I will now describe a divinatory healing session to illustrate further how Ifa acts to heal a client. The gravely ill client or family of a gravely ill child visits a babalawo diviner. Following the process already described above, the diviner casts the opele on his mat. The odu that appears is the *Obaraofun,* a sign of a serious problem. Among other verses, the diviner recites these:

> Oh, ye style-less people, ye unknowledgeable people,
> Ye who eat the pounded yam even as Obaraofun surfaces!
> Did not Ifa awaken because of me?
> Oh, Ifa, please, come to awaken this child for me.
> Oh, Ela, you resuscitated the dying one yesterday.

The verses use the term *child,* which can also be a metaphor for the gravely ill adult. Hearing this dreadful, yet promising, message—that Ifa has the power of inducing life back into the dying "child"—the client confirms that the matter brought before the babalawo for divination is indeed a grave illness. If a daughter, an *abiku* child (a child of repeated birth and death), is about to die, the babalawo reminds the parents of the taboo in serving pounded yam *(iyan)* during the period of the child's illness. Although in Yoruba society the yam is a staple of the evening meal, the verses proclaim that Obaraofun forbids the eating of pounded yam. Perhaps the taboo is a metaphor calling for sobriety, abstinence, and discipline or even fasting—and certainly refraining from indulgence, delicacies, or merriment while an individual may be on the verge of expiring because of serious illness.

After interpreting the sacred verses to the client, the diviner now prescribes the appropriate sacrificial ritual, the offering of a he-goat. It must be slaughtered, put into a calabash container, and placed by the riverbank. The diviner explains that the sacrifice is for the child's heavenly companions who will arrive to release the soul of the dying child. To confirm that the sacrifice is appropriate, the diviner performs divination again, in which Ifa confirms that all is well. The client's parents then leave to perform the curative sacrifice.

The events and stories in divinatory verses are convincing models for the clients to consider. The narratives are archetypes available for the diviner to access in order to assist the client to recover. Several of the narratives are stories of clients in ancient Yoruba city-states who consulted divination on similar issues. In the present divination session, the client is faced with primordial reality and the consequences of either rejecting or accepting Ifa's prescription. However, he is left in no doubt about the authenticity and truth of his own divination session.

As DuBois aptly puts it, in ritual speech the role of the ancient diviner is laminated onto the current diviner, as the role of the ancient client addressee is laminated onto the current client (DuBois 1994:56). The message from Ifa is plausible because of the ultimate origins of the speech in a distant place and time. The diviner decides which part of the oral narratives comes closest to the client's social world and existential situation. The diviner's role then is to interpret the client's situation through the events and meanings the Ifa text conveys and to provide meaning and direction for the client.

Therapy and Sacrificial Ritual

Once divination is performed to determine the cause of illness, healing involves a combination of dispensing herbs and performing a healing or cure. This entails two steps: (1) prescription and application of herbal medicine by the diviner and (2) the performance of sacrificial ritual to appease malevolent spirits identified in the divination process as suspected to be responsible for the client's illness. The first is done with the assistance of Osanyin's herbal medicine. Verger (1977), the most authoritative scholar on Yoruba herbal medicine, has carefully demonstrated that there is a strong causal relationship between the medicinal herbs administered for illness and their religious and symbolic meanings. What seems to differ from other indigenous medical systems is that, in addition to the medicinal leaves, the preparation of the medicine often involves the use of powerful incantations of Ifa oral text, without which the medicine will not be efficacious. The spoken incantations give the medicine its power and *ase* (vital force) that makes the medicine work. The Yoruba also believe that one's Ori plays an important role in therapy. The Ifa verses recited often contain references addressed to the client's Ori to aid in the treatment. "Ori," the Yoruba say, "aids the efficaciousness of herbal medicine."

Sacrificial ritual is the ultimate cure of illness. The diviner will prescribe to the client the appropriate sacrifice to the aggrieved supernatural being. The client may decide to perform the sacrifice alone or may plead with the diviner to carry out the sacrifice on his or her behalf. When sacrificial objects are procured and prepared according to the prescription of Ifa, the sacrifice is taken to an auspicious place. This is usually at the crossroads, junctions, riverbanks, deep forests, or open markets, and places where supernatural spirits are often found. Esu, the bearer of sacrifice, is first offered part of the sacrificial food to appease him and to ensure its safe delivery to the supernatural realm.

The purpose of sacrifice *(ebo)* is to bring about harmony between the social and moral orders. Disequilibria between the world and the heavenly realm is brought about by the individual's sins and offenses against the gods, ancestors, and witches. A good number of sacrifices are substitutes and ransoms to buy back clients whom the witches might have vowed to devour or the gods may have promised to destroy.

In the sacrificial process, the Ifa diviner identifies the particular deity or supernatural being connected with the affairs of his clients and the issues concerned. The forms of sacrifice appropriate for a remedy are related to the nature of the problem and the personality of the spiritual agent. For example, a sacrifice involving Sango, god of thunder, may require sacrificing a ram. Ogun, god of iron, may require sacrificing a dog, and so on. Once a specific sacrifice is determined and prepared, Esu is invoked, fed, and invited to see to the delivery of the offering.

If the propitiatory sacrifice involves offering an animal, the animal is presented to the god with a declaration of the client's intention. For example, a sacrifice to Ogun may state: "Ogun, this is your animal (a dog). My client presents this to you to secure the return of his health. Keep him and his family safe from destruction." The client then touches the animal's head with his own head, during which it is assumed either that the evil embedded in the client's head is transferred to the animal or that the client's inner head aids in the efficacy of the sacrifice.

Sacrificial offerings involve communal participation. Members of the surrounding community, especially the household and neighbors, must partake in the sacrificial meal and offerings. An Ifa text supports this idea. It refers to a client who performed a sacrifice to an aggrieved deity but did not realize that the neighbors must partake of the offering to the gods and ancestors. Therefore, he came back to the diviner to complain that the sacrifice was not effective. The diviner discovered that he failed to give part of the offerings to his neighbors. The text suggests that any sacrifice, be it to avert death or for healing purposes, involves a sacrificial meal shared by the immediate neighbors and households of the client. The logic is that the Yoruba people believe that one of the causes of illnesses is interpersonal crisis among neighbors. However, once a client feeds his neighbor, such a neighbor can no longer be of any harm. As a Yoruba proverb says, "He who partakes of your salt and pepper can no longer cause evil to befall you." It is assumed that such neighbors would bring curses upon themselves because of their ungratefulness.

Conclusion

This chapter explores the construct and meaning of Yoruba cosmology, religious ideas, and the facets of the spiritual and human agencies directly involved in determining the cause of illness and its remedy. For the Yoruba people, Ifa, a complex divination practice and body of knowledge, provides explanation and remedy to illnesses and misfortunes. The babalawo, a priest-diviner, casts his divination chain to arrive at the source of the client's illness and to uncover the human and the spiritual factors responsible for the state of disequilibria in his environment. The babalawo then offers herbal medicines and prescribes appropriate sacrificial ritual to cure the client. Although Ifa is one of the most studied divination systems in Africa, many aspects of it still call for in-depth study. Future research may involve the study of Ifa's encounter with modernity and how it pertains to new forms of disease and their cures—as well as the babalawo themselves and their responses to the new diseases that bring new clients.

Acknowledgments

Research on which this chapter is based was supported in part by the John Simon Guggenheim Fellowship Award and the University of California Humanities Fellowship.

II

VARIETIES OF DIVINATORY EXPERIENCES

5

Divination in
North American Indian
Shamanic Healing

WILLIAM S. LYON

D ivination is found in all American Indian cultures of North America. It appears in many different forms and is put to various uses. However, no comprehensive overview of American Indian divination has ever been published. This chapter focuses only on divination techniques used for diagnosing illnesses. The ethnographic data on diagnostic divination is rather sparse. Only a few field ethnographers have witnessed an actual healing ceremony that includes diagnostic aspects. Furthermore, diagnosis was often held in secret or when the shaman was alone. As such, most accounts of shamanic healing give little detail, if any, with regards to such divinations, with the data coming mainly from field informants who witnessed it versus performed it.

The general pattern of dealing with human illnesses usually begins with the sick person opting for a family-known ("home") remedy. If success is not obtained by this means, then one usually seeks out a professional herbalist. Only as a last resort does one go to a professional shaman who has mastered the art of healing.

The request for a shamanic healing ceremony is always conducted in a culturally prescribed manner. Quite often the request can be as simple as bringing a ritual offering of tobacco to the shaman. Whatever form it takes, the requester must follow the prescribed ritual procedures if the shaman is to be successfully engaged. Nonnatives seeking healing from American Indian shamans usually overlook this aspect and are subsequently often turned away.

Once the shaman has accepted, several other factors need to be in place before the shaman can proceed. Most important is the faith of the patient in the healing ceremony per se. In addition, the patient must also have trust in the shaman. Finally, there has to be a willingness on the part of the shaman's helping spirits to heal the patient.

American Indian shamans normally begin a healing ceremony by first diagnosing the patient's illness. All shamans have their own, personalized diagnostic techniques, and most often these techniques involve some form of divination. However, differences in techniques are of little consequence since the shaman's "diagnostic ability depends more on the intuition, sensitivity, and spiritual power of the healer than on the precision of a particular diagnostic technique" (Cohen 1998:50). The diagnosis is achieved by what Peek (1991:193) terms "non-normal modes of cognition," which "necessitate a heightening of the diviner's state of consciousness" (19).

Common Forms of Divination for Diagnosis

Some ethnographies give the impression that the shaman has not conducted any diagnosis of the patient. For example, it is recorded for a Bear River Waila-ki healing ceremony that "different songs were tried out for their potency. If a patient liked one song especially, it was sung repeatedly in the belief that it was the most powerful song for that individual patient; otherwise the shaman selected the song she judged the most effective" (Nomland 1938:96). However, this same report also indicates the existence of *isnasta* (seeing doctors) within the culture "who could see pains (the disease) in a patient but could not remove them" (96). In the case of powerful shamans it is sometimes reported that they know ahead of time that someone is coming to them for a healing (for example, Frances Philips [Tübatulabal] in Voegelin 1938:72) and what ails them.

There is at least one clear case in which psychometry was used to diagnose a patient. A Creek specialist, the *kila* (diviner or prophet), uses this technique. "His diagnosis consisted merely in the examination of an article of clothing belonging to the sick man. From this he claimed to be able to determine the nature of the disorder and he sent back word accordingly" (Swanton 1928:615). Diagnosis by examining a patient's shirt is also reported for the nearby Yuchi (Speck 1909:132).

The most common form of diagnosis involves the shaman consulting his or her helping spirit(s). The shaman first enters a shamanic state of consciousness (SSC) in order to communicate with these spirits. The record is quite clear in this regard (for example, Gifford 1936:316 [Yavapai]; Koppert 1930:86–87 [Clayoquot]; Seguin 1984:210 [Tsimshian]). Their singing, drumming, rattling, dancing, etc. are SSC induction techniques, albeit this was not realized by earlier ethnographers. Many reports simply state that the shaman seats himself beside the patient and begins to sing, sometimes accompanied by a rattle or a drum.

Information concerning the patient also comes in various ways to a diviner. One common form is the shaman's ability to "see" into the patient with a "supernatural," "x-ray," or "second-sight" type of vision (for example, Curtin 1898:513 [Wintu]; Henry Allen in Elmendorf 1993:217 [Twana]; Jacobs 1939:93 [Coos]). Some shamans cover their eyes in order to obtain such vision (Smith 1940:77–78 [Puyallup-Nisqually]). During this time the shaman is usually dancing (SSC induction) and singing (spirit calling) about the patient.

One of Fools Crow's (Lakota) techniques for diagnosing a patient was to conduct a *Yuwipi* ceremony. During this ceremony, he reported, "I see on my mind-screen the full dimensions of a person's illness" (Fools Crow in Mails 1991:170). The Inuit shaman of the Cumberland Sound and Baffin Land areas sees "through the back of his head" (Boas 1907:154). The Alsea shaman also sang and danced himself into an SSC whereby "he could see everything, all over the world" (Drucker 1939:99). In more rare cases, such "seeing" is done via a sacred divinatory object. For example, the Walapai shamans have sacred gourds whose spirit "sees the sick person and knows everything about the sickness" (Cooney Kuni in Kroeber 1935:191).

In some cases of trance induction the actual disease is seen, while in other cases the shaman sees revealing imagery. The latter case happened to Paviotso shaman Dick Mahwee. He would begin his diagnosis by smoking his pipe and passing it around to others present. When the smoking was completed, he would stand up and begin to sing and dance around the patient. It was expected that he would begin to stagger as he entered the SSC. Moaning and frothing at the mouth were two indicators that he was in this state. In the visions that came to him, a patient picking flowers or seeing his footprints were indicators of recovery, while withered flowers or no footprints left meant the patient would die (Dick Mahwee in Park 1938:54). His diagnostic trances usually lasted anywhere from one-half to two hours.

Shamans often also use their hands in diagnosing the patient, feeling about the patient's body or massaging it. For example, the Clayoquot shaman usually places his left hand on the patient's stomach while rattling with his right hand and singing in subdued tones (Koppert 1930:86). The Luiseño and Mojave shamans felt the patient's entire body (Boscana 1969:311; Stewart 1970:18), and the Pomo sucking doctor not only uses his hands but also tastes the skin to discover the nature of the disease (Freeland 1923:64). He also often sees a cloud of steam rising from the afflicted part of the body as soon as he first sees his patient. A Cocopa shaman, named Suwi, would lay the palm of his left hand on the area of the patient's body where the pain resided. If there was motion in the outer joint of his little finger, he knew that a cure was possible. In addition, his mouth would water when he was over the sick person. However, if his mouth became dry, he would tell the patient to call in another doctor (Gifford 1933:313).

The shaman often warms his or her hands before using them, such as rubbing them together, holding them over a fire or heated stones, or putting hot ashes on them. It is assumed that this increases the sensitivity of their hands (Loeb 1933:180). Flora Jones, a Wintu shaman, would vigorously rub her hands together before she felt for a sickness. "Any place they are hurting I hurt. I become part of their body," she explained. Her diagnostic trance was a full possession trance in which the spirit spoke through her giving the prognosis (Knudtson 1975:12).

Among the Thompson a similar form of trance possession occurs in which "some shamans were able to ascertain the cause of sickness, only after their guardian spirits had entered their chests. If the first guardian spirit whom they called did not give the desired information, the shaman called another one. If the guardian spirit refused to enter the shaman's body, but jumped back as soon as he approached him, it was a sure sign that the patient would die" (Teit 1900:362). When a shaman enters into such a deep SSC that he becomes possessed by a spirit (which then speaks through the shaman), he does not remember what is said. As such, afterward someone must tell the shaman what was the prognosis rendered by the spirit.

In rare cases it is reported that the helping spirit enters the patient's body versus the body of the shaman. The Walapai shamans often use a sacred gourd rattle that "sees" the illness. During the diagnosis the shaman "sings and shakes the rattle. The (guardian) spirit goes into the sick body and discovers what dead relative's spirit is in the body and tells the doctor, who names it" (Cooney Kuni in Kroeber 1935:190). The Tenino shaman also projects his diagnostic spirit into the patient's body, usually by blowing through a tube (Murdock 1965:169).

Another common form in which diagnostic information comes is through the shaman's dreams (for example, Barbeau 1958:44 [Gitksan]; Cooney Kuni in Kroeber 1925:137 [Hupa], 1935:192 [Walapai]; Opler 1959, 99 [Southern Ute]; Teit 1900:362 [Thompson]). Among the Diegueño this included "the interpretation of his patient's dreams, categorized by type" as well as his own diagnostic dreams (Rogers and Evernham 1983:109). However, in most cases it is only the shaman's diagnostic dreams that are given attention. Tudy Roberts, a Shoshoni shaman, received his diagnosis in a dream. If it became necessary for Tudy to examine the patient, he would move "his beaver skin over the patient's body; when the fur became hot he knew where the disease was located" (Hultkrantz 1992:89).

Diagnosis by Divination Specialists

Most often the shaman who performs the diagnosis is also the person who performs the healing ceremony. However, many American Indian cultures had diagnostic specialists. Such specialists would perform the initial diagnosis but would not conduct the actual healing ceremony. Among the Iroquois, they are known as the *saokata*. The saokata would call on his *oki* (helping spirit), which would enter the body of the patient and locate the problem. Among the Tohono O'odham the sick person would first consult the *siaticum*. In turn, the siaticum would refer the patient to the shaman who knew the proper songs for curing the patient's illness once the diagnosis had been made. Among the nearby Pima the diagnostic specialist is known as the *siatcokam* (examining physician) (Russell 1908:256). Among the Wappo the *yomto hintcome* (dream doctor) performed the diagnosis (Loeb 1932:108). Among the Central Miwok it was the *alini hiwêyi* who conducted the diagnosis (Gifford n.d.:24).

In some cases these specialists received their diagnosis via dreams. The Menomini *mitäwäpe* (seer) was approached with a tobacco offering and request. The mitäwäpe then "will look into the trouble overnight, seeing clearly in a vision what is the matter" (Skinner 1920:130). The patient returns the next day to obtain his or her diagnosis.

Among the Cayuga the dreamer class of shamans would be called upon to diagnose a case that proved problematic to other shamans. Either a *hadrauta* (male dreamer) or a *hodrauta* (female dreamer) would be approached by a person carrying a tobacco offering wrapped in a piece of the sick person's clothing. That night the shaman drinks a special medicine and puts the offering under his pillow. The patient then returns in the morning and receives back the piece of clothing and a prognosis (Speck 1949:124).

Not so common was the use of two diagnosticians—one to find the cause and one to find the disease. Among the Wailaki and the Pomo, "it was the sucking doctor who did the diagnosing and investigated the cause of the sickness, but it was the singing doctor who found out where the 'pain' (disease object) was located. Thus the two worked hand in hand, and split their fees" (Loeb 1932:9, 35, 81, 101). However, among the Coast Miwok it was not the *wakilapi* (sucking doctor), but the *walimitca* (outfit doctor) who "always visited the patient first and made the diagnosis" (114).

Morgan (1931:390) reported that among the Navajo "the shaman has no technique for discovering the cause of an illness." As such, the Navajo make a clear distinction between a shaman and a diagnostician. For example, one major difference is that "a diagnostician's apprentice may be ready to practice in a few months" (391), while a shaman usually trains upward of fifteen years or more. The Navajo have three basic types of diagnostic specialists: the above-mentioned stargazer, the hand-tremblers *(ndishniih),* and the listener, with the latter being the most rare. Of these three forms the most powerful and preferred are the ndishniih.

In performing a diagnosis the ndishniih (literally, "with motion-in-the-hand" [Morgan 1931:390]) sits facing the patient and prepares to enter the SSC. Each has his own particular ritual procedures (for example, smoothes the dirt floor, draws pictures in the dirt, sprinkles cornmeal, sprinkles pollen, etc.) and ritual objects (for example, stones, sticks, reeds, painted and unpainted, etc.). Once prepared, the diagnostician usually chants or prays with his eyes closed as he enters into the SSC. "Then with his arm outstretched he closes his eyes and enters a trance state. Through the mind of a man with motion-in-the-hand runs a series of visualizations of the illness and of the cause of the illness, whereas the listeners (type of diagnostician) receive auditory manifestations. These men believe in their ability to diagnose, because the trance-state seems unusual and real, the more so in that visions come to them when they are oblivious of external stimuli" (Morgan 1931:393). When the diagnostician thinks of the correct cause, it is indicated to him by an involuntary shaking of his arm. This shaking "may vary from a fine tremor of the hand to rather violent motions of the whole arm, and can become uncontrollable" (Levy, Neutra, and Parker 1987:41). When finished, the diagnostician not only identifies the illness but also names the particular chantway (healing ceremony) that must be used to heal the patient and gives the name of the shaman capable of performing the required ceremony. This ability of hand trembling comes spontaneously to people and no training is involved. The ceremony takes about an hour to perform. Members of the Shaker cult among the Northwest Coast cultures can also gain "an insight into the cause of the sickness that is being treated" when their shaking hands touch the patient during a healing (Barnett 1957:267).

Diagnosis by Special Techniques

Many American Indian cultures have special divination ceremonies for diagnosis. In some cases this ceremony is particular to only one shaman. Godfrey Chips, a Lakota shaman, uses a special divination ceremony known as the five-stick ceremony for diagnosing his patients. This particular ceremony is known only in his family and is not conducted by any other Lakota shaman.

The Pima have two types of diagnostic ceremonies. The *kúlañmada* (the application of medicine) is a limited diagnosis, while the *dúajida* (vitalization) is an extensive diagnosis (Bahr et al. 1974:122). The kúlañmada is conducted during the day, while the dúajida is conducted at night. In the Pima classification of sickness, the limited diagnosis will only reveal the upper levels of a stratified sickness, while the dúajida must by used for the "beneath sickness" (143).

Perhaps the most well-known diagnostic ceremony, and certainly one of the best documented, is the shaking tent ceremony of the Ojibwa. Although it is better known as a spirit-calling ceremony in which the audience puts questions to spirits, it is also used for diagnosing a patient (Ritzenthaler 1953:200). This ceremony is also widespread. Among the Menomini it is the *tshisaqka* (the most powerful shaman) who conducts the shaking tent ceremony to diagnose a patient (Hoffman 1896:149). The Menomini shaman also uses the turtle spirit to diagnose during this ceremony. In addition, there is also "a special type of *je'sako* (shaman) who only carries medicines and *okanûk* bones and does not build a lodge (shaking tent) nor does he always have to swallow bones (usually an aspect of the healing ceremony)" (Skinner 1915:196).

There is a fairly detailed ethnographic record of a shaking tent diagnostic ceremony performed by Chippewa shaman John King. In this case the patient, Laurence Butler, had been diagnosed with incipient tuberculosis by Western physicians. Subsequently, anthropologist Robert Ritzenthaler drove the patient and his mother, Mrs. John Butler, to see John King. Initially, John King said he could not perform his ceremony in the presence of white people, but later he consented to Ritzenthaler's attendance since he drove the patient there.

Once John King entered the tent it began to shake for a period of about five minutes before the voice of the summoned spirit was heard. (During a shaking tent ceremony the audience can hear the dialogue between the shaman and his spirits.) The spirit asked, "What's that white man doing here?" causing the others to laugh. Then the spirit asked why it had been summoned, to which Mrs. Butler answered that she had brought her boy for a diagnosis and medicine. The spirit agreed to assist, then left while the tent shook. When it returned it said that it was not a serious illness and indicated what medicine was to be taken (Ritzenthaler 1953:203–4).

Diagnosis by Special Instrument

Throughout North America there are many instances of the diviner using a special instrument. A Shoshoni shaman used a black muff stretched tightly on four sticks set into the ground, which caused the disease in the patient to glow in the dark (Hultkrantz 1992:89). A Tolowa shaman had a special, plate-shaped basket he would put on the floor, and if it danced about, the patient could be cured (Drucker 1937:258). Some Cherokee shamans used two needles afloat in a small creek-side pothole or bowl of water. Depending on how the needles drifted apart or together, a diagnosis was determined (Kilpatrick and Kilpatrick 1967:116). A Lakota shaman (Brave Buffalo) used a mirror and could see the disease reflected in it (Densmore 1918:249). Crow shamans used the skull of a former shaman named Braided Tail (Wildschut 1975:77). Many Lakota shamans use sacred stones to this day. In most cases the stone speaks directly to the shaman (Mails 1991:125). The Wailaki use string figures (Foster 1941:126–27) for divination purposes.

The Cherokee have many different forms of divination, but the "examining the beads" technique is considered to be the instrument par excellence for determining a true diagnosis and prognosis (Fogelson 1980:76). (Bead divination is also found among the Surprise Valley Paiutes [Kelly 1932:191].) The standard technique was to hold a black bead (representing death, calamity, failure) between the thumb and index finger of the left hand, and a red (or white) bead (health, happiness, success) in the right hand. The beads are then rolled around and whichever bead feels the most active becomes the indicator. "Besides rolling the beads in the fingers, they . . . may be rolled on the ground, in which case the bead that rolls furthest will foretell whether or not a patient will recover" (Fogelson 1980:76–77).

In some cases the beads are cast upon a new piece of white cloth. Each throw requires a new cloth. There is a detailed account of Doctor Mink using this technique on a boy named Charlie, who was about to die. The boy's grandmother called for Doctor Mink to diagnose the case. In tossing the beads he found that there was no hope for this boy. The grandmother proceeded to put a new cloth down three more times, and each toss of the beads gave the same result. Then it was proposed to go to the sick boy's home, where they found him unconscious. Two more divinations were conducted with the same results. His cousin reported:

> "I suggested to change the boy's name. Charlie could die, but we would give him a new name; we would call him Alick. Mink then again examined with the beads, and he found that Alick was going to get better. They tried a fourth time, and again there was hope. I then got Mink to examine to see if he would be able to cure him; but he found he couldn't. Then he examined for another medicine man, and then for another,

and another, and finally he found that Og. could cure him. We then sent
for Og. to cure him. In the sick boy's house nobody was allowed to sleep
that night. Doctor Mink kept busy about the fire, working against the
witches.

"Og. came down every morning and every night; he did the curing,
and Doctor Mink did the examining with the beads. Four days afterwards I went down to the river once more with Doctor Mink, and we
found that in seven days Alick would be about, hunting. And so it was."
(Mooney 1932:67–68)

Fools Crow (mentioned above) also used a sacred stone in diagnosing a
patient. He would roll the stone all over the patient's body while repeating a
finding song four times. Then, holding this stone, he would go under a blanket
and sing a thank-you song to the stone. "I sing this song four times, and then
I wait, holding the stone like this, in the open palm of my right hand. In a little while, the stone starts to turn red and gets very warm. Sometimes it nearly burns my hand, and I'm sure it would seriously burn the hand of someone
who did not know how to hold it. Then the stone begins to make a crackling
and popping sound, which turns into Lakota, and it speaks to me, giving me
information about the patient and what to do to cure them. When I know
everything I need to know, the stone turns cold, and we are finished. Then I
use the treatment the stone has told me to use" (Fools Crow in Mails
1991:129).

The most common instrument used for divination is a quartz crystal,
especially among the cultures of the Southwest area, where it is often worn on
a string around the shaman's neck during ceremony. The shaman usually holds
the crystal between one eye and the body of the patient and can then see a disease object within the patient's body or the witch who sent it (Bunzel
1932:533; Grant 1982:293; Parsons 1939:330). In some cases, such as at
Acoma, the crystal may first be dipped into a bowl of medicine water and then
rubbed on the shaman's eyes in order to achieve the needed "second sight."

The Tohono O'odham shaman often carries four quartz crystals for divination purposes (Underhill 1946:265, 271). He "placed it on the ground
before him. It cast a ray of light on the patient's body, showing the seat of
disease or the presence of an intrusive object. The ray might not strike clearly for some time, and meantime the shaman fortified himself by singing and
smoking" (Underhill 1946:276). Among the nearby Pima the above-mentioned

siatcokam also uses clear crystals for divination of illnesses (Russell 1908: 259–60).

The Navajo stargazer commonly uses a quartz crystal. With friends and family in attendance, the stargazer tells everyone to close their eyes and not move or speak. They "must concentrate on the illness and try to see something . . . If the illness is serious the stargazer will prescribe a ceremony and the shaman who can give it" (Morgan 1931:394–95).

There is an account of a crystal divination diagnosis made on Alexander Stephen during his study period with the Hopi in the 1890s. Stephen (1936:213) reported:

> He [the shaman Yellow Bear] then drew from his pouch an irregular shaped lump of quartz crystal, about the size of a walnut, retaining it in his hand . . . Taking the crystal between finger and thumb, sometimes in one hand sometimes the other, he placed the crystal at arm's length toward me. Then he bent over so as to bring the crystal close up to me, and thus he swayed back and forth, in silence, occasionally making passes with his arms to and fro and toward me, for about four or five minutes. Suddenly he reached over me and pressed the crystal against my right breast, and just upon the region of a quite severe pain . . . he located the seat of the pain exactly.

The Cherokee *ulunsata* (sacred quartz crystal) was used for divination (Fogelson 1977:190). This crystal is regarded as a person and is periodically fed drops of human or animal blood in return for the divinatory services it provides. (Offerings are regularly made to power objects to keep them efficacious.)

In addition to special items used by diviners, there are also special techniques. Among the Inuit there is a widespread divination technique generally referred to as the *kila* (also *krilaq* [Nelson 1899:433]). It is a form of divination by weight. Sometimes a bundled piece of clothing is used for this purpose. In most cases, a body part of the patient is lifted while he or she lies prone on the floor. As such, "the kila may be either the head or the foot of a patient, his clothes, or the clothes of the shaman himself" (Jenness 1922:217). Among the Inuit of Baffin Island and the Hudson Bay areas a substitute person (the *keleyak*) is used for such testing instead of the patient (Boas 1907:135). In all cases the shaman calls upon his helping spirit to enter the bundle or person. Usually a special cord is attached to the person's head or foot for lifting purposes. Depending on whether the weight is light or heavy, a negative or positive answer is obtained.

The Canadian ethnographer, Diamond Jenness, became ill during one of his visits to the Copper Eskimos and submitted to treatment by a female shaman. The kila was a tied-up coat. Several malignant shades (soul of a deceased person) entered the kila and were driven off by the shaman. "The bundle at once became light; all the malignant shades had been disposed of, and nothing remained presumably to prevent my recovery. A year later Higilak reminded me of this performance, and claimed that she had been instrumental in curing me of my illness" (Jenness 1922:214–15). Note that in this case the divination ritual extended into a healing ritual through the use of the kila.

The Role of Divination in the Healing Process

There has never been a comprehensive study of American Indian divination to date; however, the subject has not gone entirely unnoticed. Frank Speck (1935:127–68) undertook an intensive study of scapulamancy among the Montagnais-Naskapi. He was struck by their "unbounded zeal" for many different forms of divination and concluded "that divination is the one motive of religious ceremony that strikes our attention in the whole area to the exclusion of almost everything else . . . (it is) the embodiment of religious practice" (138). This was the case for most American Indian cultures. Divinations usually outnumber other shamanic performances such that they will appear to be the major "religious" activity on a daily basis. One reason for this is that divinations are more readily performed than shamanic healing ceremonies. Another reason is that there are more diviners than healers within a culture, since most healers are capable of divining also. Given the presence of both specialists and healers who divine, divinations are more readily available. It can be assumed that divinations played an integral role in most shamanic healings, namely in diagnosing an illness, as well as in rendering a prognosis.

In discussing divinatory forms of diagnosis it is important to understand that American Indian healing most often operates on two levels with regards to the patient. In Western medicine a physician will diagnose a patient's symptoms with the intent of getting rid of them. However, American Indian diagnosis goes one step deeper to search out the initial cause(s) of the symptoms. For example, the Lakota shaman Fools Crow made this distinction in using the terms *curing* and *healing.* In his view the patient needed to be healed as well as cured. Curing is the aspect that relieves the patient's symptoms, while healing corrects the underlying cause(s) of the illness. That is, curing takes place on the physical level, while healing takes place on the spiritual level (Mails 1991:137). Thus, Fools Crow would be heard asking a dying patient if he wanted to be "healed," knowing well the patient would soon die. This same distinction is found among the Navajo, where there are the patient's symptoms and then, even deeper, the "first causes" (Leighton and Leighton 1941:517). As such, American Indian divinations for illnesses often include a prognosis that includes changes the patient must make in his or her personal life once the cure is achieved. Otherwise, the illness (symptoms) will return.

At the most fundamental level, an American Indian healing ceremony is a wish-fulfillment process activated by human wills (minimally that of the patient and shaman). Frances Densmore (1929:45) was aware of this perspective when she wrote, "the chief purpose of the (Chippewa) *djasakid* (shaman) is to work upon the mind of the sick person, and by that means to produce a recovery." Among the Navajo, Reichard (1944:6) called it "ritualistic persuasion." Frank Speck (1935:138) came to a similar view when he concluded that Naskapi shamanism was essentially "dreaming, wishing, intention, and exercise of will." Even earlier, Radin (1914:211) summarized the salient features of Ojibwa shamanism as "endless and ceaseless repetition," "persistent fixation of attention," and "the power of complete absorption while at prayer."

It should be noted that such "ritualistic persuasion" filters down to the individual level. That is, nonshamans are versed in them as well and use them for attaining their objectives. For instance, Speck also noted that each individual Naskapi had access to *mentu' elte'ltak,* literally "spirit-power thinking," with "probably the nearest equivalent being 'power of thought'" (Speck 1935:184). So both the shaman and the patient are acting in magical ways during a healing. This patient-shaman mode of interaction leads to a subtle interplay between the processes of divination and that of healing, which remain active throughout the course of their interactions. Because these interactions operate on the level of magic, it is also a special type of personal interaction that is absent in Western physician-patient relationships.

As shown in the above examples, divination is often used for the purpose of diagnosing an illness and rendering a prognosis. The following comments pertain only to those cases in which the healing shaman also performs the diagnosis on the patient, which is the most common case in North America. Also excluded are those cases of illness that are diagnosed as a "shamanic call," which often manifests itself as a sickness in an individual, especially in the Northwest Coast area. For example, Henry Allen reports for the Twana: "So if your mother or grandmother had lots of visions in her time, you can inherit them. If you get ailing the doctor diagnoses and says, 'Your mother's vision wants you and I'll bring it to you'" (Henry Allen in Elmendorf 1993:191). When so diagnosed, the individual is not subjected to a healing ceremony. Instead, the person must undergo the culture's training in shamanism in order to be cured.

As stated earlier, the healing process begins with the patient approaching the shaman with a request for healing. The shaman's acceptance (usually determined by measuring the faith of the patient) to heal the patient is the first step in this process. The process then becomes one of increasing the patient's faith, especially in the powers of the shaman.

Once the healing process is initiated, some form of divination usually follows in order to diagnose the patient. In rare cases, such as the above-mentioned Copper Eskimo divination for Jenness, the divination process becomes the curing process whereby "the diagnosis alone is considered sufficient to arrest the evil, especially if it is reinforced by an abstinence from such articles of food as the shaman may ordain" (Jenness 1922:171).

However, most often the diagnostic divination and healing are two separate ceremonies. The shaman usually begins the divination by giving a lengthy account of his or her powers. For example, Densmore (1929:45) reports: "It has been noted that a *djasakid* (shaman), before beginning a treatment, narrated his personal dream as a guaranty of his success." What guarantees it is the patient gaining more faith in the shaman's abilities through this dialogue. That the shaman's discourse takes several hours is common. For example, "Fools Crow talked with the (sick) person for a long time about the way of curing. He patiently explained that what he would do had its roots in ancient history. The way that *Wankan-Tanka* (Creator) would use was old and proven

. . . As the person's confidence and hope started to grow, Fools Crow talked with the person about the cause of the illness, what had happened since it started, who the person had already gone to for help, and what had been done. As they talked, Fools Crow sifted through the answers and compared the situation to others he had treated that were like it" (Mails 1991:154). Fools Crow was so skilled at instilling faith in a patient that he once told Mails to watch his patient during a four-day healing ceremony and note that at some point the patient would "reach out and touch me on the cheek or the shoulder" (154). Mails reports that he subsequently saw this happen many times to Fools Crow.

Once a divination ceremony begins, the interplay between the shaman and the patient takes on an even deeper significance. At this point, the shaman's subsequent course of action is determined—which spirits are to be called upon, which altar display is to be used, and the like. Most significant is the fact that the patient (or friends thereof) can change the course of any spirit-predicted outcome at this point. If it is reported that there is little hope for the patient, it is a time that calls for persistence of will on the part of the patient and those who have come to help seek success. Such success is achieved mainly through their prayers.

This persistence of will was evidenced in the Ritzenthaler case of the boy with tuberculosis. Even after the spirit indicated a recovery, the mother of the boy was insistent on not only having the spirit work on her son but also on getting a medicine for him from the spirit. An even more elaborate example was the divination of Doctor Mink in which the grandmother of the patient continued over and over to sponsor yet another divination until a cure was possible. One of the ways this flexibility manifests among shamans is when they become suspect of a "wrong" answer during the course of a divination.

The Cherokee also guard against false diagnostic traits, called "simulators," that are often sent by a sorcerer. The diagnostician "is led astray by the sorcerer who sent the disease, and who 'made it resemble some such ailment as found by the medicine man in his diagnosis'; but the disease is of a totally different nature" (Mooney 1932:33).

The Yavapai would often call in a "ghost specialist" to divine whether a seriously ill person would recover or not. The technique involved audience participation and was subject to "wrong" answers. In this technique the shaman conducted the diagnosis in a ceremonial house. Outside of the house he would post a "fearless man with big heart" (Gifford 1936:316) who would hold intercourse with the spirit. The shaman summoned a spirit by singing inside of the ceremonial house, and the audience could hear the approach of this spirit. The man posted outside would question this spirit and get answers from it. However, sometimes the "wrong kind" of spirit came, such as a "Walapai or Mohave, or one making sound like roadrunner, etc." (316). In such cases those sitting in the ceremonial house would throw dust out into the darkness, scaring off the spirit.

From such examplés it is clear that individual human will plays a very important role in the overall success of any healing. This is not a new fact. Therefore, one of the major roles of the divination ceremony is to set the combined wills of those participating in the healing toward success and to also strengthen each person's intent for that success to manifest.

The other major role of the divination ceremony is to acquire the consent of the spirits to assist in the healing of the patient. This usually takes the form of a spirit-given course of action for the patient. As such, the prognosis constitutes a greater "unknown" to the shaman than the subsequent healing ceremony, since once the course of action has been given by the spirits, it is more a matter of simply following the proper rules of conduct.

This fact is usually overlooked in the ethnographic literature. The way it manifests itself among shamans is in the difference of difficulty of the two ceremonies. That is, it is more difficult to perform the diagnosis of a patient than it is to perform the actual healing ceremony. All shamans I have subsequently questioned have replied in the same manner—in effect, the greater the unknown, the more difficult it is to obtain.

I do not want to give the impression that divination during a healing ceremony always ends with the initial diagnosis. This is certainly not the case. Any diagnosis can change during the course of a healing. For example, the Pomo also had a special technique for suspected diagnosis. If the "outfit doctor" (or "singing shaman") makes several visits to a family to treat a sick individual and fails, he begins to doubt his original diagnosis. His first inclination is to suspect a haunting spirit. The shaman then begins a second round of diagnosis. He "consults with the family to discover . . . the probable nature of the spirit. The doctor then prepares to test the patient by reproducing the vision as closely as he can. He may himself dress as a ghost, or may construct a model of a monster . . . (it) is suddenly revealed to the patient. If he reacts strongly, struggling and then fainting, the doctor regards his hypothesis as verified" (Freeland 1923:63). The cure is founded on the Pomo understanding that "seeing a thing again takes it off your mind" (72).

In other cases the emphasis is not on an incorrect diagnosis, but on one that can change over the course of the healing. For example, Henry Rupert, a Washo shaman, received visions during the course of his healing treatments that caused him to alter his treatments: "At some time during the course of the ritual, Henry would receive visions relating both to the cause of the illness and the prognosis . . . Over the four-night (healing ceremony) period the content of these visions, or occasionally dreams, tended to change . . . The portent of the vision of the fourth night overrode those of the visions seen on the previous night" (Handelman 1967:451).

Similarly, among the Hopi it is reported "even after the taking of a thorough history and the utilization of the most complex and sophisticated diagnostic ritual, final diagnosis (usually with a crystal) may not be made until a number of therapeutic approaches have been tried" (Grant 1982:292).

From these examples it can be concluded that the divination process quite often extends into the healing process per se. Furthermore, their results will redirect the healing efforts being made by the shaman.

Conclusions

In Native North America, divination is intimately related to the healing process, mainly during the diagnostic phase. The outcome of the divination is influenced not only by the shaman but also by the patient, then the family and relatives, and even by those assisting. Little attention has been given to this factor, whereby human will directs, in part, the results of a divination process. No doubt this is due to what is known in quantum mechanics as "the observer effect," whereby human consciousness plays a significant role in what comes manifesting into reality (that is, the basics of magic). It is for that reason that divinations continue right through the healing process per se, as the shaman, patient, and participants all send their prayers to effect the outcome of reality. That is to say that reality is fluid, and our observations on it play a significant role in its manifestation.

The process of divination also helps to instill the necessary shaman-patient bond needed for success. Included in this process are various techniques, such as the shaman relating his or her powers, recalling other successful healings, touching the patient, etc., that contribute to the shaman-patient bonding. The divination process also serves to secure the aid of spirit helpers to be used in the healing.

We are gradually beginning to understand not only that divination is efficacious, but also that what we call miracles actually take place in American Indian healing ceremonies. No longer can anthropologists ignore the recent collapse in materialism (see Walker 2000) brought about by what many physicists now claim to be the greatest discovery in the history of science—namely, that God does play dice with the universe and Einstein was dead wrong on that point. To this end, all future research on healing and divination must take into account the quantum leap in worldview that has most recently taken place. The observer effect is the basis for magic and provides us with an understanding of how it operates. Most important, magic can no longer be regarded as superstition.

6

Ways of Knowing
and Healing

Shamanism in the Republics of Tuva and Buryatia in Post-Soviet Russia

EVA JANE NEUMANN FRIDMAN

Shamanism in the Inner Asian areas of Tuva and Buryatia is practiced primarily as rituals for the well-being of the kinship community and healing for the individual person. Common to these areas is a cosmological belief system that sustains all the various means of divination and healing processes. This belief system relies on the ability of the shaman-healer, through his or her powers of entering into an altered state of consciousness (ASC), to make a connection with the spiritual world, with the divine, and hence use that information and knowledge to heal. In many processes of divination common in Buryatia and Tuva, shaman-healers may use traditional methods and objects to come into communion with the divine and may also be influenced by newer methods of healing. After the interruption in traditional shamanistic practice during the Soviet period, younger shaman-healers, in particular, have acquired new points of view, but with respect to their practices of divination, their abilities to "see clearly," to foretell, to see the soul of a person, show the strengths of tradition and continuity.

Historically, the hallmark of shamanism is the ecstatic ASC leading to a connection to the spirits, which then allows the shaman to aid and cure members of the community. This religious or spiritual aspect, a connection through the shaman's intercession with the spirit world, links the members of the community with the spirits and hence brings about healing for the individual and well-being for the community. Shamanism is deeply grounded in the cultural, religious, and spiritual beliefs of the community and takes its validation and much of its curative effectiveness from that connection. ASCs of the intensity reportedly experienced prior to the Soviet period may be a phenomenon of the past, but the communal belief system that supports shamanistic healing is still a vital component of healing effectiveness.

Without the connection to the world of the spirits, and the guidance from this otherworldly source, shamans would not have the information, power, and ability to heal members of their society. Entering into an ASC, which only a person who has been given the gift of shamanizing by the spirits can do, is a prerequisite for accessing the spirits in order to understand the causes of a patient's illness and receive the necessary guidance. Indeed, there are a number of ways divination is employed by shaman healers in Buryatia and Tuva: as diagnosis (a means of diagnosing the disease or problem causing the illness); as a way of teasing out the (evil) forces of witchcraft and malignant energies sent by bad spirits; as a way of understanding spiritual or ecological forces at work which need to be appeased; for foretelling the future; and even for help with predicting the course of more mundane concerns such as work, school, and future economic endeavors. Healing and divination are closely bound together by these shamanic interventions since no healing can take place without prior consultation with spirits—hence there is always a process of divination that must be set in place a priori. Often, shaman-healers will, once they have returned from an ASC, tell the fortunes of those people gathered around them, based on information learned from the spirits during the ASC. The benefit of healing for the patient(s) gained during the shaman's ASC is augmented with subsequent knowledge offered to help the patient in decisions concerning future activities.

Divination in healing among the shamans in Inner Asia is based in their connection to spiritual forces, operative through their own singular links to these divinities, and is used in the service of healing. In the actual healing sessions, emphasis is on communication with spirits particular to the shaman or to the locale itself, so that these spirits may be engaged in arriving at a helpful solution to the problems the patient is experiencing. Often shamans will

communicate with the spirits of the patient's deceased relatives who are continuing to trouble the patient and hence cause the illness. Shamans use their
own special protector spirits to engage with other spirits or to lead them to
the correct understanding of the solution to the patient's disorder. Divination is a practice where a supernatural means is used to reestablish a rational
order within the patient—that is, the shaman-healer makes the connection
to the spiritual world in order to discover hidden knowledge so that the
patient may receive the benefit of this information and then follow the correct
procedures to straighten out psychological problems. These healing procedures could be drinking certain water, making invocations with vodka to the
appropriate spirits, using physical objects to learn the diagnosis from the
spirits (such as mirrors or stones), using the shaman's hands in a bioenergetic
manner to understand the problem, and especially, while in an ASC, consulting with the spirits of the locale or ancestral spirits. Often important in the
healing of a disturbed patient is the shaman's understanding through divination of the requests of an unappeased ancestral spirit; the patient is then
directed to the appropriate relief of the situation.

This chapter describes the healing practices of shaman-healers observed
in Buryatia and Tuva between June 1996 and November 1996, when shamanism was undergoing regeneration in the former USSR. Therefore, this is a
snapshot at one point in time. It is noted that divination is a process that
becomes more prevalent in times of social instability and change and is seized
upon by the public under these circumstances to provide assistance and aid
in making life decisions. In other words, given the turmoil and daily crises of
the post-Soviet period, people are flocking to shamans for their skills in divination and healing. The opinion of the shaman, in consultation with his or
her spirits, gives weight to the decisions of the individual by appealing to a
higher authority, especially in this case, where the temporal authority—the
State—has shifted its bases of power so markedly and the previous ideology
has been discredited. Examination of selective representative shamanistic
healers from each area illustrates similarities and differences in their practices and the changes that have occurred as a consequence of acculturative
influences, as will be noted in the conclusion.

There are substantial differences between the practitioners studied in
Buryatia and Tuva during this period of 1996 and the traditional and cross-cultural patterns of hunting and gathering shamanism as explicated by Winkel-

man (1990, 1992). One of the problems is to clearly differentiate between shamans and shaman-healers. Using the schema developed by Winkelman (1990:316, Table 2), shamanistic healing in the Inner Asian areas does not fit neatly into one or another of these constructs but exhibits aspects of both. This is probably due to the fact that historically the Tuvinians and Buryats were nomadic pastoral people rather than embedded primarily in a hunting or agricultural social complex. Therefore, the association of shamans with hunting-and-gathering conditions and shaman-healers with agricultural subsistence is not as clearly demonstrated (316). Healers also show characteristics of shamans (part-time practitioners; selection and training consisting of visions, dreams, illness, and spirit's requests; training involving trance; and magico-religious activity consisting of healing and divination). There is not a predominance of male or female practitioners in any of the areas researched. They also demonstrate some of the shaman-healer aspects such as moderate social status, no political power, and sometimes a specialized role as healer. Therefore, the terms generally used here are *shaman-healers* and *healers using shamanistic methods* (since they are not possessed but do use ASC as a basis for their divination and healing practices). The term *shaman* has also been employed because that is the same word used in this part of the world. There are differences in the intensity of shamanistic experiences and the use of purely shamanistic or combined Buddhistic and shamanistic means for divination and healing. By comparison with Mongolian shamans observed in 1999 and 2000, shamans in Tuva and Buryatia lack the intensity of their ASC experiences. Tuva, the area presented first, shows more intense and more traditional aspects of shamanistic practice.

Tuva

Information in the Tuvan museum of regional studies, named "Aldan Maadir" (Sixty Heroes), in Kyzyl states that January 21, 1992, was the official registration of the Shaman Society of Tuva Dungur Society (*dungur* means drum). Thirty-seven shamans from all the corners of Tuva registered with the society. On October 15, 1993, shamanism was established as a health system by a presidential decree and old-age pensions for shamans were established. They now have a house for the Dungur Society at 41 Lenin Street, in the center of town, where shamans can practice healing. In 1993 the first official shaman ceremony, sanctification of the Scythian stone figures with smoke from mountain alder trees, occurred in the courtyard of the museum. In 1994 the government established a Scientific Center for the Study of Shamanism. Shamans who are members of the Dungur Society receive a *kham* (shaman) I.D. card with their name and number, as well as a document to practice healing, perform rituals, and divine.

Healers in Tuva who practice according to a shamanistic philosophy and use shamanistic methods call themselves shamans. There seems to be no doubt in their minds that they are shamans, even though they admit that they cannot enter an ASC as well as their predecessors did. Therefore, in this section these healers are referred to as shamans, since their way of reaching the spirits involves an ASC, often using drumming or music to achieve this state.

Rituals can be addressed to the sun, moon, sky, earth, water, mountains, bear, and to the big bear (the Big Dipper constellation). Prayers are implemented with ritual sprinkling of milk to the sky or to the spirits of fire. Tuvan shamans pray to five types of spirits: the spirits of the shaman's own family ancestors; the spirits of heaven, who live in the sky; the spirits of evil; and the spirits of earth and water. These spirits can help the shaman in his ritual to cure the sick patient. When a person trains to be a shaman, the evil spirits come to him. He beats his drum, talks to the spirits, and asks them for help. He prays and sings, and as he continues in his interaction with the spirits during his years as a practicing shaman, he develops a collection of *eeren*. These are physical representations—in the form of animal parts, pieces of fabric, wooden dolls—of spirits that are the shaman's helpers in the spiritual world. When the shaman does *kamlat,* meaning that he goes to the other world with the help of a drum, mirror, jaw harp (a mouth instrument commonly used by shamans in Inner Asia), or staff, he also needs his special shaman's song, anthem, or incantation.

The role of song and sound in creating a shamanic whole has been noted in many accounts of Tuvan shamanism (see Kenin-Lopsan 1993a, 1993b, 1994, 1997; Kyrgys 1993). Sound and music are vital components of the healing practice, with the shaman's hymn or incantation the only force sufficiently powerful to bring a lost soul back from the evil spirits. Shaman hymns to the lost soul may illustrate the interweaving of nature and humans in the Tuvan landscape of the spirit.

What captures the spirit of shamanism in Tuva is not just the intimacy of individual healings but also the relationship to the whole of nature. One may be out herding sheep and meet the low-level spirits of earth and nature. A person can perform a ritual alone or find a shaman to make the connection with the spirits. But at any and all moments there is a connection to the spiritual world that can touch one and heal.

A Ceremony in Nature

"The spirits are all around and this is why there are so many shamans in Tuva," said Rosa, "because there are so many spirits." Rosa, using a wooden spoon with nine hollows in it, was sprinkling tea from a bowl in the four directions of the compass. We were standing on a hilltop and around us was an undulating steppe landscape, hills piled upon hills in shades of beige fading to a more distant purple. A clouded sky reigned overhead. Beyond a hill, about two kilometers to the north, was a creek, invisible below a small herding farmstead. At a far distance to our east it was possible to see some of the buildings of Kyzyl, rising like a mythical white city from the plain, and a glimpse of the glitter of the Yenisey River, but only if we made an effort to look for these points. Silence reverberated. A few crows flew overhead. The landscape, in the Western sense, was empty. No roads, cars, habitations, people. Only yellow steppe grasses, more and more hills stretching into the infinity of snowcapped mountains and sky.

Rosa had planned this open-air, in-nature ritual especially for my benefit. Unable to connect with several other shamans with whom she had previously made arrangements and anxious to have at least one other shaman participate with her, Rosa went to the Dungur Society house, where she found Duu-Dori. Duu-Dori was afraid to come with Rosa, afraid of being photographed and afraid she would be thrown out of the Dungur Society. With difficulty Rosa hauled her onto our bus, and there she sat airing her worries and anxieties in Tuvinian to Rosa on the trip to the ritual location.

A small *obo* (cone-shaped stone structure dedicated to the spirits of the place) sat on the brow of the hill where Duu-Dori, wearing a brown crocheted wool beret and a dark green silk coat with groups of braided fabric snakes hanging down the back, took her drum and began to call the spirits. She went to each point of the compass, drumming into the landscape and calling forth the spirits, joined by Rosa, who offered libations into the air. She told

Rosa that she felt a spirit come to her. It was Rosa's drum that she was using. This was a round drum, approximately fifteen inches in diameter, covered with the skin of a castrated male goat. The reverse side of the drum had two crossbars, from which hung three bells—one of them a large cowbell—on the left side and five small bells on the right-hand side of the horizontal bar. The baton for the drum was like a wooden spoon with rings inside the hollow on one side and fur covering the other side.

Duu-Dori cleansed Rosa with the smoke from an Artemis (juniper) branch before Rosa could sit down to drum. Duu-Dori called the spirits, moving her hands, and Rosa drummed. Rosa wore no headgear; her only special garment was a pink sleeveless silk vest embroidered with yellow thread in geometric designs and totally lined with sheepskin, given to her by a grateful client. As she drummed she heard the spirit of the creek speaking to her.

Rosa said afterward that when she comes here, she usually invites this spirit to speak with her. She says she is in an ASC when she listens to this spirit, who speaks to her in Tuvinian. After the spirit has spoken to her, she has no memory of what the spirit said. Rosa herself has questioned this process, suggesting that her thoughts are simply coming from her own unconscious. After the spirit left Rosa, Duu-Dori, having taken off her shaman robe, cleansed Rosa again with Artemis. Then we gathered together and had a picnic, like any normal early fall outing. Rosa brought food—bread, fish, candy—and we had tea. Eventually, as we rode back to Kyzyl, Duu-Dori settled into a litany of complaints about other shamans.

Duu-Dori is a traditional healer, relating to spirits in nature, using plants, as her shaman grandfather did, and specializing in a few illnesses in which she is an expert. Rosa, on the other hand, a much younger woman of thirty-four, is representative of a new generation of shamans—more flexible, given to self-doubt, and critical of shamanistic practice as a valid method of healing. Having lived through the Soviet period, however, they both inevitably reflect some of the changes that have occurred in shamanistic practices in Tuva.

Duu-Dori Bair-oolovna

Duu-Dori claims that healing in Tuva has not changed from practices prior to the Soviet period. The methods are the same, as is the specialization of the shaman function. As of June 16, 1994, she is member #125 of the Dungur

Society of Shamans. Her identity card, like a driver's license, is replete with a photograph and the signature of M. Kenin-Lopsan (famous Tuvan folklorist and ethnographer of shamanism). Duu-Dori, age seventy-one, was born in 1924 in the Bai-Taiga region. She began working as a shamaness in the early 1950s. She became ill and was diagnosed with gastritis; but instead of going to a hospital, as the doctors advised, she tried to heal herself, gathering herbs from the mountains. She spent a whole night drinking herbal tea and her gastritis was gone.

Duu-Dori's maternal grandfather was a shaman who used herbal teas, and she believes she received her gift of healing from him. Her paternal grandmother was also a shamaness. She remembers that when she was a small child her grandmother took her out onto the steppe and said, "You see this thing; you see those things." Then she went home and told her father and her grandfather about it, and her grandfather beat up her grandmother for telling her. Duu-Dori also heard and saw the spirits her grandmother heard.

Duu-Dori told us that after that she met a woman suffering from sharp gastritis pain. The woman came to her for a year for Duu-Dori's prepared herbal tea. Then the woman came and said the pain was gone. Some time later she asked for the medicine again, but afterward she was fine. After this, people began to come to Duu-Dori for healing. She healed secretly (since this was during the Soviet period) with herbal teas that she still uses today. Although she does not know the name of the plant used to make her tea, she knows it by sight—it looks like a carrot. Using the roots and the leaves, she prepares this herbal tea for skin diseases and for allergies; in addition, she helps heal people with osteoporosis and women who have problems lactating. She also talks to spirits, one of whom is a man who, by rattling her tea cups, tells her whether or not to go healing somewhere.

Duu-Dori says that her healing practices are unchanged from those of her grandparents. Although she inherited her gift of shamanistic healing, she only began to employ these methods after being ill herself. This was true of every shaman or shaman-healer I observed; they all inherited their gift of healing from a direct ancestor and, moreover, went through an inexplicable illness—only to be cured by beginning themselves the practice of healing in a shamanistic manner. Duu-Dori is therefore very typical of shamans, whether old or young, in these aspects. Moreover, it can be noted that her ASC is not very strong. She appears to have one specialized method, healing with an herbal tea, which she uses for patients with certain illnesses. Her powers of divination, of communicating with the spirit world in order to diagnose and understand the patient's problems, do not seem to be evident. Hence, her connection to the spirit world is weak and her powers for shamanistic healing are limited. Other shamans and shaman-healers, as noted later, have reported the specific ability to "see clearly" (an important method of divination), as mediated through the spirit world, and hence can tailor their healing techniques to the particular problem presented by the patient.

Rosa Nasyk-Dorjou

Rosa was born in Bai-Khaakh, directly south of Kyzyl, and grew up in Mongun-Taiga in the southwest corner of Tuva. She is from shaman lines—grandfathers and grandmothers on both sides of the family were shamans. Rosa's life history is replete with signs that indicated that she was to become a shaman. At age fifteen the first incident occurred when she saw a sick woman one evening. Suddenly she could not see her, and she had a feeling like someone made a tube of this woman's body and the woman had crawled out of her house. The next morning the woman died. Following this event, Rosa visited her sick uncle in the Bai-Taiga region. She felt some kind of invisible power dragging her soul out while the shaman sang a healing ceremony. She said he sent a black ball to her that got stuck in her throat, so that she could not breathe, and she tried to throw up the black ball. Something yellow, like a ball, went out of her mouth and broke; a week later her uncle died of lung cancer.

Such incidents occurred repeatedly until 1991 when she saw the spirit of the mountain at Arzan Shivilig, a sacred natural spring west of Teeli, a town in western Tuva. At first she tried to refuse it, but eventually she realized she could not deny this "gift"; it was part of her life. She was walking down the street when an invisible power threw her into a big pail of snow. A group of faces told her, "If you don't communicate with us, the ceiling of the university (where she was studying to become a teacher) will fall down on your head." She became like a slave to them, and they told her different things. Feeling like a slave made her angry, so she started to do her own work.

People came to her for help and healing and soon she no longer had time to teach. The spirits that helped her disappeared and other spirits showed up, among them a very wise Chinese person and a powerful buffalo with red eyes.

When she went to the United States a few years ago, she saw a Native American shaman in a sweat lodge turn rocks red hot, and she received nine brown bears from him as a gift. Now she has no animal spirits; during the time we were speaking, Rosa had sent her spirits away. She decided that she had too many personal problems and could no longer help people with their difficulties.

Rosa is a strong shaman with great powers of healing but is plagued by self-doubts about the actual process of shamanism itself and what is really going on. Is she sensing, seeing, and hearing spirits, or are they simply projections of her own internal state of mind? She fluctuates between Buddhism as a spiritual path, psychotherapy in the Western sense as a healing modality, and shamanism as a worldview and healing practice. For her, this was not just a philosophical discussion but a gripping drama. At one moment she was rushing off somewhere in the Tuvan steppe to heal someone who had called to her; at another moment she was landing chaotically in her apartment, renouncing shamanism and swearing that from now on she would only practice according to Buddhism.

Rosa goes to people's homes for healing, or people come to her apartment. When she goes to the outlying village of Kyzyl-Dag she heals in the Khure (Buddhist temple) there. Speaking about her work, she says she performs healing like psychotherapy. There are shamans who forecast and say a person will die. She considers these to be bad shamans; she does not work like this. People come to her with their problems: husband and wife or mother and children. They might have fears (phobias), like a fear of a big dog. She helps them overcome their fear little by little (like behavior therapy in Western psychotherapy). She explains that often when people do not feel well, they label it as a problem in their stomach, but the difficulty really comes from their head, from the unconscious.

She often treats the problem of a lost soul. Rosa can tell if a person has lost his or her soul—the person will become sick and possibly die. Rosa finds the person's soul and brings it back. She also performs the seven-day and forty-nine-day ritual after the death of a person, a ritual that is traditional and obligatory in Tuva. This ritual connects the soul of the deceased person with its living relatives. She, the shaman, is the mediator between them. She speaks to the spirits of the deceased; she tells them that the family is sad, weeping. The spirits tell her to tell them not to weep, and she passes the message back to the family. It is necessary for the soul to feel free to fly, move, without boundaries of walls or buildings. For forty-nine days after a person's death, the soul flies around and observes problems in the family and in the world and reports on them to the shaman (Rosa), who tells the family. When a person dies, the soul goes into an animal or bird or insect, such as a dog or a chicken or a cockroach. In order for the soul to be reborn as another human being, she has to do the ritual of seven and forty-nine days and then the soul will settle into a human being. This is a clear example of Rosa's use of divination—communication with the spirits—in order to diagnose and find a lost soul, and in order to help heal emotional pain. She serves as the mediator between the grieving family and the spirit of the deceased person through divination.

Although it is traditional and hence expected that a shaman will make a fire to facilitate communication with the soul, Rosa said she does this only to please the family. She does not feel the need for a fire in order to put herself into a short ASC. She may use her drum and then, while in an ASC, speak with the soul of the deceased person. She told me that the first time she saw the soul of a dead man was some years ago when she visited an apartment where nine days previously the husband of the woman had died. She was saying hello to her and suddenly she saw the man sitting in the armchair. She said hello to him but then saw no one. When she sat at the table, the man (spirit) came up to her and told her different things and gave advice; he told her how he died and what he did not like at home. She told the family what he said and the relatives asked questions, which she then asked the spirit. She was the channeling person for him. After this she began doing the seven-day and forty-nine-day rituals for families.

Rosa says she can heal in three different ways: shamanistic, psychotherapy, and Buddhist. She heals by nontouch massage, energy-giving, and talking to a person. For example, one morning a woman arrived at Rosa's apartment with her six-year-old son. They sat and talked in the living room, and Rosa later told me that the boy has a problem with being very aggressive against his mother, other children, and other people. He is depressed and angry because his parents separated, came together, and then separated again. Now the father lives in the countryside with his sister in a little village near Bai-Khaakh. Rosa counseled the mother to go to her husband and persuade him to live at home again. If the father is at home, the situation with the boy

will improve. Rosa also gave the boy a nontouch massage, giving him bioenergy.

Rosa says that in her work as a shaman she works by feeling, how she
feels inside. She used to think she was schizophrenic, seeing things. She was
very relieved when she read in a Buddhist book ideas similar to hers about
spirits, and she realized she was not schizophrenic after all. As a child she had
these ideas, but she only started to shamanize at age thirty. She would see a
person and the person was not there. She would see an animal in the house,
such as a beautiful cat, but the family did not have a cat. Rosa says 80 percent
of people in Tuva have this potential, but they cannot handle it well. They get
crazy; it is like a nightmare.

When she joins a group of people, she understands their thoughts and
sometimes sees different spirits around a person. At one time she could not go
onto a bus because it was too difficult: she saw big nails and she had to hold on
to them and squeeze them. She has seen a person on the street with a bear or
a dog (not real) and a person walking with one leg going in one direction
and the other leg in another. Sometimes she sees a person with only part of a
body; as she explains it, she sees only the part that has energy. These people
have energy that is twisted. According to Rosa, if a man is sitting and she
does not see his legs, it means that he does not have a connection with the
earth or want to live in his house. Because the problem of negative energy is
a most important aspect of the mind, she will try to talk to the person and
fill him with hope, so that his legs will fill up with energy. She can restore the
person not only by talking but also by touching. But if the person does not
want to go somewhere or be in the house, then the problem will remain.
The individual has to learn to squeeze out the negative energy, and Rosa's
therapy provides anchor and hope.

One of the major problems Rosa (and indeed all shamans) deals with is
bad or negative energy. She can feel bad energy in a house, how people suffer, and how difficult it is to live in such a building. When she comes into
such a situation, she immediately cleans the place using her own energy in
order that the place will be a good place for her and it will be easier to help
people. You have to establish a good atmosphere in order to work, she says (a
basic principle in Western psychotherapy also). One of her helping spirits, a
Chinese person, showed her an energy form that eats out the bad energy.
She can clean energy from everywhere—even clean the sky.

Rosa, as can be seen in her descriptions of her healing practices, is adept at various forms of divination, including the ability to find lost objects. By putting herself into a brief ASC through drumming, she reaches her helping spirits and discovers through them the patient's problem. In a similar manner, she is able to communicate with the spirit of the recently deceased person and tell his family what he said, and what they should do. She can also foretell using knucklebones. In her healing work, she uses a number of techniques, many of which she seems to have developed for herself.

In a time previous to the Soviet era, such a person who saw miraculous things and had all kinds of unusual insights would have probably been close to the true idea of the shaman with powerful ASC or trance states. However, in many respects Rosa fits the description Winkelman (1990:316) puts forth with respect to the shaman: in her selection as shaman she experienced visions, dreams, illness, and spirits' requests; her training involved ASC; her status is recognized by clients; she has powerful animal spirits as allies; she uses physical and empirical medicine and massage and employs a variety of methods of divination to assist in healing and fortune telling. She does not do malevolent acts (or hunting magic, since this is not requested). It is important to note that one of the hallmarks of shamans in other societies is their power to do malevolent or evil acts, but in the Inner Asian complex examined here, no shaman or shaman-healer would admit to malevolent acts. In fact, they occasionally explained an unfortunate occurrence, or death, as caused by someone else's evil act or witchcraft, but all the healers I observed and spoke with, whether in Tuva or Buryatia, emphasized that they only performed positive, healing measures for people.

In Rosa's practice changes due to modern times can be seen overlaid upon her more traditional practices. She uses bioenergetic methods of healing, and she consults with patients as a psychotherapist, searching to understand their problems through discussion rather than through methods of divination—communicating with the spirits—only. Even though she calls herself a shaman, her approach to healing seems to fluctuate between modalities of shamanistic healing, Buddhist-oriented healing, and Western methods of psychotherapy—perhaps partly explained by the fact that she has traveled to the United States, where she was exposed to alternative forms of healing. Her horizons have widened beyond the steppes of Tuva, and this may, indeed, become more typical of the younger shaman-healers in Inner Asia.

Kirgis Khavendaevich, singing and drumming, calling his spirits to heal Rosa;
Shagonar, Tuva (photograph by Eva Fridman, 1996)

Kirgis Khavendaevich

The use of many media to create a total landscape of shamanic healing was nowhere better illustrated than in the case of Kirgis Khavendaevich. Kirgis was a shaman for whom geometry and nature were interlaced. He was also an artist, capturing in his apartment nature and magic, spirit representations *(eeren),* and artifacts, animals and aspects of landscape towering over him and lending him their power.

About one hundred kilometers west of Kyzyl, the town of Shagonar appears on the steppe. In a rather unprepossessing apartment building, we entered into Kirgis's home and office, glowing with painted imagery on every wall, filled to every corner with Tuvan designs and portrayals of nature. The floor of his office was a brilliant dark brown, painted with beautifully stenciled designs of circles, Greek frets, birds marching in rows, and branches and leaves. The walls had Greek fret designs in blue and red on gold; the edge of the doorway was painted in gold. The designs continued out into the hallway in a riot of colors.

Even the ceiling held attention with a lotus-shaped design in green around the base of the hanging lamp, centered among other green geometric designs of intricate knots and interlaced lines. The lamp itself was not spared decorative treatment, embellished with a pale pink silk shade with golden metallic-like petals attached and three golden fish with silver-threaded tails hanging from the light cords. In one of the hallway corners was a picture of a Tuvan shaman in traditional feathered headdress with snakes on his garment, holding a large round drum and balancing on one leg on a large tree stump, with a red desert and a small mountain in the background. On the door to this, his consultation room, hung a sign with a picture of Kirgis himself dressed in a shaman outfit and holding a drum. Listed were all the shaman healing services he could provide.

On the left-hand wall hung his feathered headdress, his large brown drum with twelve white circles painted on it, and his eeren, among them a sable, a claw of another small animal, a bear claw, an arrow, a shaman's whip to chase bad spirits, a horse-hoof eeren, a drum stick with a face of a spirit on it, and a squirrel skin. In addition, he had a flag or a fan that was made of fabric and showed the sun, a horse, and the moon. He used this for chasing black spirits away and to fan *artish* toward a person. His coat, which he put on together with his feathered headdress, had bells and snakes on it. His headdress featured a red and green band and feathers standing upright, exactly like the Plains Native American headdress. Bells decorated the lower edge of the headband, and snakes twisted around it. A Buddhist altar with small and large paintings of various Buddhist deities and even a floor wall panel painted with images of the Soviet hammer and sickle, one with a laurel branch depicted beneath it, completed the curious mixture of ideologies in the room.

Kirgis started to practice as a shaman when he was fourteen years old. When he was herding sheep he saw a rainbow after the rain stopped. The rainbow went through him, and he started to faint. He went home and told his mother, and she told him, "Your ancestors were shamans so you will be a shaman also." After this experience, he became a shaman. When he did not work as a shaman, he felt sick. When working, he felt well and could heal others.

In his present practice, Kirgis performs a variety of shamanic rituals. As his list of shaman services on the door notes, he chases away bad spirits and invites happiness, he helps people with mental problems and with family and child-behavioral problems, and he looks into the future. A variety of divination methods are used. With the help of a mirror he sees what will happen to a person, and he also cleanses houses, sanctifies fire, and sanctifies animals. He can check the pulse and the palm to analyze a health problem and can check blood pressure. He heals alcoholics, drug addicts, and smokers. He helps women who cannot become pregnant, and he can heal gastritis and cancer. If children are sick, he uses artish smoke to help them. He does seven- and forty-nine-day after-death rituals. He uses his own songs for healing, preferring them to the songs Kenin-Lopsan has collected that are available for shamans to use. He and his wife played and sang one of his own songs, using the Bizanchi, a stringed instrument.

If we compare Kirgis's shamanistic attributes to pre-1917 shamanistic objects collected and displayed in the museum in Kyzyl, many of the same artifacts can be seen. Moreover, an archaeological collection of shaman objects dating back to the sixth to eighth centuries B.C. from Kurgan Ardjan, including a bronze mirror and amulets from the fang of a wild boar and the jaw of a horse, indicate there has been very little change in shamanistic artifacts over several millennia.

The shamanistic complex in Tuva is a remarkably stable complex, even allowing for individual differences among practitioners. Kirgis's practice, which includes depictions of nature and animals and a copious collection of eeren denoting his relationship to the forest and to nature, give evidence of a deep attachment to place, essentially undisturbed despite his imprisonment during the Soviet period. His various abilities at divination and ways of reaching the spiritual world for guidance and assistance also attest to his capacity as a traditional shaman still working within a belief system that offers contact with the spirit world.

Buryatia

Buryat shamanism has to be understood by its relationship to physical locale and kinship structures. Although perhaps not obviously related to healing practices, these essential concepts underlie healing by shamans because they appeal to these spirits of locale and kinship for assistance; hence, the form of divination most important for Buryat shamans is the connection to the ancestral and locale-related spirits, a connection made through a number of techniques, as evidenced in the cases discussed below.

Shamanism has always been stronger among the Buryats living on the western side of Lake Baikal. The Buryat who lived on the eastern side of Lake Baikal (the Selenga and Khori clans) came under the influence of Buddhism in the early eighteenth century. Their attachment to shamanism was weakened by the Buddhist lamas, and they have continued to be much more strongly Buddhist than the Buryats living to the west of Lake Baikal and on Ol'khon Island in the Baikal. With the conquest of Siberia by Russia, missionaries from the Russian Orthodox Church Christianized the western Buryats, but their adherence remained superficial. Underneath a Christian veneer, the Buryats continued to maintain a shamanic worldview.

In Buryatia, shamanism has become more organized. In 1992 Nadejda Stepanova founded the Khese Khengereg Association of Shamans to organize shamans living in separate villages and to give them a sense of community. At the first formal presentation of the association, fifteen or sixteen shamans gathered from the Irkutsk, Buryatia, and Aginsk regions (areas that were all included in the original Buryat republic in the early 1930s). Gathering in a quasi-group is unusual for Buryat shamans. This response to changing times indicates shamans need more than their clan adherence to have community approval. Formerly, Buryat shamanism was clan shamanism, with the shaman as the most important person in the clan because of his or her ability to communicate with deceased clan ancestors. Now, although these concepts are still operative, the sense of community has expanded and a broader identification with a community may be necessary.

Nadejda is a powerful and active shaman. In 1996 she was president of the Khese Khengereg and an active spokesperson for shamanism in Buryatia and abroad, having connections with spiritual healers in Italy and Brazil. She comes from a family line of shamans and as a child had visions. She could read thoughts, particularly bad thoughts, and could foretell bad events in the future. She became a shaman at age thirty-six after suffering from a number of "shaman sicknesses." Her process of divination is as follows: when she heals, she goes into an ASC and talks to gods. Shamanism, she says, is a "gift from God and Nature." After consulting with her spirits, she has the ability to heal and cure, to help the sick, return what has been stolen, and to correct mistakes. She cured a boy who suffered from cerebral palsy and could only lie in bed and did not speak. After her cure, he was able to speak, sing, and walk. The family claimed he had improved greatly.

Nadejda cures with her hands, words, and the feeling of connection between herself and the patient. If the patient sits in front of her and thinks of other things, the treatment will not work. She has been able to cure people with growths on their head and people covered with eczema. If a young family wants children, they come to her because they need to know which gods to address and at what time. She performs a special ritual and then children come to these families. Nadejda stresses the need for a psychological connection between herself and the patient, saying that it is the relationship that is important. Her practice utilizes divination in her abilities to call upon her gods to diagnose illnesses and to determine what is necessary for healing. She calls herself a shaman, although perhaps the category that would best identify her, as well as other shamans in Buryatia, would be that of shaman-healer.

Valentina Baldakhinova

Valentina is a respected healer with a very busy practice in Ulan-Ude, the capital of Buryatia. Valentina was originally a biologist and worked at the Medical Institute in the teachers' training department but was taught by another

Valentina Baldakhinova, using her tools to divine patient problems; Ulan-Ude, Buryatia (photograph by Eva Fridman, 2001)

Buryat shaman and now practices healing full time. She has a particular mark on her chest, which, she says, is due to her paternal grandmother Sangali, a famous shamaness who practiced fearlessly throughout the entire Soviet period. As a member of the Shemaiten clan who grew up with her grandparents on the holy island of Ol'khon in the Baikal and in Bichura she was surrounded by relatives who were initiated as shamans and practiced healing. Valentina was able to maintain an unbroken connection to her ancestors and ancestral spirits with no break in tradition during the Soviet period. Her family had not moved away from their clan locale on the Baikal, and the spirits were still available to her. This created great efficacy in healing, as witnessed by the large numbers of patients who came to see her daily. In her ancestral line there are forty male and female shamans. These shaman ancestors include her grandmother; her paternal grandfather, defined as a strong shaman because he could lick iron; her mother, a shamaness in that she made rituals; and her father, who is a shaman and does blessings.

Valentina uses divination by the method of "seeing clearly," which allows her to diagnose the cause of a patient's problem. Her ability to see clearly, in

a special way, began when she was nine years old; she thought all people could
see like this. But even her classmates at school realized she had special vision.
She can look at a person and determine their disease by "shaman's sight." The
difference between a healthy and a sick aura reveals the location of a person's
problem. According to Valentina, when a person is sick, the aura moves; every
disease is different. She has to determine whether the person needs shamanistic or conventional medicine and, if the latter, what conventional medicine is
necessary. She also may use astrology to diagnose and examine the aura of a
person to determine his or her problem. She treats eye and ear diseases,
bone diseases, and almost all illnesses except venereal diseases. She uses
bioenergy and shamanistic healing, not herbs.

Valentina has been in Mongolia a number of times and has developed a
strong connection to shamans there, going on extended healing expeditions
with them to a sacred area northwest of Ulaanbaatar, where there is a shaman
mountain with burials of shamans. Valentina experienced the enormous energy from the mountain that makes it a strong healing source. Nearby is an
area with 108 springs for different diseases. On one side of the mountain the
springs are very hot; on the other side, cold. A special map shows which
springs should be used for specific diseases. Valentina tried four springs (for
herself), for women's diseases, kidneys, eyes, and teeth.

She was inspired by the landscape there, the mountains and the desert,
and the strong spirits of the locale whom she had encountered. While she
was there, one of the people she healed was a young Khalka Mongolian boy
who had epilepsy. She divined that his illness was caused by his ancestral line
and also by the spirits of water. The boy felt well after she performed two
ceremonies—the first was a *tailagan,* an offering of a sheep to his ancestors;
the second was a ritual at the sacred spring where he was originally taken
when he was three years old. Due to this successful healing, the local people
began to invite Valentina to do healings, and seventy to eighty people came
to her for individual healing and treatment. They also asked her to make rituals for rain in an area where there had been no rainfall. After the people
offered tailagans to the spirits of nature, they were told that rainfall had come
and the grass needed for flocks was growing. Valentina's work of divination
in Mongolia indicates how her close association with the deities of the
locale—mountains and water—inspired her in healing people, and this,
indeed, encouraged more people to come to her and ask for individual and

communal help. Without her ability to divine through the guidance of the spirits in that locale, she would not have been able to find the power to heal.

Although a good part of Valentina's healing practice was performed in a
communal way with tailagans, in Ulan-Ude she sees individual patients. She
works every day, all day, at a hostel at the edge of the city. Patients come to her
from all over. Whenever I was there, she had as many as twenty patients waiting to see her, many of whom she had helped before.

I visited her Ulan-Ude office in 1996, 1999, and 2001 and observed how
she analyzed the nature of patients' problems and treated them. Valentina sat
at her desk with stones, incense sticks of juniper, matches, dishes for pouring
water, and other objects, such as a small drum with bells that she uses to call
the spirits. Hanging on the wall was a bear claw, a gift, which she uses for healing breast tumors (she rakes the claw over the breast of the patient). She
wore her usual working clothes: a special dark blue silk vest with gold trim,
a blue scarf (the type used for offerings), prayer beads around her neck, an
iron bracelet (which protects female shamans from bad spirits), and a small
black cap. She also wore a shaman's mirror when working, which she would
not let me photograph her wearing (nor could I photograph her while she was
talking to her spirits, for fear of offending them and making them angry). At
the other end of the room was a wall upon which she threw vodka to read
what its patterns foretold.

Her first patient was an older Buryat man who walked with some difficulty into the room and spoke with her in Buryat. Valentina began to pray,
moving liquid with a spoon from a smaller bowl to a larger one. She opened
a window and threw a cup of liquid to the local spirits outside in order to
bring them into her room. She shook her drum and prayed to the spirits while
wearing her mirror and cap. Then she struck three matches, put them on a
metal plate, added vodka to the flame, and prayed. She added a whole cup of
vodka to the plate and threw the vodka on the wall. It was a good sign because
the vodka splashed up to the ceiling. She then offered a plate of vodka and
bread to the spirits outside the window. She blew into a vodka bottle the
patient brought, gave him the bottle back, and spoke prayers into a piece of
rolled-up paper. She then instructed him on what he should do at home. This
patient had a paralysis, she told me. Every sickness has its own reasons, she
said. In this case the reason was coming from his *utkha,* his ancestral core.
His ancestors were making a problem for him because they had been forgot-

Valentina Baldakhinova, foretelling by reading the patterns of vodka thrown onto the wall; Ulan-Ude, Buryatia (photograph by Eva Fridman, 2001)

ten. If no ritual was made, the problem would continue.

A middle-aged woman brought Valentina a white item wrapped in a blue cloth. It was a *tele dux*—the body of a spirit, similar in appearance to raw pastry. With a small knife, Valentina cut holes in it and inserted incense sticks, which she lit. She then rolled up the tele dux, put it in a jar with herbs and grasses, and wrapped the whole thing in paper. This procedure cleansed the energy channels of the woman. Valentina understood from her spirits that during a ritual for a dead person the patient had received a negative force; a ritual of cleansing and burning of cloth was necessary to eliminate the negative information.

In subsequent visits to Valentina, I noted similar appeals to her spirits, mostly in the service of helping her heal patients who came to her with various physical ailments such as curvature of the spine. Valentina, having diagnosed the problem, healed using bioenergetic means, raking the patient's chest with her bear claw, and nontouch healing encircling various parts of the patient's body. In her shamanistic healing of individuals, she always appealed to the spirits first, in order to know the diagnosis, and then was able to determine from that information what procedure to follow, whether bio-energetic or prayers and entreaties to her spirit to help the person with his or her dilemma.

Duyar Dordjiyevich

Duyar Dordjiyevich's shaman *utkha* (roots) go back thirty-seven generations. He can hear his ancestors in his head when he enters an ASC. When speaking to his kin shamans, he may go back thirty-five or thirty-six generations, but only to male shamans, although there are women shamans in his lineage. He says that his shaman kin told him that he became a shaman nine generations ago. From the time he was three years old he was warned about forbidden activities and forbidden places. His father, a very strong shaman and soothsayer, followed all the warnings and rules, held rituals, and was clear-sighted (that is, he had the ability to see the future). Duyar also sees very clearly. A clear-sighted person, according to Duyar, can read another person's program of life.

His divination skills show that when he does healing he can see every organ in the body and diagnose what organ needs to be treated. Every organ, he said, is like the yoke in an egg—it has its position. The lines in the hands that show the positions of the organs can be moved, spread, and deformed. After a woman has a child, her organs should be repositioned. Doctors here, he said, put a cold pack on the woman's stomach when she is having a child, but that is exactly the wrong thing to do. In the village, old wise women used to massage the stomach of a pregnant woman. Recently, Duyar was asked to come to a new maternity hospital where a young woman had just delivered a large child and could not walk. He saw breaks in the lines in her hands, so he massaged her, placing the organs back in their correct positions. In three hours the woman walked to the telephone and called her mother.

Duyar also often heals witchcraft problems. He said that during the seventy years of Soviet power there were executions of lamas, shamans, and orthodox priests. Before that time, these three balanced the powers of witchcraft, but during the Soviet years witchcraft people grew like wild herbs.

In his dreams, Duyar flies to heaven, where he speaks to spirits and goddesses. There he has spoken with a woman whose young son will be a great person in the future, and a young woman who will be a famous person. He speaks with Buryat gods and goddesses who talk to him about cleansing the Barguzin area (the northeastern side of Lake Baikal). He talks not only to his ancestors and kin, such as his deceased older brother, who gives him advice, but also to contemporary powerful shamans. He is greatly concerned with the ecology of Lake Baikal and associates shamanism strongly with responsibility toward nature and locale. The body is a microcosm of the larger field of nature, so the healing of the body and soul is just one aspect of caring for the well-being of the whole environment. Due to the Buryat focus on kinship and locale, the shaman's sense of healing has extended beyond the individual person to a total healing of the natural landscape. Duyar's ability to divine, to see clearly and communicate with so many spirits, has brought him the power to heal not only individuals but also the natural world around him.

Piotr Khartakhaevich

Connecting problems of ecology and the natural environment is a logical outcome of present concerns of shamanistic healing in Buryatia. Other shaman-healers emphasize clan affiliation and long-unbroken connections to shamanic lineage, especially when tracing their roots back to the Buryat tribes west of Lake Baikal. One of the western Buryat shamans I visited, in the western Ust-Orda region, was seventy-two-year-old Piotr Khartakhaevich, head of the Kharanutski clan, which is a subsection of the Bulagat tribe. When Piotr falls into an ASC, he prays to spirits living on the land, calls them by name, speaks with them, and asks them for the health and well-being of the people who come to him. He knows secret places not far from Ust-Orda that he can use for prayers, depending on the problem. He uses divination to connect to the spirits of the locale and to entreat them to intervene in his patients' problems.

According to Piotr, before people come to him they must go to a *galdaka,* a fortune teller or diagnostician, who says how many sheep or vodka are necessary for his ritual. On the western side of Lake Baikal the shaman functions are separated—divination or diagnosis and healing—and they are performed by two completely separate people, the galdaka and the shaman. There are two galdakas in Ust-Orda. They write a note to Piotr prescribing how much milk or meat and how much vodka (one bottle or ten) is necessary to offer the spirits for a particular problem. Piotr then performs the appropriate ritual. He does healings in his house only for relatives. For other patients, he visits their homes after they have consulted a galdaka for the correct diagnosis and the correct spirits to address.

Conclusion

Shamanism in Tuva and Buryatia has been practiced primarily through rituals for the well-being of a kinship community and healing séances for the benefit of an individual. Shamanism in this area underwent a regeneration following the dissolution of the former USSR. Common to the areas under discussion is a belief system that sustains all divination and healing processes. This belief system involves the shaman's ability to act as a liaison between the spiritual world and the natural world. Historical accident, political necessities, and the pressures of other religions have, however, altered the shape of shamanistic practice, if not its inner core (see also Fridman 2004).

However, it is noticeable that among the shaman-healers of Tuva and Buryatia there are many commonalties in divination practices. In Tuva, shamanistic practice demonstrates a close bond with nature and an intense connection to the spirits with very little admixture with Buddhist practice. The examples of Tuvinian shamans emphasize different traditional Tuvinian approaches to shamanistic healing, all strongly underlaid with the uses of divination in order to make connections to the spirits. Kirgis Khavendaevich had a great array of helping spirits, and in his comprehensive healing practice he used various eeren, such as a bear claw, arrow, and animal parts, as divination tools in order to connect with his helping spirits. Musical instruments— drum, jaw harp, and his own songs—were an important means of healing and connection to the spiritual world.

Even in Tuva, an area of traditional practice, there is evidence of new approaches to divination and healing. The practice of shamanistic healing has changed since pre-Soviet times; even the shamans themselves say they are not as powerful as their ancestors, although they are rehoning their skills and hope to achieve more effective power. Duu-Dori saw and heard the same spirits her grandmother heard, but in her practice, taken up at an older age, she relies upon herbal remedies for healing one type of illness without going into a strong ASC and without further consultation with the spirits. Rosa, an example of a new shaman and one with strong divinatory powers and insights, although she has many traces of traditional shamanistic thinking (in her vivid imagery and drumming to call upon spirits), doubts herself. She is not clear in her own mind whether she is truly experiencing a communication with spirits or whether this is a figment of her own mind. The external world has entered into the Tuvan cosmos and has begun to make its mark on the practice of divination and healing. Rosa, as well as other healers in Buryatia and Khakhasia, have been affected by influences from the world beyond Inner Asia.

Buryat shamanism, as I observed it in 1996, was regenerating very vividly. Not only were shamans working as healers, as noted above, but communal rituals or tailagans were also beginning to be performed for the benefit of a particular community. In their use of divination, Buryat shamans also used eeren and other material objects—bear claws, drums, matches—such as noted in the case of Valentina. Like Kirgis, she treated a variety of disorders, always consulting with her spirits through an ASC. She used bioenergetic methods and foretelling by throwing vodka on the wall. Duyar Dordjiyevich was remarkable for his ability to see clearly and to see each organ in the body in order to diagnose ailments and heal his patients. He also seemed to have very close spiritual connections, flying in his dreams to heaven and speaking to spirits and other people. Dreams are powerful divinatory tools that give the healer access to the spiritual world.

Piotr Khartakhaevich presented an instance in which divination is separate from healing; his patients first visit a galdaka for diagnosis and information as to the exact amount of vodka or sheep to use in the healing ritual.
However, he himself went into an ASC to connect with local spirits to heal
his patients. In this instance, divination was used by two people in order to
effect a healing.

It is important to stress that in a shamanistic world where a human being
relates to the power of nature and the spirits that reside therein, healing is
not only an individual enterprise between shaman and patient; it is also necessary on the larger-scale communal map. The well-being of the whole human
group, the benefits of rain and good pasture land for cattle, are part of communal health. Considerations of communal well-being have now extended
into an active concern with issues of ecology, particularly surrounding Lake
Baikal and its ecological treasures. Shaman-healers have joined with ecologists
from outside of Russia to work together on joint projects of restoration and
preservation. This may indeed be the window to the future for shamanistic
healing of people and nature.

Divination and healing, whether in Tuva or Buryatia, have worked together to help ameliorate individual and/or communal crises and to bring about
well-being in times of economic and personal stress. Methods of divination,
although somewhat varied and individualized from one shaman to another,
cannot be said to be markedly different in Buryatia and Tuva, both of these
areas responding to the same worldview and cosmological orientations. After
a long period of interruption of traditional shamanistic practice during the
Soviet period, younger shaman-healers, in particular, have acquired new
points of view. However, with respect to their practices of divination, their
abilities to see clearly, to foretell the future, and to see the soul of a person
show the strengths of tradition and continuity.

7

Divination in Multireligious Southeast Asia

The Case of Thailand

RUTH-INGE HEINZE

T he Thai have produced elaborate systems of ritual behavior around divination since prehistoric times. Using data from my fieldwork in Southeast Asia (1960, 1971–72, 1975, 1978–79, and several shorter visits later on), I report on divinatory systems in Thailand and describe the different diviners—Brahmins, astrologers, shamans, and other folk practitioners. Combining the data accumulated during my forty years of fieldwork in Thailand with the results of other researchers illustrates the psychological aspects of the process of divination and the pro- phylactic, therapeutic concerns that are the main reasons for divination in Thai- land. Pervading Southeast Asian countries is, furthermore, the concern about the "essence of life" *(khwan)*. Rituals to restore the essence of life are performed as a precautionary measure to avoid disaster and reinforce well-being (Heinze 1982). Performing these rituals also generates merit that is another reinforcing element for the individual for whom the ritual is performed, as well as for the community that is supporting and/or performing the ritual. The concept of khwan is important because it is present in all aspects of divination.

Because Thai beliefs manifest in the broader context of four world reli- gions—Buddhism, Hinduism, Islam, and Christianity—as well as indigenous animist beliefs, I first review the historical development to illustrate the rel- evance of these belief systems for divination.

Historical Background of Divinatory Belief Systems in Thailand

Records show that the Thai were already Buddhists when they were still living in Yunan, southern China. They began to migrate south in the sixth century of our millennium. In 1287, a Thai kingdom consolidated around Sukhothai, the first Thai capital of the territory, now occupied by the Thai nation. At that time, Theravâda ("Word of the Elders"), the earliest form of Buddhism, was declared the state religion. Thai armies then conquered, in 1431, Angkor Wat and invited Cambodian court Brahmins to perform important rituals in Thailand. For example, the Hindu god Shiva was evoked to descend into the Thai king during coronation. This act can be compared to the anointment of European royalty during coronation when an archbishop bestowed the "royal touch" on a monarch. European royalty was, indeed, approached and asked to touch those who sought healing (Heinze 1982:112).

Presently, 93.6 percent of all Thai claim to be Buddhists; that means ethnic Thai may adhere to Theravâda Buddhism and ethnic Thai-Chinese to Mahâyâna Buddhism that was introduced by Chinese traders who settled down in Thailand. Over 10 percent of the Thai population (including the Thai king) are Chinese or have Chinese ancestry (Heinze 1988:35–36). Furthermore, 4 percent of all Thai nationals are Thai-Malay who, with a few exceptions, are Muslims. The Thai-Malay are a minority, but they are the majority in southern Thailand (Heinze 1988:37). We also have to take into account the many animistic belief systems that have survived because the Thai elite adopted beliefs they found to be useful and imposed a reinterpreted version on the people. In sum, it can be said that at least five major belief systems are operative in Thailand. Thai divinatory practices are, therefore, based on the following:

1. The Hindu belief in the Law of Dharma, the "Universal Law." Dharma was established at the time of creation to maintain order in the universe. The belief in dharma was introduced to Thailand early in this millennium by Indian traders and later, in the fifteenth century, by Cambodian court Brahmins.

2. For Southeast Asian Buddhists, the *dhamma* (Pâli, the language of early Buddhism) is also the Buddha's teachings. He talked about the

"Eightfold Way" to end suffering. When all attachments are removed, one can enter nirvâna (Pâli: *nibbâna*). For over two thousand years, Thai have, therefore, also accepted the Buddha's dhamma as an immutable law.

Buddhists, furthermore, believe in the Hindu/Buddhist Law of Karma (Pâli: *kamma*)—that is, the quality of past thoughts, words, and actions that determines the present quality of one's life. Interestingly, the Law of Karma allows some modifications. Although everybody suffers the consequences of past negative behavior, everybody also reaps the fruits of past good thoughts, words, and deeds and can improve one's present and future life with cultivating one's behavior. The Buddhist ideal is not to accumulate karma anymore. This can only be achieved by leading a life of complete equanimity, which is very difficult because it requires one to think, speak, and act always without attachments to the outcome. The Law of Karma allows the belief that the "future is not considered to be immutable, it is rather a configuration of events that can be modified provided enough information is available and this is the secret of the popularity of divination" (Goodman 2000).

3. Since time immemorial, Southeast Asian Buddhists and Hindus believe also in the Akashic Records—that is, mystical books in which all past, present, and future events have been recorded—that means one's fate has been predetermined by a higher source. Thai therefore attempt to find somebody who knows how to access these records and can assist in exploring the nature of past, present, and future.

4. Muslims and Christians in Thailand firmly believe in the same God, whose word is considered to be the final authority. Muslims as well as Christians know they depend on God's grace. They pray to God and are also convinced that moral behavior will positively influence their fate. They also want to explore their future and thus use divination to alleviate existential anxieties.

5. Most important, at the bottom of all belief systems in Asia there are still animist beliefs. These indigenous beliefs attach a soul not only to humans and animals but also to rice, trees, house posts, pillars, mountains, etc. Rituals based on these beliefs are still performed in Thailand, a Buddhist country that absorbed Brahmin customs over time (Tambiah 1970).

Each khwan (soul) has to be taken care of and prevented from
leaving its body. Souls may even have to be propitiated to not disturb other people or the environment. Consequently, the concept
of khwan appears central to the conceptual framework of divination
in Thailand, regardless of whether clients and diviners declare to be
Christian, Muslim, Hindu, or Buddhist.

Thai Experts in Divination

When Thai want to consult a diviner, they will look for the most efficient
practitioner and will cross ethnic, cultural, and religious lines in their search.
Even though textbooks on the different forms of divination are readily available, not only in bookstores but also on open markets, it is considered to be
safer and more effective to consult a knowledgeable expert. The experts may
be the following:

1. Astrologers of any ethnic group and religion are expected to be scientifically accurate. They are publicly known and so are their fees.

2. Brahmins are prestigious and considered to be highly knowledgeable in using astrology and other divinatory methods. They are
   sought because they facilitate the "presence of the Divine" by calling, for example, a god into a statue, and talking directly with the
   god. Brahmins, however, are expensive and there are not many genuine Brahmins in Thailand. No one can become a Brahmin by choice
   or through study; the office is hereditary—that is, in Hinduism one
   has to be born into the Brahmin caste. Nevertheless, I met several
   Thai practitioners who acted and dressed like Brahmins without
   having the necessary qualifications.

3. Thai Buddhist monks are consulted because they are considered to
   be more reliable, not only because they have studied religious books
   but also because their monastic vows prevent them from exploiting
   their clients. Appreciation for a consultation is expressed by a dona-
   tion, which may be food or other necessities for the divining monk
   or an optional sum of money.

4. A wide range of shamans and other folk practitioners belonging to
   various ethnic groups and belief systems are selected based on their
   reputation—that is, their success rate. Spirit mediums, for exam-

ple, are approached because they can call a deity into their body. Their clients seek the presence of the Divine and want to hear their fate directly from a god's lips.

5. An elder (of the family, the village, or the government) may perform a *tham khwan* (making of the khwan), since not many Thai can afford to invite a Brahmin or other experts into their house.

Divination Rituals

The most popular form of divination in Thailand is astrology that is a noninspirational, deliberate form of divination. Astrology plays a part in every aspect of Thai life. Because the predominant system of astrology in Thailand originated in India but has absorbed earlier indigenous concepts, it is worthwhile to look at the content of present beliefs.

According to Wales (1983), who extensively studied ritual behavior in Thailand, the number and position of planetary deities (seven to nine), for example, can inform about fate. Brahmins will show how to adapt to cosmic influences. For example, after a child is born, it is important to care for the afterbirth, or placenta. For children born in the fourth, fifth, or sixth month, the placenta should be buried north of the house. If the child is born in the seventh, eighth, or ninth month, the placenta should be buried north or northeast of the house but not to the east, because in that case the child would be hard to rear. If the child is born in the tenth, eleventh, or twelfth month, the placenta should be buried south or northeast of the house. If the child is born in the first, second, or third month, it will live long, provided the placenta is buried to the south or southeast (Wales 1983).

An astrologer will also predict a child's fate by the name of the lunar year in which it is born—the year of the rat, ox, tiger, hare, large snake (or dragon), small snake, horse, goat, monkey, cock, dog, or pig. This belief obviously was influenced by Chinese customs brought by Chinese traders who migrated to Thailand.

For the twelve months, as well as the days of the week, an elaborate numerical system has been worked out (Wales 1983:24–32). Astrologers will explain the quality of each aspect and provide information about the length of time a specific aspect will influence a client's life. To be aware of one's position on an astrological chart greatly enhances the possibilities of well-being, because necessary precautions can be taken.

Astrologers are also consulted to assist in selecting marriage partners; to determine the right time for building a house or starting any action in agriculture or trade; and to give general advice for becoming successful in one's work and relationships.

Numerology, another form of deliberate, noninspirational divination, is quite popular in Thailand. To determine the probability of a couple having children, it is suggested one take the age (in months) of the older partner and subtract from it that of the younger. Divide by seven; if the remainder is one, two, three, four, five, or six, it is positive. But if there is no remainder, the answer is negative. Once pregnant, to know whether the child will be a boy or a girl, one writes down the mystic number forty-nine (seven times seven), adds the number of months since conception, and subtracts the age of the mother from the total. From this, one subtracts one, then two, and so on up to nine. If the remainder is odd, it will be a boy; if it is even, it will be a girl. Other techniques determine whether the child will be easy to rear, and there are other concerns about which to consult a numerologist (Wales 1983:3).

Other practitioners specialize in interpreting physical phenomena—for example, portentous pimples—which is another noninspirational, deliberate form of divination. Facial pimples, unlike those on the body, are more often unfortunate than the reverse, especially for men. Good ones are black or vermilion, not so are red, white, and yellow pimples. If slight, the ill effect will be mild. Those in groups of seven or five are especially favorable. If on the left side they denote wealth; if on the right side, they indicate promotion. A pimple on the left eyebrow indicates prosperity, on the right longevity. A black spot in the hair suggests prosperity, still more so if it is prominent. When a group of seven pimples is arranged on the forehead in the W-shape of the constellation Cassiopeia, this is considered to indicate great fortune. A pimple on the earlobe signifies intelligence, and long life when inside the ear. Between the eyebrows, pimples indicate prosperity. If the pimple is on the tip of the ear, the prosperity will continue. A pimple on the eyeball means that this person will be grateful to parents. When the pimple is situated above the middle of the upper lip it is lucky, especially when black or red; otherwise it is only moderately so (Wales 1983:48). Such interpretations obviously are influenced by Chinese customs introduced by Chinese who became Thai nationals.

Wales (1983:52–62) offers ample descriptions of the Thai system of palmistry. This noninspirational, deliberate form of divination does not differ much from methods of palmistry practiced in other countries. The lines on the inside of each hand allow the diagnosis about strengths and weaknesses of a client's physical and mental state. The head line indicates his or her present mental state; the heart line, the present emotional condition. Lines in the left palm indicate inherited dispositions, and lines in the right palm point to faculties that have been acquired during this life. Many lines around the left wrist, for example, indicate the inherited disposition for a long life and, on the right wrist, the acquired disposition for a long life (personal communication during numerous interviews with Western and Asian palmists).

Another form of inspirational divination is the art of interpreting dreams. Relevant books can be bought in stores or open markets. Only when the interpretation of premonitory dreams is complicated may a competent soothsayer of any ethnic group or religion be consulted.

The simplest method to divine one's fate is sortilege. Thai go to one of the numerous Buddhist monasteries to employ this inspirational form of divination. Next to the altar are containers with small, wooden sticks. Whoever wants to know his or her fate takes one of these containers and kneels in front of the altar. After an appropriate prayer, the container is shaken until one stick jumps out, with a number printed on it. Next to the wall, there is a shelf with small strips of paper filed under their respective numbers. These small strips of paper usually contain excerpts from the Buddhist canon. They are supposed to offer advice on how to face one's problems in a Buddhist way. Although such advice appears to be predictable, I was surprised by how many people, every day, in each monastery I visited were vigorously shaking these containers as if they could influence their fate by their ardent prayers. Again, the belief that a power can be evoked with sacred words is reinforced. It may be a placebo effect; in any case, it produces satisfactory results.

During my research in southern Thailand, where large portions of the population are Thai-Malay, I observed divinatory practices of *bomohs* (Malay practitioners). Most of them are devout Muslims. Allah does not allow any other god or spirits besides him, so how do the people reconcile their faith with their practices? When in Singapore, I asked the mufti (religious leader of Muslims) about the numerous bomohs in his area. He answered, "If they pray to Allah five times a day and go to the mosque on Friday, we look the other way. They are good circumcisers and help our people in many ways" (personal communication 1978).

When asked to divine, bomohs will cut lemons into four pieces. When the majority of the pieces fall cut-side up *(buka)*, the answer is "yes." When the majority of the pieces fall cut-side down *(tutup)*, the answer is "no." When half of the pieces fall cut-side up and the other half cut-side down, the oracle refuses to answer. The bomohs will then suggest asking again at a later time.

I was present when an elderly woman inquired about her health and the bomoh (a woman) used a wooden knife to diagnose. She inserted the four-inch-long knife between the second and third toe of the client's right foot and pressed her toes together. She wanted to find out whether a spirit caused the illness. It is assumed that the spirit will feel the pain and cry out loud. In this case, no spirit interference was diagnosed, and the obesity of the woman was considered to be the result of too much *angin* (Malay word for "wind").

When the pressure of angin builds up in the body, it destroys the balance of the four elements—earth, fire, water, and air—from which the world is made. The spirits must be sent back to their place of origin so that the division between darkness and light and spiritual and human realms become clear again. Excess must be allowed to escape from the body so that balance can be restored (Laderman 1991:64–85).

Malays are, indeed, not supposed to express emotions. When frustrations accumulate, they produce "wind" in the body. On September 11, 1978, I witnessed a *main puteri* ("calling of the spirit princess") performed for a young worker in Kelantan. He had been angered by an incident at his job and was now suffering from excess angin. To cure his *sakit berangin* (sickness from wind), the bomoh evoked first the guru (mystical teacher) and then began to count rice kernels—two kernels each for earth, fire, water, and air—to determine which of the four humors was in excess.

Procedures may differ from bomoh to bomoh, but the basic elements are similar. Bartlett (1931), for example, recorded the sequence of such divinatory ritual:

> When there is sickness, there is requested medicine of the datoe [folk
> practitioner]. . . . there are to be taken one egg, of rice one cupful, of
> palm-leaf stalks seven, bound up with thread of three colors . . . To be
> invited is the soul of the sick person. . . . There is to be taken with thumb
> and two fingers rice, an even number (of grains). If it is the right

amount, it will be an even number. If it is uneven, not divisible by two, it is to be taken a second time.

The rice is then boiled without salt and held over the head of the sick person. At this time, a cooked egg is given to the bomoh, who examines it and formulates a diagnosis.

I observed a similar form of diagnosis among Chinese spirit mediums in Singapore who move an egg around the head and body of clients and then break the egg. A client may also bring a coconut that the spirit medium blesses and puts outside the door of his house. When the coconut breaks open naturally, the curse is considered to be broken (Heinze 1988:170).

To ascertain the presence of helping spirits, some bomohs tap their arms from the elbow to the wrist, the left arm with the second and third finger of their right hand, and the right arm with the first and third finger of their left hand. When the bomohs feel a vibration, they announce the presence of the spirit (Heinze 1988:251).

A bomoh in Patani confirmed his findings by reading the flame of a wax candle (Heinze 1988:242). Other Thai practitioners may look into a glass of water or invite the client to use the water like a crystal ball (Heinze 1988:251). Carol Laderman (1991) summarized the functions of bomohs by explaining that the healing shaman opens the floodgates of emotion and exorcises the demons of disease. Rather than merely being a by-product of a magical ceremony, the bomoh's cures are the result of conscious psychotherapy. Because the concept of angin is a powerful therapeutic tool, Laderman thinks that the healing role of the shaman is not likely to be filled by someone trained in another medical tradition soon.

Some bomohs, however, also read medical books and may take the pulse of their clients or use a thermometer. Most of them have large collections of herbs, different kinds of bark, and minerals for their concoctions. Some showed me books in which they recorded the most favorable times for diagnosis and healing (Heinze 1988:255).

The "Essence of Life" (Khwan)

Because the khwan plays such an important role in Thai life that includes divination, I want to offer more detailed information about how it is perceived.

Thai will say a khwan is "the 'essence of life,' a principle vital and essential for all sentient beings. Insubstantial and indestructible by nature, the khwan is supposed to reside in a physical body, which it can leave during sleep, illness, or death. Without a khwan, a person would not be complete" (Heinze 1982: 17). If a khwan leaves a human body for more than three days, the owner will die. It is believed that a sudden fright, an upsetting experience, or the changing of one's residence, especially a trip abroad, can cause a general weakening of a client's condition that results in the leaving of his or her khwan. Moving away from one's familiar environment and support group will, indeed, upset the khwan. Good wishes and blessings from a person's community are therefore important.

Thai also may use the word *vinyan* (Pâli: *viññāna,* "knowledge") "to denote a more abstract soul. . . . It is believed that the vinyan is that which transmigrates and, in rebirth, enters a mother's womb" (Heinze 1982:18). In Thailand, souls of the deceased—that is, souls without a material body—are called *phi* or *peta* (hungry ghost). The *chai,* another word for "soul," represents the khwan of the heart (see Heinze 1982:19). Thai know of a large range of different souls; the presence of the khwan, however, is the most important.

The khwan is distinct from the Chinese concept of *chi,* which circulates through the body and whose harmony has to be restored and maintained. Khwan is considered to be either one entity or a group of over thirty-two "souls." There are marked differences also to the Indian concept of *prana* (life breath) or the Greek *pneuma* (soul, spirit). Each khwan has to be considered in a context that may be sometimes difficult to recognize for an outsider.

The belief in the khwan and other spiritual beings is still quite visible in Thailand. For example, small spirit houses rest on poles in front of private houses, even hotels (for example, the Erawan Hotel in Bangkok) and government buildings. The spirit of the former owner of a lot of land or the spirit of the land itself is invited to reside in a spirit house nearby but outside a house. This spirit is honored each day with offerings of flowers and food. Thai believe that when a spirit is satisfied, it will not disturb whoever lives now on the land and may even protect the present residents (personal observations over the past forty years).

Opposite Wat Phra Keo, the monastery of the Emerald Buddha in Bangkok, stands a small temple dedicated to the Pillar of the City. It is believed that the spirit of the city resides in this pillar. Every day, people of

all walks of life, including intellectuals and students, fill the temple to propitiate the khwan of the city and to ask for blessings, healing, and fulfillment of
various kinds of wishes, such as passing an exam (personal observation over
the past forty years).

The care for an individual khwan is the responsibility of parents, children,
relatives, friends, and neighbors, who perform rituals to call back, to fasten,
and to strengthen the khwan. When necessary, such rituals can be performed
at the spur of the moment. More effective rituals, however, may require
lengthy preparations because the correct performance of each detail in such
a "life-restoring" ritual is of vital importance (Tambiah 1968).

The making of a khwan (tham khwan), an animist custom that has been
performed since time immemorial, is practiced in a Buddhist context to
which Brahmin features have been added over time. Survival considerations—
that is, precautions to avoid future disaster—permeate all belief systems in
Thailand.

I have observed tham khwan rituals performed for quite a few reasons.
The textbook I bought on Sanam Luang, which is the Sunday market in
Bangkok in front of the Royal Palace, lists ten occasions for performing a tham
khwan: (1) for a one-month-old child; (2) when the top knot is cut; (3) when
a new house is built, for the house posts; (4) during a housewarming; (5) for
a future monk; (6) during a wedding ceremony; (7) when making merit (paying respect to the Buddha or making donations to monks); (8) after a cremation ceremony, for the living; (9) for a Buddha image ("to open its eyes," "to
activate its essence"); (10) for the rice (Heinze 1982:49–50).

But even this textbook does not list the wide range of ceremonies where
the essence of life has to be propitiated, such as when winnowing rice, when
somebody goes away or returns from a trip, and other situations when the
essence of life must be assuredly restored. The precautionary ritual assures the
well-being of all participants.

Ritual Components of a Tham Khwan

Each tham khwan requires seven basic steps (Heinze 1982:69–84):

1. Everybody agrees on the purpose of the ritual
2. Everybody enters the sacred space ritually—for example, in a home
   special care is taken to demarcate the space and purify it and all participants with incense (other sacred places seem to have natural

markers to distinguish the sacred space from ordinary reality)

3. Deities are evoked from different realms

4. Lights are waved *(wien thiang)* to welcome deities from different realms (Heinze 1982:75–76)

5. Feasting of the khwan and the deities, including feeding the person for whom the ritual is performed, takes place, with food from the different levels of the *bai si* (auspicious tray, Tree of Life) representing the different realms of existence (Heinze 1982:69–75)

6. All participants' wrists are tied *(phuk khwan)* (Heinze 1982:76–84)

7. The deities are sent away and everyone leaves the sacred space ritually

The tying of the wrists has especially prophylactic value because (a) it protects one from outside negative influences, (b) it prevents the khwan from leaving the individual, and (c) it seals the contract between the participants and the spiritual world (Heinze 1982:76–84).

A tham khwan is performed at any occasion where there is concern about the condition of an individual's essence of life. I have attended the following three kinds of tham khwan rituals.

THAM KHWAN. On January 4, 1977, I attended a tham khwan for a one-month-old child in Bangkok-Thonburi. The ritual was performed at the parents' home by the father, who was a boatman of the British Naval Attaché in Bangkok. He called himself a Brahmin and wore Brahmin-like clothes, but he was also a practicing spirit medium (Heinze 1982:1–5). The second tham khwan was performed in Bangkok-Thonburi at the home of the father's colleague, by the colleague's mother, in the presence of three Theravâda monks, whose chanting increased the merit (Heinze 1982:5–9).

PHUK KHWAN (TYING OF THE ESSENCE OF LIFE). On July 15, 1972, I witnessed a ritual performed for the freshmen on the Chiangmai University campus by a Roman Catholic rector assisted by other faculty and senior students (Heinze 1982:9–11).

THAM KHWAN NAG (MAKING OF A NOVICE'S ESSENCE OF LIFE). On July 21, 1972, in Chiangmai, I attended a tham khwan nag ritual, which is performed to assure a novice's khwan accompanies him into the monastery. The ritual was performed inside the mother's grocery shop, which was emptied for this purpose. The ritualists were two *mo khwan* (spirit doctors) from Bangkok (Heinze 1982:11–16).

Conclusion

Divination is required to determine the right time for any ritual. Whatever divinatory practices are chosen, the decision will depend on the abilities of the individual doing the reading or creating the chart, thus providing valuable information beyond generalizations. In the West, diviners and other practitioners often meet culturally programmed prejudices; in Asia, individuals with extraordinary faculties are sought after enthusiastically. Practitioners need not advertise their services; their psychic abilities become known through word of mouth.

Each Thai is more or less familiar with astrology—for example, the course of the planets and astrological charts. Most Thai also have some knowledge of other divinatory practices. But, as I said before, Thai will be inclined to use the most efficient way to prevent future misfortune. This gives divination another twist. Thai know they cannot change their past, but they can prevent the accumulation of unnecessary karma in the present, and good or absent karma may influence their future positively.

While Westerners may not be concerned about the quality of their thoughts, words, and actions and how it influences the quality of their future, these concerns are very important in Asia among the elite, the royal family, and the government, as well as the general public. They believe divination can locate the source of an impending misfortune and so allow preventive measures to be taken in time to counteract negative effects of bad karma and other outside influences. Divining the source of an illness may be too late; therefore, it is more important to practice prevention, almost blindly, not to miss any opportunity to improve one's well-being.

No matter what the cards or charts say, an individual's future is open to interpretations and change. Learning the future is, after all, why most people seek diviners in Thailand, but it appears to be the least accurate focus of psychic perception. Nobody really knows whether the future will be changed, and individuals may make decisions incongruous with the information they receive. No matter how truly precognitive a practitioner is, once the future is predicted, the client can alter the prediction through different choices. The interpretation is up to the diviner, but the future for the client moves on from that point, and he or she can make or break those predictions. On one hand, Thai believe in predestination; on the other hand, they also believe the future is mutable. Everything is in flow, and they do not want to miss the opportunity for a better turn of events.

In sum, a wide range of techniques has been developed in Thailand, with the goal of recognizing the causes of imbalances. It is of great importance to Thai to perform precautionary rituals before a situation deteriorates and more substantial damage may occur. The first of such considerations will be the reinforcement of the essence of life. Divination in Thailand, therefore, attempts to take care of fears at their roots.

Thai, whether they are Buddhists, Hindus, Malay-Muslims, Christians, or animists will employ as many techniques as possible to restore and maintain balance and harmony in life.

III

DIVINATION AND HEALING

8

Healing through the Spirits

Divination and Healing among the Jaunsaris of Uttrakhand, India

KRISHNAKALI MAJUMDAR

Fieldwork and research for this study was conducted among the Jaunsari Paharis—the mountain people of Jaunsar-Bawar in the northwestern mountainous terrain of Uttar Pradesh in North India. Typically, a Jaunsari hamlet is built along the contour of a hillside or a ridge (with altitudes ranging from 1,500 meters to 2,300 meters above sea level) with terraced fields and cattle posts surrounding it. Each hamlet consists of fifteen to twenty-five households, with the dominant caste groups, the Rajputs and/or the Brahmins, occupying big houses in the center of the village and the other castes, Bajgi (the drummers), living in smaller houses surrounding the big houses. The caste groups who occupy the lowest rung in the caste hierarchy are the Doms and the Koltas, who usually live in a hamlet of their own on the outskirts of the land-rich hamlets. The households are maintained and reproduced through fraternal polyandrous unions, but polygynous unions are also common.

Beyond the village and the terraced fields, in the higher altitudes, are the forests, locally known as *danda*. To villagers, the danda represents the wild, where spirits live and men go to hunt. Beyond the danda is the terrain of Indralok, which is associated with supreme divine beings. The movement between the domain of domestication (the hamlet and the terraced fields) and

183

that of the wild and undifferentiated is carefully governed and is of fundamental relevance to Jaunsari perceptions of well-being and affliction. The
domain of domestication is centered upon the promotion of fertility in
women, livestock, and field; both women and men are equally involved in
the upkeep of this domain. The danda is dangerous, higher, and beyond the
control of humans. It is where wild animals are hunted by men and spirits have
the power to control mortal beings.

The Interpretive Practices and Structures of the Divination Process

There has been a narrative turn in writing on illness experience. The narratives of illness, Bryon Good argues, have little to do with affective dimensions of experience (since these sensual and affective dimensions resist
objectification to symbolic forms). He suggests that anthropologists focus on
how dimensions of the perceived world are unmade, broken down, or altered
as a result of serious illness, as well as on the restitutive process of the "remak-
ing of the world" (Good 1994:131). The narratives of spirit possession discussed in this chapter are approached from a critical phenomenological
perspective, as espoused by Good (118). In my analysis of Jaunsari culture and
divination rituals, I am especially interested in the way the narratives are
organized, their particular syntax and meaning order. I also show, through an
analysis of divinatory and curative séances, the necessity of understanding
spirit possession in terms of its therapeutic nature and the dynamic meanings
this has in the ongoing lived world of people.

  In choosing to explore spirit-based diagnosis and healing in narrative
form, I borrow concepts from Good's interpretive analysis of the restitutive
process of epilepsy. The restitutive process, according to Good, involves two
linked interpretive practices: symbolization and narrativization. He shows in
his study of chronic pain experience that the diagnosis itself is a form of symbolization. It is in the interpretive process that the origin of suffering is
invoked. Narrativization, on the other hand, is a process through which "the
life world is reconstituted" (133). The narratives I have collected are inevitably
derived from the Jaunsari's lived experience and life world, which are filled

with spiritual forces, cosmological prescriptions, moral codes, and other such practices and ideologies that regulate structures of social relations and power. As a number of anthropological studies have pointed out, an illness event is held as a moral event and accordingly invokes "moralizing judgments" and becomes a source of "contested judgments" (134). The ethnographer's task, then, is to uncover and anticipate the underlying symbolic structures in cultural terms, to elucidate potential meanings, and to illustrate how these structures and meanings give form to distinctive forms of lived experience.

In my analysis of divination process in Jaunsar, I discuss three significant concepts of narrative from Good's analysis of Turkish epilepsy narratives (135–64). These concepts are emplotting, subjunctivizing, and positioning. The emplotment of an event refers to the plot through which an ordered story is constructed and authored; there is an underlying structure to a story and there is an engagement of the reader in the sense-making of the story. In the case of an illness, the plots are about predicament, a continuous endeavor, and suffering. These stories give texture and meaning to the larger life story, uncover the various ambiguities and contradictions that exist in culture, and at the same time bring coherence to events.

As the story unfolds from one event to the next, the story becomes more diversified and multireferential; new episodes introduce new twists and open up potentials for reevaluation of the past events and hence the motives, intentions, and context. This is what Good describes as the subjunctivizing of illness narratives. The subjunctive mode of narratives is maintained by the provisional quality of the story in which new events alter the story or a new angle is thrown in by a different narrator or the story is told in a different way. All these give a creative potency to the story.

The narrative positioning of suffering refers to the pragmatic of illness narratives. The narratives are intersubjective and dialogically constructed. The stories are positioned among the authors, narrators, and audience and reveal the structure of the divination and healing. Analysis of narratives of divination séances shows how healers and their patients interpret and articulate problems and negotiate solutions. A focus on these narratives exposes the cultural logic underlying spirit-based diagnosis and the centrality of the role of divination in managing social integration and protest against social ascriptions.

Symbols and Cosmologies

In order to understand the cultural logic behind healing through spirits, it is necessary to understand the social landscape and the nature of the key actors involved. The social landscape, according to the Jaunsaris, is stratified, with the Indralok (upper world) above, Mrityulok (underworld) below, and the Prithvi (people world) in the center. There are a number of worlds between the upper world and the underworld (seven below the center and seven above the center), but to most Jaunsaris, Indralok, Prithvi, and Mrityulok form the three-tiered indigenous cosmos.

Each world has its respective spirits, which in turn have their own hierarchy, and its denizens define each world. The upper world that is above the high mountains is the home of the major deities. The mountaintop is closer to the upper world and is the home of the lesser deities *(matris)*. The underworld is inhabited by nefarious spirits, while earth is where humans live. The inhabitants of the underworld are the spirits of humans who died a premature death or died unfulfilled, a condition variously known as *masandh, bhutpret,* or *heyrdh.* The cremation grounds, which are considered to be continuous with the underworld, are areas where malevolent spirits roam free. The shaman or diviners, who reside in the people world, are seen as the mediators between the beings of the upper world and the underworld, and he or she acts on behalf of the humans inhabiting the earth.

In addition to the three worlds, the Jaunsaris also recognize nine *graha* (planets) that affect inhabitants of the people world. In accordance with the Hindu astrological system, a villager priest will develop a horoscope upon the birth of a child. The horoscope is calculated by taking into account the date of birth, the time of the birth, and the first two letters of the child's name. Two levels of analysis develop for use with this chart: the ruling number and the relation between the planets. The date of birth, according to certain rules, is calculated/manipulated to determine the ruling number. The time of birth helps to calculate the asterism *(naksatra)* under which a child is born. The particular asterism one is born under is therefore defined for the person from birth and determines the planetary influence *(rashi)* on his or her life. Each planet has certain attributes that affect the mental, physical, and spiritual strength of the person.

The birth chart is consulted for major decisions and for finding out the cause of suffering and misfortune. It also helps to predict anxieties and problems that might afflict the individual and finds solutions to them. Each year, a number of publishing houses release an almanac *(jantri)*, which is vigorously and extensively consulted by Brahmin/religious specialists of the community.

The Jaunsaris believe that the human body is made up of elements that affect a person's personality and that an imbalance in the elements will bring about physical and social ailments. This belief is in accordance with the *tridosha* theory (humoral theory) from the ancient Indian medical tradition of Ayurveda (mentioned in Hindu classical texts of *Charaka Samhita* and *Susrata Samhita*). The visible component of the body, capable of sustaining an independent existence, is also influenced and affected by the inhabitants of the various worlds. The Jaunsaris conceive of an image of the body that is made up of five elements *(dhatus):* ether, wind, fire, water, and earth. For the well-being of the body, these elements must be kept in balance. Digested food generates elements and refuse. The elements are further invested with subtle qualities, and their imbalance affects the elements. Clearly, then, disruption is caused by inappropriate intake. In order to bring the person back to his or her initial state of balance, counterbalanced intakes are prescribed. Balance therefore characterizes the logic underlying the healing approach in Jaunsar.

Jaunsari Understanding of Affliction and Healing

The learned power of communicating with supernatural worlds is almost always exclusively the domain of the Brahmin caste—the *Bamons* (Heinze, in this volume, refers to them as astrologers and Brahmins). The Bamons are official religious specialists who gain their power to heal or alleviate afflictions by learning to use the *Bagoi* or *bhagyabahi* (the Book of Fate) and are the representatives of the community.

The *Mali* (male diviners) or *Matriya* (female diviners) are healers who have gained power as a special gift and are selected by the spirits known to possess them (Turner, in this volume, calls them tribal doctors). They are considered to be mediators between humans and other inhabitants of the three worlds. There is another category of practitioners known as *Masandhya*. These practitioners usually belong to the lower castes, the untouchables, and are assumed to communicate with nefarious spirits of the underworld. They are considered to be powerful mediators between the human world and the world of the dead.

The divinatory process primarily involves identifying the cause of suffering at various levels: (1) Is the cause of suffering natural or supernatural? If supernatural, which particular force or spirit is causing the suffering? (2) What are the reasons for possession by the spirit? (3) Were any humans involved in this process?

The Jaunsaris recognize several kinds of affliction, depending on the cause: (1) *bimari*—an imbalance in the elements of the body because of natural causes or supernatural involvement; (2) *dosh*—an imbalance in the body's relationship with the "behavioral environment," resulting in divine punishment; (3) sorcery *(jadu-tona);* and (4) witchcraft *(daag ki shakti).*

In this research, I found dosh to be the central organizing metaphor in shaping experience and making sense of the world. It is particularly a significant metaphor around which the people's narratives were built and gained coherence. In fact, many of the narratives explicitly ordered their experience in this form.

The Jaunsaris consider dosh to be a curse that is given or attached by supernatural forces when an individual fails to maintain certain cosmological prescriptions. Dosh brings suffering. It is a diagnostic category that reflects how Jaunsaris tend to explain or understand the problems of everyday life and suffering. It reflects and symbolizes the change in the behavioral environment and in the individual's body and manifests itself in internal and external transformations. A change in the behavioral environment or the proportions of elements that form a body has a tremendous impact on the constitution of the self and personhood. That is to say, dosh is the central metaphor related to the Jaunsari understanding of suffering and healing. Dosh has multiple meanings; it is polyvocal.

The healing process involves either driving out the spirit or appeasing or integrating the spirit. The Jaunsaris believe that spirit possession can be symptomatic of an illness, or the divine call or divine selection. In either case, intrusion by a spirit into the body of a human endangers transformations in the life of the host. In the case of possession, there are two contrasting responses: (1) exorcism *(jhar-phunk)*—driving out the spirit; and (2) andoricism *(bonth)*—appeasing or integrating (habituating) the spirit and cultivating a viable and enduring relationship between the host and the spirit.

Divination and Diviners:
General Considerations

Jaunsari diviners are part of a great pan-Indian tradition of shamanistic practices. Ancient classical Indian scriptures contain frequent mention of *muni* (Eliade 1974:407), and in various oral traditions of Indian aboriginal people there is mention of ecstatics, called *ojha,* who may be male or female. There are several categories recognized in Jaunsar that show important continuities with pan-India Hinduism. Every diviner has tutelary spirits who inhabit his or her body. Their primary duty is divination. In case of sickness, the cause is sought through an altered state of consciousness. It is believed that the diviners are chosen by deities or other lesser spirits to be conduits or a mouthpiece of the particular deity, for whom he or she acts as the medium in the diagnoses of suffering and misfortune. The divination occurs when the supernatural force enters into the Mali's or Matriya's body, possesses it, and speaks through the entranced host. The Mali then becomes the mediator, able to communicate with the divine forces and other spirits not considered benevolent.

The diviner's status is legitimized by the blessings obtained at the temple of Mahasu at Hanol—the most scared pilgrimage place for all Jaunsaris. However, diviners differ in terms of their divinatory objects, style of divination, language, and area of expertise, as well as their caste affiliation. Becoming a diviner is not automatic after having been chosen by the divine (a special calling). Usually such calls from the spirit world would come in possession episodes, prophetic dreams, or visionary encounters, and a person may appear deranged or ill until the spirit is calmed. This stage is known as the untamed stage *(bawala),* during which one does not have any understanding, much the same way a young child cannot speak. Once the spirit is ready to be tied permanently to the host (which is expressed during divinatory and curative séances), one goes through the process of habituation (bonth). This process can sometimes take months or years. The habituation ritual confers the legitimate status of a Mali or Matriya and they subsequently have immediate access to the world of spirits.

For the Jaunsaris, divination is a process of obtaining knowledge about past, present, or future events, as well as a way of knowing the causes of affliction and suffering. It may involve one or more of the following divinatory techniques:

1. Possession involves seeking the guidance of the tutelary spirit who it is believed will reply through the diviner when he or she goes into an altered state of consciousness.

2. *Anad-ganad* is a mechanical divinatory procedure where a Bamon consults the Bagoi with the help of a solid rectangular bone, locally known as *pasa* or *goti* (dice), which has four sides, each side having one to four dots. The dice is flipped three times and the sum of the numbers is used to calculate and search (anad-ganad). The sum of the numbers refers to the location of the page that reveals the nature of the dosh and the ritual required to rectify it. The Bamon interprets the real meaning inherent in the verses.

3. *Grahadosh* involves interpreting astrological signs by a Bamon. The Bamon also use *jantri* or *panchang* (yearly astronomical calendars) in conjunction with the Bagoi to offer remedies and suggestions. For instance, dosh resulting from the conflicting influences of planets—grahadosh—is calculated from charts in the jantri that maps the movement of various planets.

4. Reading *motia* (rice grains) involves interpreting the spatial arrangement of rice grains thrown in the air and caught while singing hymns or mantras. The number, spatial location, and design of the rice grains caught in the palm of the hand are interpreted.

5. *Chui-chalana* is a divinatory technique used in severe cases of dosh. A Bamon will invoke his tutelary spirit to help him locate the source of dosh.

6. Necromancy involves Masandhya, who are believed to divine with the bones of the dead and with the Masandhya spirits of the underworld. Their divination style involves awakening the masandh and/or calling the dead to impart information about the causes of unnatural deaths. The Masandhya are known for possessing evil powers obtained by meditating on a moonless night in cremation grounds. Some Masandhyas possess a book of figures *(yantra),* which they use to make charms *(bujhri)* and designs used during rituals of exorcism.

The diagnosis process involves the healers engaging in a dialogue with their guardian spirit, or *devata,* and the afflicting spirit. From their dialogical space, they communicate for resolution as well.

The life histories of Mali/Matriyas I collected reveal another feature common to all of the healers: the state of bawala. This state is described as frightening and uncontrollable and features considerable physical uneasiness. However, it was followed by the "opening of the tongue" *(bocwan)*—a state of maturity. It is interesting to note here that these stages, reflecting the development of the novice, are very similar to those stages that shape the development of a person from infancy to adulthood. Bawala is very similar to the state of an infant—not knowing where one is or where one is going. In contrast, bocwan is a state of enlightenment—one with vision—and able to articulate (speak) what one can see in this light.

In terms of the power objects and ritual paraphernalia used by the healers, there is a certain amount of mimicking of Hindu rituals—sprinkling Ganga water around the space in which the healer sits, burning incense, applying vermilion on the forehead, etc. Whether conscious or not, it does establish a link with orthodoxy and gives the healer an official legitimacy. A number of healers hang pictures of local politicians and famous people they claim to have cured, which also creates an image of official status.

The séances begin with prayers that evoke the power of sacred sites and powerful spirits. Drumming and chanting mantras are the most common ways of invoking the spirits to manifest themselves. Jerking movements of the body to more controlled movements, as in *khel,* signal that the spirit wants to communicate its presence and/or its desires. Falling to the ground rigid signals the departure of the spirit. Whether or not this departure is a permanent one is by no means predictable. The spirit can manifest in the body of a person at its own will, without any invocation.

The curing ceremony typically involves a contractual relationship with the spirit. During the ceremony, the healer, with the help of mantras and rhythmic drumming, invokes and invites the spirit to introduce itself. The patient enters into an altered state of consciousness and starts to dance. The spirit, speaking through the patient, identifies itself and makes its demands known. With the promise of fulfillment of demands to satisfaction, the spirit agrees to restore the patient's health. This concludes the ceremony but by no means puts a closure to the contractual relationship. The spirit can intrude upon the host at will and make new demands.

The contractual agreements are infinitely bargained and negotiated. In some cases, the spirit may decide to make the body of the patient its home *(vas)* in return for certain privileges. Rituals of habituation (bonth) are performed to tame the spirit and "tie" the spirit permanently to the host. In such cases, hosts become healers and, depending on their gender, are known as Mali or Matriya.

Once a person has been identified as being possessed by a spirit, curing entails developing a viable relationship with the spirit. Close observations of the rituals and discussions with several healers and hosts reveal there is a common theme, a "grammar of therapy," that involves two processes that structure spirit possession in Jaunsar: transaction and transformation. The elaborate transactional and transformational culture of Hindus has been well articulated by Marriott (1976, 1980, 1989) to indicate the idea that, for South Asians, the self is essentially nondiscrete and fluid.

In the contractual relationship, the spirit makes demands on the host (food taboos, sacrifice, taboos on activities that are polluting, ritual bathing), and the healer, on behalf of the host, bargains for restoration and maintenance of the well-being of the host. The conditions set out by the spirit bring about some positive changes in the life of the host. For example, a ritual bath makes a person holy, having had all her sins washed away by the sacred river. The Jaunsaris call such people *nainu,* or the holy people, and interact with them with reverence.

The experience of possession itself is therapeutic. I have heard women say, on leaving an altered state of consciousness, how the ritual made them "feel light" *(halka)* or "at peace" *(man mey shanti),* affirming that the state itself has "intrinsic remedial powers" (Boddy 1988). The curative power of possession is derived not only from the experience of possession but also from the healer's interpretation of the possession that provides a new meaning for the affliction.

Mediumistic Healing Practices

I attended several healing sessions as an observer before asking permission to interview and photograph the participants. At these divinatory séances, I systematically documented the interactions between the healers and their clients.

This was done in order to understand the therapeutic transactions and the role of the diviner in recasting the reality for his clients, which I argue brings about a transformation that is therapeutic. The following four cases have been select-ed as representative divinatory and curative practices to illustrate the theo-retical generalizations made earlier in this article. In these next cases, I examine the healing process, which further reflects the underlying principles that characterize the divinatory process.

Case I: Rani, Who Would Be the Matriya

This case describes how a middle-aged woman becomes a Matriya and a heal-er. During my twenty months of fieldwork, I accompanied Rani to a number of meetings with her healer and was fortunate to document her habituation ceremony. Rani's initiation to healing was very similar to that of many other women healers. She suffered from excessive leukorrhea *(safed pani)* and pain all over her body; consultations with the local midwife and the doctor at the Primary Health Clinic could not ease the pain or the bothersome discharge. In the next few weeks, she experienced involuntary body movements fol-lowed by a total loss of sensation on the left side of her body. One night she dreamed about a woman sitting on a roof who asked her to join her. All this happened during the harvest season, a very busy time for agriculturists. Her family members were especially worried, as she was unable to work in the fields. They summoned a well-reputed Bamon, who diagnosed the symptoms to be the working of a *matri* (spirit).

Rani Devi decided that she must consult with matri specialists—the Matriyas. Every Friday for the next three weeks she visited the Matriya who later initiated her. During one such meeting, the spirit demanded to be "tied" (bonth) permanently to the host, at which time Rani Devi began to dance to the rhythmic drumming of a brass plate. This demand of the spirit created a lot of tension in the family despite the fact that this was a divine call and Rani was the chosen one. She began to experience an array of emotions that she could not relate to other experiences in her life. She informed me that this is locally known as bawala—a state of mental uneasiness, instability, and uncon-trolled possession. She was conscious of what she was doing, but had no con-trol over her activities.

With the help of her family Bamon, Rani Devi observed a series of habit-uation rituals in which the matri afflicting her was tamed and permanently bound to her. In the series of rituals, the spirit matured. The maturity of the spirit is indicated by the fact that the host is able to communicate with the spirit. Rani was now a bocwan and could effectively communicate with people and conduct divination on her own. She adds, "now with the gift *[vardan]* of vision *[prakash]* I am able to see and discern the problems." The following year, Rani made a pilgrimage to Hanol, where she obtained a blessing and a silver coin from the Mali at the temple.

Every Friday, before her séance, she puts the silver coin on a silver chain and wears it around her neck. As she sings hymns urging *Matri* to manifest herself, she places the silver coin on her forehead. She then enters into an altered state of consciousness and is ready to communicate on behalf of the people who come to her with their problems. As she puts it, "every Friday I dance [khel], after which I feel light and I experience peace." She hopes one day she will initiate women in becoming healers themselves.

DISCUSSION. This case illustrates the transformation of a simple Jaunsari woman into a healer. The themes of selection *(bulava),* vision (prakash), and the gift (vardan) were the primary organizing features and the primary plots that frame a narrative of the healers' experiences. In the transformation of a simple person to a healer, the host acquires a new identity, an identity that has power. In most all the fifteen life history narratives that I collected, the healers were keen to point out the legitimacy or the genuineness of their status. Through the process of habituation (bonth), the taming of the spirit, and the final initiation at Hanol, Jaunsaris believe that the spirit transmits power to the healer. This power enables them to see, discern, and heal, to take control of their lives and the lives of the others. These observations about healers' lives and practices reveal how indigenous conceptions of power and its generative capacities inform the workings of the divination and healing system. The fact that the majority of the healers in my sample refer to their selection as a "special calling" suggests that it is power that is out of the ordinary—beyond everyday life. It also suggests that the healer's journey reflects the emergence of a new self in a manner similar to the process of the development of the self from infancy to adulthood.

Case 2: Roshni and Her Spirits

Roshni is one of my principal informants, and of all the women I met she seemed to understand my project the best and became a willing collaborator and confidante. She enjoyed sharing her past experiences with me as much as she envied my life as a single person free from any obligation or responsibility. At the time I met her, she was the second and last wife of two husbands and the mother of six children ranging in age from four to seventeen. It was her story that made me aware of how more than one spirit can possess a body. Her somatic discomforts were attributed to possession, and the healing process involved a continuous and persistent attempt to make this possession experience a meaningful event.

During my field research, on several occasions, I was able to witness Roshni when her spirits possessed her. One evening when I was preparing to go to bed, I heard piercing cries from Roshni's house. I ran out to find a crowd had collected in front of her house. Inside, I found Roshni lying flat on her back on the floor with her head on her co-wife's lap. Her whole body was jerking slightly, but her head was shaking violently. Bijma, her co-wife, was having a hard time holding her to avoid her head being bumped on the hard wooden floors. All this time Roshni was breathing very heavily and making grunting noises. The women around her were watching very closely, and her co-wife was trying to pour some water into her mouth. Soon thereafter Roshni lost consciousness and fell stiff onto the floor. Outside, the men were discussing what needed to be done. They decide to call a Bamon this time. Her youngest husband summoned the Bamon from the neighboring village for anad-ganad, to predict witchcraft and to offer an exorcism ceremony. But this proved unfruitful. Roshni was frequently visited by her spirits. So her family decided to consult a Mali. The Mali divined that not only did a matri spirit possess her, but also a *cheradha*. Cheradhas are the souls of very young children who die at infancy or at the time of birth and whose final funeral rituals were unsatisfactory. They are under the control of a witch and are known to be her followers. He pointed out that the matri was trying to drive the other spirits out, and when such a battle rages inside one's body, the body shakes, and hence the jerking movements. The Mali, with the help of his tutelary spirit, exorcised the cheradha and requested the protection of the matri.

I accompanied Roshni to a number of curing ceremonies. A curing ceremony would last several days, and Roshni and I would stay at Mali's place. Roshni repeatedly lost and regained her consciousness and spoke in tongues when under the influence of the spirits. Mali advised her not to have meat or any kind of "hot" food. Roshni had no more possession episodes in the last few months of my stay there. Later, Roshni recalled her last visit to Makhti.

This was my last visit to Makhti. Remember that you were there. Hari Mali—Makti ka Mali—wants to make sure that there are no remnants of cheradha left in my body. I danced [khel] for matri, after which I passed out. When I woke up my body felt heavy but I felt better—peaceful. Our Lineage Bamon—Jagat Ram Joshi of Dwiyna—will perform a *pujan* (worship) just to protect me from the witch from village Laccha (my natal home). Mali told me that when a pujan was performed, the witch would come to know about it. The witch lives in Laccha; she is the eldest wife—has never borne a child. She has a thick nose and is fat. She wanted me to remain in Laccha and serve her. She has even poisoned her co-wife.

DISCUSSION. Roshni's possession narratives and her various physical symptoms are very typical of women's stories that I collected. They reflect their understanding of the problems that plague them. The physical symptoms, however unrelated they might be to their experience, give them a legitimate reason to seek help. In most of the cases, the initial symptoms they report are stomachache, headache, loss of appetite, or nausea. This process echoes what Good (1994) has described as the symbolization of illness narratives in reference to the need to "localize"; it is a "struggle for a name," an image around which a narrative can take shape.

This narrative reveals that women themselves link fertility and childbirth complications to possession. Roshni saw the link between childbirth and possession by spirits, as exemplified by her opening statement, "possession by spirit started after I started having babies." The second episode she recalled was when her daughters, Kavita and Namita, were two and a little over three years old, respectively. Because there is a high incidence of infant mortality in the area, women fear the loss of their children. This may call into question their femininity and womanhood, as the ability to reproduce is a natural function of womanhood. Witches are thought to be ugly, childless beings who enjoy eating unborn fetuses. Jaunsari women believe that possession by a witch or even a glimpse of her evil gaze can cause miscarriage or sterility.

Roshni also repeatedly drew upon certain metaphors that give us certain insights into her everyday reality. She used religious metaphors and popular images in Hinduism, such as the goddess battling with a demon for the soul of her host and winning. First of all, possession by both a goddess (in this case matri) and a demon, and later the eradication of the demon, leaves Roshni with the good spirit. The possession by a demon puts the body of the host in a polluted state, and inversely the possession of the body by a benevolent spirit makes the body pure and thereby divine. Matri also represents the ideal role of a woman—to protect and be responsible for the well-being of the family. In contrast, Roshni's representation of a witch as childless and ugly emphasizes what is nonfeminine—infertility and undesirability. This also reveals the resentment that might build up against a woman who has been unable to reproduce and is branded a witch.

As the story of Roshni unfolds, it became very clear to me that there were several plots to her story. The process of narrativizing thus reveals potential ways of interpreting spirit possession and finding alternative approaches to alleviate the problem and bring it closure.

Case 3: Punni and Her Ancestors

Punni was married for many years but never once became pregnant. So her husband Ram Lal Thakur married another woman, Namita. She too failed to conceive. Ram Lal Thakur's family is one the richest households in the village, so he could afford to take his wives to a number of "fertility clinics" in Dehra Doon and Delhi. This went on for five to six years, but the trips to fertility clinics proved fruitless and expensive. The family, now desperate, turned to Malis and Bamons for their expertise. They agreed that the nature of their affliction was a severe dosh that had "taken birth" a few generations ago. To propitiate and appease the spirit and encourage it to help the family (identify the exact nature of dosh), the family, with the help of their lineage Bamon, organized a three-day pujan. On the third and final night, Punni became entranced and started speaking. The entity that had possessed her introduced itself as a matri spirit and revealed that the nature of dosh was a kind of a *paap*. The term *paap* literally means "sin," and it is believed paap is passed on from generation to generation and is, in a certain sense, an ancestral cult. A paap is born from hurt feelings caused by exploitation, torture, and/or neglect experienced by a person, which feelings drives him or her to commit suicide.

This "sin" was in later divinatory séances found to be emerging from Punni's natal home. Punni's grandmother shared her four husbands with three other women. That is, she had three co-wives. It is the norm that a woman should devote herself to all of her husbands with equal love. But one of Punni's grandmothers liked one brother best of all. They made a promise to live together. Such an act is known as keeping *niym dhoram* (rules and obligations). Under this agreement, a couple promises to be faithful to one another for the rest of their lives, with God as their witness. This family was divided later on. Unfortunately, this couple was separated during the course of this division, and, as a result, the agreement was broken. The grandmother felt very bad about it, but it was not under her control. Distressed, she committed suicide. As she was pregnant at the time, a "sin" was committed.

Under the guidance of a Mali, Punni's father made an idol (a silver block with three female figures engraved on it) and took it to the banks of the River Ganga and gave it a ritual bath. The idol was brought back to the village and given a home—a miniature house in the family field. Punni's affinal family took her to Hardwar where she took a ritual bath. Thereafter, a number of children were born by her.

Very recently, the family witnessed a heavy loss of animals. Besides this, a number of family members had died. It was thus evident that either some serious dosh was involved in all of this or someone had put a hex on them. They had approached Hari Mali to reveal the source of their afflictions. It was at the Friday clinic where I met them. Mali divined that a hex was in operation and recommended that a Bamon perform the ritual of chui-chalana to relieve the effect of the curse.

DISCUSSION. This case narrative highlights how divination serves as a way of making sense of current events through a reanalysis of past events. It is in the interpretive process that the ultimate original cause was invoked, what Good calls the symbolization process, which is the first crucial step in reconstructing a reality that opens up more alternative solutions. Thus, this symbolization not only named the original cause but also became a reflection of the disorder in the social structure. First, it reinforced the moral code, and, second, it provided a set of responses that could be therapeutic. It is interesting to note that the kind of paap that resurfaced was related to the unnatural death of a pregnant woman. This suggests that the repercussions of one's action can often hurt future generations and can lead to the end of a lineage. The source of paap throws light on what Jaunsaris regard as constructive functions of polyandrous families. This dramatic event is then a moral event and hence invokes, as Good suggests, moralizing judgments.

This case also illustrates how a Mali might manipulate prior knowledge of the clients or overheard conversations in order to provide a solution. The Mali knew this family and was perhaps aware of this lineage's history. Although it was never stated as such, villagers would gossip about Ram Lal's impotency. The fact notwithstanding, the wives were held responsible for it. In the search for impotency (or the women's barrenness), that was seen as a bimari, the first step was biomedicine and herbal remedies. Finding no cure, Ram Lal turned to indigenous healers for remedies. Locating the cause of impotency and sterility in some kind of cosmic transgression eased the stigma for the people involved, and at the same time it conferred a new meaning to the situation.

Case 4: Usha's Teenage Dilemmas

I met Usha on the first day of my fieldwork. Usha, also of the village Bisoe, was in the tenth class in school and was preparing for her first public exam. She was born second in a family of seven. On my first visit to Matriya of the village Khati, I was surprised to see Usha along with a few other girls from the village Bisoe. They knew I was researching about matri and women healers but had never mentioned their participation in matri-related rituals. In fact, they had actively denied any knowledge about matri and matri possession. Such a denial is not surprising since belief in possession is considered superstitious by many, and some (especially those with a high school education) openly ridicule and mimic body movements associated with possession. I imagine that Usha, who was a high school student, felt that she should not be indulging in "backward" beliefs and customs.

At Khati, the Matriya invokes her tutelary spirit and Usha starts to dance and stutters.

> Matriya: Yes, your highness, do tell what upsets you.
> Spirit #1: She is my baby. I will look after her.
> Matriya: So be it. Please leave her body in the right form.
> Spirit #1: I can not leave her body. She is my baby, I have to protect her.
> Spirit #2: I will not leave her, either. She is my baby as well. I will not leave her.
> Matriya: Who are you? Manifest yourself.
> Spirit #1: I am matri, I will protect her. I am protecting her from the other spirit—the *bhut-pret*.
> Matriya: Hey, bhut, leave her alone, or do you want me to bring the iron tongs that are heating up in the hearth?

> Spirit #2:   Okay, I will leave her body, but I need to eat meat and sweet
> things.
> Matriya: So be it.
> *(Usha slowly calms down but falls on the ground stiff)*

Since our encounter at Khati, I had accompanied Usha to other such traditional healers. Usha opened up and narrated the reasons for her visits to the Matriya at Khati. She told me that once she was collecting firewood in the forests on the danda when she fell off a branch. She was unconscious for a few hours. She was only nine years old at that time. Another time, she was returning home after collecting firewood, and, as her load was very heavy, she was lagging behind her group. The sun was setting, so she started to walk faster, but then she fainted. She recalled another incident when she was cutting grass along with her friends from her village. When they were taking a short respite, she fell asleep while her friends were amusing themselves creating new songs. One of her friends screamed into her ear to wake her up. This frightened her and she fainted. When a Matriya was consulted, she divined dosh and possession by matri. Matri had entered her body to protect her. Matriya told her that when her body jerks violently, it is so because matri is waging a battle in her body against the attack by bhut-pret.

I probed if her symptoms were signs of epilepsy *(mirgi)*. She said even though the symptoms might look the same, in her case the jerking movements were resulting from matri trying to drive the bad spirits out of her body. A few months later, on a visit to see her brother, who is in a school in Dehra Doon, she was shown to a physician who gave her pills for her fainting spells. Usha pointed out that the doctor had lamented that her illness could not be cured. I asked her if the physician had diagnosed her with epilepsy, but she did not answer me and left the room.

In the months that followed, Usha avoided any encounters with me. Then one afternoon she knocked on my door. She was visibly very upset and asked if she could speak with me. She told me that what she had feared all along had come true—she had failed her public exam. She said: "I never find any time to study. All day long I collect firewood or cut grass for cattle. Who will want me now? I am useless. Nobody can leave me to do any work on my own. If only I had passed my exams, like Bablididi, I could have studied further. Now this. No one will ever want to marry me. I am of no use to anybody.

I cannot look after children, not knowing when I might have a fit." This was the first time she had ever used the word *fit,* the Jaunsari word for epileptic convulsions. She recalled her conversation with the physician in Dehra Dun who had informed her that her illness was incurable, and then she left abruptly.

The next day was Friday. I was getting ready to catch the bus to Makhti to document and follow-up on cases at the Friday clinic. Usha was waiting for me at the bus stop. Although she sat next to me on the bus, she said nothing. Her older brother Dinesh was escorting her.

At the Friday clinic, when Usha's turn came, the Mali looked at her nails and asked her if she was ever frightened. She told him of incidents that she had never told me. She said she was frightened when she was returning home one night from another village where she had gone to see a film. Hari Mali, true to his divination style, made her breathe incense and started drumming on a brass plate, invoking the spirit to manifest itself. Usha started to dance and speak in tongues. When she came out of her trance, she opened her eyes as if she had just woken up from a deep sleep. Her brother noted the suggestions made by the Mali—restricted diet, bath in the Ganga River, and three more visits with him. When I left the field, Usha was still on her restricted diet and had successfully passed her public examinations. She was making arrangements to move to Dehra Doon (a nearby township) for higher studies.

DISCUSSION. Usha's story is narrated from different points of view, providing alternate readings of the same experience. It clearly indicates that no single point of view (religious healer, biomedical healer, or family) adequately renders her experience. This multiplicity of interpretation embodies the fact that possession experience cannot be represented from a single vantage point. According to Good (1994), this narrative structure is the subjunctivizing quality of a narrative. Usha's views about her experience radically change from one encounter with the healer to the next. This is revealed in the ambiguity inherent in her narrative. Hence, as I have tried to show in this sample, there is no way to envision a definite encounter. The framing of the story using a different account of the cause of illness presents a very different meaning to the same experience. In fact, each potential alternative interpretation casts doubt on the other interpretations.

This contingent element of the interpretation of possession experience introduces a quality that is potent with creativity. The creative aspect is clearly exemplified in this case study, which deals with the stigmatizing nature of several diseases, not only for the individual but for the family as well. Usha knew that if her fainting spells were diagnosed as epilepsy her family would have a hard time finding a groom for her. If the label of "epileptic" were stamped on her, it would mark her for life, even after remission. Her seeking out Makhti ka Mali was a desperate attempt to escape the label and create a meaning that would help her cope with this situation.

At the same time, this case represents the stress of a young woman at the crossroads of her life, for what she accomplishes at this point will determine the rest of her life. She is torn between striving toward the womanhood defined by her society versus that defined by the images in the mass media of successful, educated, working women. Her anxiety about her future is intensified by the physician's diagnosis of epilepsy.

Body, Suffering, and Spirit Possession

As an object of analysis, the body condenses a network of meanings. The body is the starting point in the study of culture and self (Csordas 1990). It is the existential ground of culture. Scheper-Hughes and Lock (1987, 1990) have suggested the body as the central object of analysis in anthropology. The body is seen as the ultimate medium that connects the personal, the social, and the political, thus creating a space where social truths are contested, negotiated, invented, or reproduced.

When the body in Jaunsari communities is possessed by one or more spirits, it becomes a space for interaction with the spirits. The body becomes the vehicle for the spirit; it is under the control of the spirit. The narratives of healers' lives and women's possession experiences highlight how the body emerges as a locus where issues of struggle and suffering are inscribed.

This emphasis on the body draws our attention to the cultural understanding of suffering. Suffering is often seen as a divine experience in Hindu culture. In the case of possession, the body as possessed and controlled by another spirit becomes the locus of suffering, yet another prevalent theme. The healers were quick to point out that becoming a Matriya or a Mali is not automatic after having been chosen by a divine spirit. The habituation process transforms the body as a locus of suffering, which serves as a temple (as the spirit resides in it) capable of healing people. This habituation process can take months and sometimes years. I was told that during the habituation process the host loses a lot of weight. Women healers also pointed out that considerable labor time was lost as well. Recalling her memories of her bawala state, Rani told me that she would go into uncontrolled possession, and when she came out of it, she felt as if she had been beaten over her entire body. Like most healers, Rani rationalizes her suffering as a test given by the divine to judge her capabilities as a healer: "One needs to be strong morally, ritually, and physically to be a vehicle for the divine." Here, she is alluding to suffering as a meaningful and purposeful emotion, a significant part of religious experience.

These notions of body and suffering draw on religious metaphors rich in shared images and symbols from popular Hinduism. For example, Roshni described her experience of spirit possession and her physical symptoms (violent jerky movements) as a consequence of the goddess battling with a demon for her soul and winning. Here she is referring to a very popular legend wherein the goddess Durga waged a battle against the buffalo demon, vanquished him, and saved the world from annihilation. Punni, who had difficulty bearing children, made references to treatment in her affinal home where, she said, she had to swallow her pride and sometimes wished that the earth would split open and swallow her. Punni is drawing from a popular episode of the epic Ramayana in which Sita, the heroine, humiliated by her husband Rama, calls upon the mother earth to open up and give her shelter.

Spirit possession is not just a culturally meaningful construction of suffering but also the focus of remedial and redressive action. By using this concept, Jaunsaris are not merely struggling to give a clinical name to a person's pain and misfortune; they are drawing attention to a complex network of metaphorical association to which the terms are meaningfully connected. Condensed in the concept of spirit possession is a semantic network that links individual distress to a social world where inequality and injustice are an integral part of social relationships. Spirit possession aims not just to alleviate symptoms but also to address the vulnerability of women—a core experience. As Rani so poignantly articulates, "This is our fate as women, everyone controls us, we (our bodies) do not belong to ourselves."

When one examines the body's meanings and metaphors, one observes a gender distinction related to the issues of power and struggle implicated in spirit possession. While Malis evoke vardan, a gift from the divine, as an essential part of spirit possession and as a key to healing, narratives of Matriyas and the women possessed by spirits typically concern issues of struggle. While women healers were anxious about their ability to fulfill their role as a mother, wife, and field laborer, the narratives of *Mali* lacked such considerations. In her narrative about her fainting spells, Usha expresses her understanding of this experience as a struggle between matri and bhut-pret—a struggle between good and evil. Rani vocalizes about her predicament as a tug-of-war between her loyalty toward the family and her desire to be a healer. Thus the experience of possession and its consequences mirror the power differential between the two genders in Jaunsari society.

The social-structural forces supported by a cultural ethos of polyandry create tension between the genders and sustain a gender hierarchy that manifests itself in the healing séances. The narratives poignantly express the centrality of gender conflict to their suffering. I see the healing rituals as providing women with a strategic means by which they hold members of their family responsible for any injustices or abusive behavior. This interpretation of spirit possession in the context of gender politics reveals the creative aspect of spirit possession.

This view of spirit possession, the identity of the healers and the realities of the lives of the sufferers, reveals the therapeutic processes of spirit possession. In all the narratives of possession and divination, there were multiple layers of meaning attributed to various events. In considering the unfolding of events in the sufferer's life, one observes that there were several themes in a story. Interactions with different healers also help in shaping how the story may turn out. With each new turn of events, there are new potential outcomes. The actors themselves are engaged in shaping their world with different members of the therapy management group having their own agenda. Their quest for different desired outcomes makes the narratives resist closure. This opens up possibilities and potentials for multiple interpretations of the possession event and alternative ways to seek therapy.

There are certain aspects of narratives that help maintain this subjunctivity and permit alternate thematic structures without a definite closure. The Jaunsaris have access to pluralistic medical systems, and this facilitates a hope with multiple potentials for cures. Within each healing system, different healers have access to different powers. Each reading presents the sufferer with a different interpretation and a different meaning that opens up more possibilities, providing alternate thematic structures with potentially more desirable outcomes. Each interpretation draws on a particular concern, making available additional thematic structures. People draw upon these alternatives, stretching and molding them to accommodate multiple readings to make sense of their experience. Even organic diseases (for example, tuberculosis and epilepsy) have supernatural explanations, furthering possibilities for cure without the stigma associated with the disease. Ambivalence toward traditional beliefs also sends people to biomedical arenas, where many more stories are created to understand their experiences. Each narrative, embodying contradictions and a network of multiple perspectives, has a creative potency to recast reality.

Conclusion

The idiom of spirit possession articulates suffering and provides interpretations that help people make sense of their world. The narrative form of divination and healing is important in understanding the transformational role of spirit possession in bringing about the patient's well-being. These divinatory narratives also reveal the tensions and contradictions in the social order and are enriched with metaphors, proverbs, and allusions that go beyond individual experience. They expose Jaunsari people's desires and frustrations, their memories, and their fantasies. Within the space provided by spirit possession, men and women discuss, articulate, and make sense of crises and the unattainable objectives of life, and, invariably, they tell us something about gender relations, household dynamics, and their existential dilemmas. By tapping into their cosmologies to deal with the harshness of the realities of their everyday world, they strive toward healing through openness to change and through the creative potential of spirit possession.

Divination through possession by spirits can be comprehended analytically as an example of embodiment through which everyday life and action become subjectively meaningful to the actors themselves. It is also a critical commentary and evaluation of the trials and tribulations, frustrations and desires, sentiments and feelings of the people concerned. This commentary is an objective evaluation, which is articulated and mused through language.

Possession by spirits, like anthropology, is a reflexive discourse (Boddy 1988:22). It is a medium through which one can step outside of one's life world and gain a perspective on it. In this sense, divination through spirits is a meta-commentary about society—disclosing, orchestrating, and revealing what is implicit in it.

9

The Laibon Diviner and Healer among Samburu Pastoralists of Kenya

ELLIOT FRATKIN

aibons are male diviner-healer-prophets found among Maa-speaking peoples of East Africa including Maasai and Samburu pastoralists of Kenya and Tanzania.[1] Born with an inherited ability to "see" events or forces normally concealed from others, laibons practice divination with "stones" (actually, many types of objects) thrown from a hollow gourd or cow's horn, and have the ability to make mystically powerful medicines used to protect against physical and supernatural harm. Their divination and protective medicines are widely sought by jeopardized individuals, including barren women, warriors traveling to dangerous places, and people who suspect that neighbors or kin are trying to harm them with sorcery.

This chapter locates the Samburu laibon within a general analytic framework of divination and healing and within the ethnographic context of East African pastoralist societies. In the course of this description, I wish to make several points about laibons, including their historical and cultural location, the therapeutic value of the laibon's healing, the language and shared meanings of the divination process, and finally their role as mediator between the human community and powerful unseen forces that act on them.

The institution of laibon is unique to Maa-speaking cattle pastoralists of Kenya and Tanzania, although it is situated within a larger "prophet complex" found among pastoral and agropastoral groups of East Africa (Waller 1995). Laibons are said to have appeared mysteriously among Maasai several centuries ago, when a founding ancestor, Kidongoi, appeared as a boy among Purko Maasai and founded the Lo'onkidong'i lineage, from which modern Maasai laibons claim descent. During the internecine Maasai wars of the nineteenth century, laibons played important roles as prophets and war leaders, where the defeat of the Laikipiak Maasai by the Purko and Kisongo Maasai was attributed to the more powerful medicines of their laibon, Mbatiany. Following this war, the Laikipiak and their laibons dispersed into various groups, including the Samburu, who are closely related Maa-speaking cattle herders living north of Maasai in present-day Samburu and Marsabit Districts in north-central Kenya.[2]

Laibons (from *ol-oiboni* [*il-oibonok,* plural] in Maa) have an inherited ability to "see" or predict *(a-ibon)* past, present, or future events ordinary people cannot see. These predictions are achieved while dreaming *(a-detidet),* while in inebriated states, or by divination, through throwing stones and other objects from a divination container, the *nkidong.* Not all members of a laibon family become laibons, only those who demonstrate a gift for prediction and who gain a following of clients. While both men and women may possess this ability, only males are permitted to practice divination with the nkidong gourd, and only a very few laibons reach the stature of great prophets such as Mbatiany.[3]

In addition to their ability to divine and prophesy, certain laibons acquire secret knowledge to prepare powerful medicines *(ntasim),* which are worn as charms or bracelets and protect against physical dangers, such as diseases, wild animals, or human enemies, or against personal attacks of humans using sorcery to inflict harm. Only a laibon's divination can determine the presence of sorcery, and only a laibon's ntasim can protect an individual from sorcery's effects. Ntasim protective substances are made from the roots and barks of particular plants; but so too are sorcery poisons that one can buy from sorcerers or unscrupulous laibons. Thus, divination, sorcery, and healing are viewed as a battle between laibons who know each other's identity, although this is never revealed to the public. The death of a laibon is almost always attributed to the sorcery of a rival laibon.

As a cultural anthropologist, I studied the Leaduma family of Samburu laibons living in Marsabit District, in northern Kenya, for eighteen months from 1974 to 1976, for six months in 1985, and during six summer visits during the

1990s (Fratkin 1979, 1991, 2004). The most powerful laibons in this family were Lekati Leaduma (born circa 1932), his son Kanikis (born 1966), and Lekati's uncle and rival Kordidi Leaduma (born circa 1922). Lekati Leaduma's great-grandfather Charrar was a Laikipiak Maasai laibon and refugee from the Maasai wars who, around 1875, moved to Marsabit Mountain in present-day Marsabit District and joined the Lorokushu section of Samburu. He fathered several sons who became leading laibons, including Somanga, Lekati's grandfather, and his great-uncle Ngaldaiyo, who achieved notoriety in the late 1920s for his participation in the ritualized murder of the white rancher Powys (Duder and Simpson 1997). Lekati's father, Kimojikole ("Six Fingers," a trait found among some laibons), and his uncle Kordidi lived among the Ariaal (mixed Samburu/Rendille pastoralists) in Marsabit District, where Lekati was raised. Lekati learned about divination and ntasim medicines from his uncle Kordidi, a more powerful laibon than Kimojikole; Kordidi in turn learned it from his uncle Ngaldaiyo (the one arrested by the British), who in turn learned it from Somanga. Thus, both the divination technique and knowledge of ntasim medicine were directly passed for several generations from Laikipiak Maasai origins.

When Lekati's mother was pregnant, it is said she had dreams that came true (a feature also said about Lekati's son Kanikis). Lekati gained a reputation for his prophesies as a warrior, but for various reasons (including conflicts with his father) he rejected his role as a laibon and tried to live a normal life as a young man. By the time he married, however, Lekati, persuaded by Lorokushu clan elders, resumed his practice of divination and healing. Throughout his career, he was known for both the accuracy of his divination predictions and for the power of his ntasim medicines in combating sorcery. When Lekati Leaduma died at the age of fifty-five in 1987, many attributed his death to the sorcery of a rival laibon. Today, Lekati's son Kanikis, a man in his mid-thirties, is emerging as his father's successor.

The Laibon as Diviner and Healer among the Samburu

Samburu are a population of 100,000 who live in acephalous lineage-based settlements in Samburu and Marsabit Districts in north-central Kenya. They are Nilotic cattle and small stock (goats and sheep) pastoralists closely related to the Maasai. Samburu share Maasai cosmology, which holds that their world was created by a supreme being *(En-gai)*, a distant force appealed to by elders in prayers, blessings, and sacrifices for rain, peace, and the fertility of their families and livestock herds. In addition to blessings, Samburu can appeal to En-gai to punish a wrongdoer by invoking the curse *(l-deket, l-deketa)*, a moral sanction most effective against close relatives, although it is rarely used. For those Samburu lacking moral justification but who, acting out of jealousy or greed, wish to harm someone, one turns to sorcery, a powerful and immoral means of supernatural retribution. Samburu believe that sorcery is used by neighbors or kin to bring harm or misfortune to a person, his or her family, or their livestock. While the occurrence of sorcery is not discussed openly, it is nevertheless held by many people to be widespread and potent.

Sorcery is achieved by using sorcery poisons *(nkurupore, nkuruporen)*, which are mystically powerful substances in the form of powders ground from certain plants and animals such as snakes and chameleons (described in Fratkin 1996). Acquired secretly, these substances may be surreptitiously placed on a person or his house, or on a stick that is thrown into a cattle enclosure. Once ensorcelled, a man may lose his cattle to illness; a woman may have successful pregnancies but lose all her children after birth; or a victim may be driven mad, become blind, or even die. The only effective treatment against sorcery is to seek a laibon who can determine the sorcery through his nkidong divination and combat it with his ntasim protective medicines.

The laibon's divination and curing rituals may be a public or private event. Public divinations are held for the community as a whole, particularly when the laibon has dreamed about or divined the presence of enemies, diseases, or other dangers. But divinations and healing performed at the request of individuals for personal problems are done privately, although not in secret, in the house of the client(s) and with their close kin (for example, wives/husbands, children, brothers).

In both public and private divination sessions, clients and "followers," male elders or warriors who often accompany the laibon, are able to participate in "reading the stones" with the laibon. The nkidong divination has particular rules of interpretation based on the number of objects thrown, the type of stones cast, and the configuration with which the stones are cast. To a limited degree the followers of the laibon understand these rules.

Lekati Leaduma's nkidong gourd contained over five hundred objects, including polished pebbles, glass marbles, seeds, cowry shells, teeth, horns, pieces made from leather and bone, and metal objects such as coins, bullets, and even a toy car from a monopoly game (see table 9.1). Many of these pieces have explicit meanings that are known to regular observers. For example, a hyena's tooth signifies Turkana enemies; two leather rings tied together means twins; a glass thermometer means hospital. Most important is a red glass ball, which indicates the presence of sorcery. Marbles and polished stones are categorized by color and signify opposition or conflict when thrown in opposing sets: red/yellow, black/white.

In addition to the specific *type* of stone thrown, the *number* of stones cast also has specific meanings, where each digit from zero to nine has a name and meaning. For example, if three separate throws of the stones are cast that add up to thirty-two objects, two is the meaningful number and has the same value as two, twelve, twenty-two, and so forth. Much attention in the divination ritual is paid to counting the objects, and the laibon often has the participants help in their count. The meaning of Leaduma's *nkidong* numerology is listed below; this system is shared by other laibons in the Leaduma family.

0   Nothing *(me-ata).* A negative response to the question

1   The ear *(n-kiook).* News, information

2   The leg *(n-keju).* Someone is coming

3   Cattle stick *(e-seki).* Pertaining to cattle

4   Strength *(n-golon).* Good fortune, ritually propitious

5   Journey *(e-lototo).* Someone is going on a journey

6   Meeting *(n-kiguena).* An important discussion or argument

7   Meat *(n-kiri).* Ritual feast or reconciliation

8   Peace, laughter *(n-kuenia).* Peace, safety, joy

9   Supernatural force *(n-golon o-leng).* Mystical danger, sorcery, ntasim

Although the divination participants may understand the number and type of stone thrown, the ultimate interpretation rests with the laibon's inherent ability to assess their meaning based on how they are thrown, their configuration. "When the laibon sees the stones, it is like a hunter reading animal tracks," said one follower of Leaduma. "He can see movement and can tell what is happening. We who follow the laibon know how to read the stones, but

Table 9.1

Contents of Leaduma's Nkidong Gourd

OBJECT	SIGNIFICANCE
77 white stones	Numerical object
123 glass marbles	Numerical object
227 small colored pebbles	Numerical object
20 miscellaneous crystals	Numerical object
3 coins (East African shilling, 5 cent, 50 cent)	Money
3 red glass balls	Sorcery
8 small cowries	Pregnancy
2 large cowries	Pregnancy
3 *se'eki* seeds (*Cordia ovalis* R.Br.)	Crying
2 *rankau* seeds (*Acacia gerrardii* Benth.)	Sorcery
1 *medimokon* seed (*Viscum tuberculatum* A.Rich)	Insanity
13 *lokorosho* seed (*Caralluma speciosa* N.E.Br.)	Sorcery
1 *lokore* (*Obetia pinnatifida* Baker)	Death, illness
1 lion skin knot	Danger to livestock
1 camel skin knot	Danger to camels
1 cow tail hair knot	Danger to cattle
1 cow skin knot	Danger to Samburu
2 goatskin pieces *(Lekiritin)*	Blessings
1 goat tongue	Blessing
1 lion's claw *(lkardati)*	Nkidong blessing
1 beaded piece *(bulibuli)*	Danger to Rendille
1 lion fur ball	*Extreme* danger
1 rhino horn tip with ntasim	Ntasim protection
4 dik-dik horns with ntasim	Ntasim protection
3 plastic pens with ntasim	Ntasim protection

1 ivory piece	Danger by elephant
2 clear crystals	Water
1 lion skin cross	Danger to children
5 goatskin crosses	Children
1 blood arrow *(lkuret)*	Blacksmiths
1 metal cylinder	Blacksmiths
1 metal ball	Unknown
1 hollow metal piece	Peace
1 metal lip plug	Turkana people
1 metal chain	Unknown
1 metal ring	Blacksmiths
2 brass bullets	War
1 threaded brass cylinder	Peace
3 crystals (green, orange, clear)	Water
1 white oval stone	Good fortune
1 red *mparua* bead	Women
1 pink crystal	Women
1 hyena tooth	Turkana people
1 plastic piece	No meaning
2 thermometer glass pieces	Hospital
1 pottery piece	Good fortune
1 lion's canine	Lion
5 wood pieces with ntasim	Good, protection
1 ring of red and yellow beads	Rendille people

TOTAL: 538 pieces

only the laibon knows what will happen." It is the laibon's ability to "see the unseen," whether in dreams, spontaneous prophecy, or reading divination stones, that sets off his ability and power.

Case 1: *The Fainting Girl*

A family asked Lekati Leaduma to treat their child, a twelve-year-old girl who for some time had been listless and uncommunicative. Her refusal to eat had only grown worse as her parents beat her in frustration. She became weak and withdrawn and developed fainting spells, sometimes three or four times a day. Initially, the girl's father consulted an herbalist to treat the girl, who proclaimed the man's daughter was suffering from measles, although eruptions did not appear on her skin. The herbalist treated her with strong emetics to purge her of the illness, but the girl's condition worsened. Finally, the family sought the intervention of the laibon Lekati Leaduma. The laibon performed a public divination outside the girl's house, attended by the girl, her parents, her father's brother, and five neighbors, men and women.

Leaduma sat on an elder's stool, his back to the house. The client and her family sat facing him. Leaduma spread out his blue cloth and placed his *l-mane-ta* (objects to "tie" the divination, discussed below), which are two cowry shells and black and white rocks, on the left and right side of the cloth. Holding his divination gourd, Leaduma asked, "Who is going to open the nkidong divination?" The father gave his daughter a shilling to place on the cloth, and Leaduma gave the young girl yellow ntasim to sniff up her nose. He said, "This nkidong knows truths and lies. Tell me the truth. What happened to this girl?" He then spit air into the opening of the nkidong gourd. Shaking the gourd vigorously, Leaduma removed his hand in quick succession from the mouthpiece and shook out three sets of "stones" onto the blue cloth. The father and Leaduma counted the stones and put them in a pile. Thirty-nine pieces were thrown, including a bullet, a hyena's tooth, and a clear crystal.

"What do you see about this girl? Tell me truths, not lies."

He threw sixty-two pieces.

"Tell me what has happened to her. Is she cursed?"

He threw nine stones.

To the girl's father he said, "She has been cursed by a woman who lives with Longieli clan. Two teeth are missing from her mouth."

Immediately the mother, who had been threatening to slap the girl for being unresponsive, put her arms around the girl's shoulders. It was now apparent that it was not the girl's problem alone.

Leaduma, to the nkidong gourd, asked, "Is it true?"

He threw three stones.

"Is it true this person is cursed?"

He threw thirty-seven stones.

"Is it true or not?"

To the father Leaduma said, "The nkidong sometimes gives false information. But all I can do is tell what it says to me, and what I've seen is she is cursed by a woman."

The father said, "When the girl was young, I used to leave my animals in a place where there were two women from a *laisi* family *[Samburu and Ariaal families with powerful blessings and curses]*. One is still alive, and the other is dead."

Leaduma then asked the nkidong: "Who actually cursed this girl?"

He threw seven stones.

"Is it the woman from Longieli clan? Is it true?"

He threw thirty-five stones.

"Someone has traveled to make this curse," he said.

The father answered, "Yes. It was the old woman who died."

"Yes, she cursed the girl before she died. Who is this without any teeth? A woman or a man?" Leaduma asked.

He threw six stones.

The father answered: "The girl was very young, walking with others to the wells, and a woman who was passing just spoke to her *[that is, cursed her]*."

Then the girl said, "I feel like I am going to faint."

Addressing his daughter for the first time, the father asked, "What happens before you faint?"

She answered, "I feel pain on my ribs." (Although she did not faint, she looked ill and scared.)

Leaduma asked the nkidong: "Was she cursed while walking to the wells?"

He threw five stones.

"Is this person known? The stones say you know this person. That you knew her before you were married, when you were a warrior."

Leaduma threw ten.

He asked the father, "Do you know we can make people quarrel, we can beat a bad person who won't admit he is bad. Even some people might say I'm a bad person because I reveal secrets. But the nkidong shows this woman cursed the girl. She will be all right because I will give her ntasim. The person who cursed the girl is from Longieli clan. The stones show she came and went back (from the cattle watering area), cursing the girl on the way." Then he asked the nkidong, "Is it true it is that particular woman?"

He threw seven stones.

"This group of stones shows you know her, and the girl was cursed near a small hill."

The father asked, "It is true? Because we were living near a small hill."

Leaduma asked the nkidong, "Is it true it was at this hill?"

He threw four stones.

"Is it true? Is it true? I ask you."

He threw ten stones and asked, "Why?"

He threw eight stones.

Leaduma then gave the nkidong gourd to the girl to blow into the gourd's mouth. He took back the gourd and threw six stones.

"We are finished. This girl will be given ntasim medicine, and she will not be ill."

Immediately following the nkidong divination, Leaduma poured "yellow" ntasim and gave it to the girl to snuff in her nose. He told the family that he would return in the evening to give them all ntasim.

Later, after the cattle were milked, Leaduma entered the house of the family, spread out his blue cloth and small gourds containing ntasim, and marked "yellow" ntasim powder that he placed on the forehead of the girl, as well as on the foreheads of the mother, father, and father's brother. A second ntasim preparation of "yellow" powder mixed with honey was placed on the tongue of each family member. The next day, the girl was looking much better, smiling and carrying on as if nothing had happened.

Later, Leaduma confided in me: "This family has been cursed for many years. It was not a matter of the child; it was a problem of the father and another woman [not the mother]. The father knew it was the woman but wanted to see if I knew as well. The nkidong asked about a man but showed it was the woman after all. Why was she cursed? Many people curse others in this place, but not by the mouth [l-deket], but by sorcery [nkurupore]. This woman was angry with the girl's mother and father from long ago. She loved the husband when he was still a warrior. When she saw that the mother had this young daughter, she was jealous and tried to hurt her. This is not the first bad thing to have happened to them. This problem happened long before this child was born. But my medicine is strong, and she will recover this time. That woman, who did this thing, she is no longer around to hurt anyone else."

This divination affirmed to the family that sorcery was indeed the cause of their problems and that its cause lay in a rivalry between two women that occurred long ago. A hyena's tooth thrown early signifies sorcery, as does the number nine appearing in response to the question "Is she cursed?" The divination reveals social tensions within the group, in this case the jealousy of a jilted lover, which had opened old wounds. Perhaps the husband's infidelity contributed to the problem. (Leaduma said during the nkidong: "Some people might say I'm a bad person because I reveal secrets.") The conflict was real, brought to light of day by the divination process. But the divination may have also helped heal this conflict by its public exposure, leading possibly to a transformation in the husband's relationship with his wife, which may have been a factor in the girl's own illness.

The divination and particular attention by the laibon also validated the girl's illness. This was not just a problem she made up, but the result of a much larger conflict of which she was an innocent victim. Once the cause of their daughter's illness was revealed to be due to the sorcery of a jealous woman, the father and mother moved to protect their daughter, putting their arm around her and paying attention to her complaints. "What happens before you faint?" the father asked his daughter, possibly the first time he had addressed her directly about her illness. Social tensions were revealed and exposed, and the family was able to reunite again. Moreover, the divination exposed tensions of an old love affair (that may not in fact have ended), and the divination and ntasim served to reunite the family and make them whole again.

The Laibon's Ntasim Medicines

Where divination and prophecy are the hallmarks of a true laibon, it is the laibon's ability to heal and protect from misfortune with ntasim medicines that brings many clients to him. The knowledge of ntasim preparation is secret, and a laibon learns most of his medicines from his father or another mentor through a long apprenticeship. Ntasimi are ritually powerful substances in the form of ground powders made from roots, bark, leaves, and, rarely, the burned remains of certain animals. They are usually worn by a person in small leather amulets tied to their neck beads, or they are carried in a horn or shell container, as the warriors do on raids. A laibon may wear over a dozen ntasim amulets around his neck; Lekati Leaduma wore amulets made from dik-dik horns and crocodile teeth.

Leaduma's medicine bag contained fifteen ntasim preparations in small gourd containers. Classified by Leaduma based on their color (for example, red, yellow, and black ntasim), these medicines are made principally from the roots of the "yellow" lparamunyo tree (*Toddalia asiatica* [L.] Lam.), "black" lkokolai (*Rhamnus staddo* A. Rich.), and "red" reteti tree (*Ficus wakefieldii* Hutch.). In addition to the ntasim powders, the laibon also carries ritual paraphernalia used in the ntasim ritual. Leaduma used a blue cloth, on which he placed the medicines; a large dish made from a seashell, which he used to mix the medicines; and a long metal spoon. Surrounding the dish and gourds are the l-maneta, the "tying ones," which are large objects that encircle and ritually bless the ntasim. These include a cord made from lion's skin, a white rock and a black rock, and two large tiger cowry shells, one female (light) and one male (dark), filled with ntasim and sealed with tree gum. "Tying" is a form of ritual blessing asking for God's protection. By ritually tying an object, a dangerous situation can be averted. For this reason, an essential feature of the laibon's medicine is wearing or carrying a l-maneta object, such as a small bag tied to one's necklaces or carrying a cow's horn filled ntasim. Often a woman will tie an ntasim amulet around a milk gourd belonging to her son, daughter, or husband if they are traveling in dangerous areas.

Case 2: Treating a Woman's Infertility

In another divination and healing session, Leaduma is asked by Lekule (a pseudonym) to perform a divination to determine why his cattle have been ill (they have been suffering from a respiratory illness) and why his first wife is barren. The first wife is childless, while the second wife, perhaps ten years younger, has three children. Leaduma conducts a nkidong and determines that the family has been cursed with sorcery (described in Fratkin 1991). The divination revealed arguments and tensions between the two intermarried families going back at least to Lekule's and his first wife's wedding day. Sorcery was revealed by a red stone being cast. During the nkidong Leaduma threw thirty-seven stones (seven = feast) and asked, "What is this meat *[that is, feast]* for?" He threw fifty-three (three = cattle) and asked, "Is this a fight over the wedding ox?" Nineteen (nine = mystical power) stones reveal that the wife will go see another laibon for ntasim and that Leaduma will later also provide ntasim for the family and their cattle.

Leaduma later confided to me: "This family had been cursed for some time. Someone had cursed the woman with nkurupore who was later arrested and beaten up by the police. He had marked a small stick with nkurupore and threw it near her gateway where she walked over it. Later when her daughter died, and her cattle died, she knew she was cursed. There were problems between her and her husband's family. But that was not the cause of her troubles. This woman lies, while the second wife is good and does not cheat. This woman is the cause of these problems; she has brought on this badness herself."

Later that evening, Leaduma returned to Lekule's house to dispense the ntasim medicines. Inside were Lekule, his two wives, his sister, and his sister's husband. As requested by Leaduma, Lekule had cut the tail hairs from twenty-seven cattle.

On a blue cloth placed in front of him, Leaduma laid out his ntasim paraphernalia: a large shell in which he mixed the ntasim powders, five ntasim containers, two large tiger shell cowries filled with ntasim, and a black and white stone. All of these items were encircled by a long cord of lion skin.

Leaduma separated the cattle hair into eighty-one strands and then tied them into nine separate rings about five centimeters in diameter. Each ring was soaked in a solution of ntasim mixed with milk, bound in leather, and presented to all the assembled adults to tie around their neck beads or placed on their personal milk gourds and containers.

Leaduma said to Lekule: "Never give away these cattle, although you may continue to milk them or slaughter them for the *lmugit [Samburu age-set rites]*. Do not bleed any of these cattle for four days." To the women, the laibon said, "Do not borrow or lend any of your hearth fire for four days." When the ntasim amulets were completed, the laibon and Lekule went outside to prepare a ritual fire (*ntasim laisar,* "of the burning") inside the cattle enclosure using four ritual woods, which were sprinkled with ntasim powders as they burned. The ntasim ritual was completed, and Lekule later paid the laibon one heifer cow for his services.

The ability to "tie" is a special gift inherited by members of laibon families in which an object or person is "bound" by ntasim to protect them from future dangers. Just as Leaduma ties his ntasim and nkidong rituals with the cowry shells and lion skin rope, he also ties a protective web around individuals threatened with sorcery. The symbol of tying is found in other aspects of Samburu culture. The village (nkang) ties together the homesteads in a continuous circle; a mother ties a string of green beads around her infant's waist (green being a color of life and good health); a warrior ties his girlfriend with a gift of beads and wire to wear around her neck; one who has killed a lion ties a cord made of lion skin around his arm to protect him from avenging lions; a warrior ties a strip of the ox he kills at circumcision around his arm to tie him to his age mates and age set.

In addition to tying, the numerology of the ntasim is also significant. In preparing the ntasim amulets, the laibon ties eighty-one cattle hairs from twenty-seven cattle into nine rings, each number a multiple of three and nine. The number nine (or three) distinguishes the laibon from the wider Samburu community. In the divination numerology, the numbers four and eight show peace and blessings, but the number nine reveals power and danger, indicating the presence of sorcery, ntasim, or other laibons. In public ceremonies such as weddings, elders use even numbers in ritual blessings, where prayers are repeated two or four times ("May god grant you children–En-gai! May god grant you children–En-gai!"); ritual fires contain four types of wood; ceremonies are held on the fourth, eighth, and fourteenth (full moon) day of the month; and so on. Where even numbers imply the moral community, led by the male elders, odd numbers are dangerous and represent mystical power. One does not journey on the fifth day of the week (Wednesday) or hold life passage rituals (birth, circumcision, marriage, and funerals) on an odd numbered day of the month. The laibon, represented by the dangerous number nine, stands outside the moral order of the lineage elders and society; he is an intermediary, not between the human community and God (En-gai) but between the human community and the dangerous world of malevolent supernatural power.

Discussion and Summary

Samburu laibons are not priests "speaking for men to God," nor are they prophets "speaking from God to men."[4] Rather, they are particular members of an "outsider" family of Maasai who have mystically powerful gifts of prophesy, divination, and protection from perceived supernatural attacks. Although Samburu laibons occasionally perform public divinations and prophesize future events for the welfare of the community, their predictions are in the main concerned with determining the cause of misfortunes, particularly those believed to be caused by sorcery. Unlike Maasai laibons who play a leading role in the large age-set rituals of warriors and in the past commanded large armies (Lamphear 1998:87), laibons among the Samburu lead a quieter, less public life.

Although feared by some for their association with sorcery and suspected by others as charlatans, the laibon nevertheless plays an essential role in Samburu life. At a community level, he acts as an early-warning system of impending dangers, including epidemic diseases, armed attacks, drought, or other disruptions. At the individual level, the laibon plays an unequaled role in combating the effects of sorcery, a dominant if hidden medium of expressing jealousy, fear, and social conflict. Mary Douglas (1970:4) pointed out that beliefs in sorcery are more common among acephalous, decentralized polities lacking courts or police than among centralized or state-structured societies. The Samburu, living in seminomadic lineage-based communities, often at great distances from police posts and towns, have little recourse to higher authorities to settle interpersonal and local disputes. In these communities, one seeks powerful intermediaries, independent from the lineage-based authority of the elders, to intervene in social conflict. Moreover, the society needs someone capable of determining the presence of sorcery or supernatural threat and competent in fighting these forces with his supernaturally powerful medicines. Seeking the laibon's divination and ntasim medicines is a fundamentally operational way for Samburu to seek control over normally uncontrollable events, utilizing the laibon's ability to reveal "unseen truths" and effect control over them through his supernaturally powerful remedies.

To Samburu participants (and to this anthropological observer), the laibon's divination and healing is a rational system, even if it uses nonrational means (see introduction, this volume). This rationality is demonstrated social-ly, cognitively, and psychologically. At the level of social structure and func-tion, the laibon's divination and healing serve both therapeutic functions (for example, the reduction of anxiety and psychological stress) and sociological functions (for example, the reestablishment of social order). People come to the laibon for a variety of problems—stress about a family illness, infertility in marriage, bad luck in love, or an inexplicable misfortune such as a cattle disease that affects one person's herd but not another's. Sometimes problems are manifested as psychosomatic pain or fatigue, sometimes as anxiety disor-ders, sleeplessness, or worry. Occasionally these problems are severe and may involve psychotic episodes—a mother cannot understand why her fifteen-year-old son rails against her with a machete blade, or a spouse remains mute, uncommunicative, and shut up in his or her house for days on end. As the lai-bon's divination unfolds, these problems are seen as the result of social con-flicts within the family—jealousy of a brother's success or, in the case of the fainting girl, tension about a husband's previous lover.[5]

Victor Turner, drawing on his classic studies of rites of affliction among the Ndembu of Zambia, described the importance of revealing social ten-sions as a means of combating sorcery acts in the healing process: "It seems that the Ndembu doctor sees his task less as curing an individual patient than as remedying the ills of a corporate group. The sickness of a patient is mainly a sign that 'something is rotten' in the corporate body. The patient will not get better until all the tensions and aggressions in the group's interrelations have been brought to light and exposed to ritual treatment" (Turner 1964:262).

The effectiveness of the laibon's divination and medicines lies not in his confirmation that the person is ill (this is already known); rather, it his vali-dation of the internal conflicts a client and his family are undergoing, and the fact that these conflicts have their root in a larger social drama. This reduces the feelings of helplessness, alienation, and powerlessness that may be the cause of the health problem, which, in the case of the fainting girl, were probably rooted in depression and psychosomatization). By taking seriously the ailments presented by the client, the laibon promotes self-respect in the patient and enlists respect and protection of her and the wider family (and, at the very least, dissuades further beating of the girl).

Peek (1991:11–12) has pointed out that divination embodies a society's epistemology, but it does so through its own particular semantic structures and shared meanings, providing both a way of knowing and a way of think-ing. In linguistic terms, divination as practiced by the Samburu laibon has an internal logic and structure that the laibon, and to some degree the partici-pants in the divination, understand. The laibon interprets the cast stones according to a particular grammar consisting of three components: the num-ber of items thrown *(n)*, the type of individual items thrown *(i)*, and the con-figuration of the items thrown *(c)*. The interpretation *(I)* of the divination throw is based on the composite of the meaning of the quantity thrown *(Mn)*, the meaning of the type of individual objects thrown *(Mi)*, and the meaning of the geometric configuration of the stones once thrown *(Mc)*. The laibon's reading of the stones, or interpretation, is based on a combination of recog-nizing the meaning of each of these three components, where

$$I = [(Mi)] + [(Mn)] + [(Mc)]$$

However, the laibon has the option of disregarding or refusing to disre-gard elements in the composition of *i*, *n*, or *c*, or even the entire category, such as (Mc), so that the brackets are optional. The laibon may focus only on the quantity of items thrown, or even on only one or two objects in the quanti-ty.[6] By understanding at least the meaning of the number *(n)* thrown and the item *(i)* thrown, the laibon's clients participate in the divination's unfolding and its revelations and thus both the laibon's abilities and the message that is being communicated.

"Sometimes the stones lie," said Leaduma, suggesting that the stones are testing him in a dialogue and pressing him to dig deeper for the truth. While some may argue this is an escape mechanism that allows a laibon to commit errors, it actually allows the laibon to carry out his divination with further throws. Like the hunter interpreting animal tracks, he must look deeply into patterns that are obscured by wind, sun, moisture, and time.

Finally, the Samburu laibon needs to be located in the wider ethnogra-phy of African divination and healing systems. Unlike trance healing or spirit mediumship found among Bantu-speaking agricultural societies of Africa (Beattie and Middleton 1969; Janzen 1991), divination and healing among the Nilotic Samburu is neither an emotionally charged nor highly dramatic encounter. Neither the laibon nor his clients show much affect during the div-ination or healing procedures; they do not engage in crying, shaking, trance drumming, or dancing, as is found in spirit possession healing in other soci-

eties in Africa. Rather, the laibon's divination and healing have a cool, intellectual character to it, like an interview between a police officer and a crime
victim, or a physician recording a patient's family history. In a comparative
study of illness and healing between Kenyan herders and farmers, Robert
Edgerton (1966, 1974) found a "pragmatic and rational" approach to psychiatric and somatic illness by Nilotic pastoralists, compared to the highly emotional and interventive actions taken by Bantu farmers. This comparison may
be a bit essentialist—both Kamba farmers and Samburu pastoralists in Kenya
may attribute illnesses and misfortune to supernatural causes, and both societies have healers capable of intervening with the supernatural world. Still,
their approaches are different—one highly charged and dramatic, the other
quiet and private. The institution of diviner-healer is shared by Samburu and
Maasai with other Nilotic societies in Kenya and Sudan, including the Nuer,
Dinka, Atuot, and Turkana. These societies are similar in that they are all pastoralist or agropastoralist, they are organized by decentralized segmentary lineage organizations, they have age-grade organizations of warriors, and they
share beliefs in sorcery and the power of divination to determine it. As Burton
(1991:44) describes for the Atuot of Sudan, "An interpretation of what Atuot
see as an essential human proclivity, to seek to gain at another's expense or
suffer misfortune because of some other's anti-social behavior, is fundamental to an understanding of Atuot divination."

Samburu believe misfortune and illness may result from the malevolence
of other humans. The laibon's power of healing is based on his ability to predict the presence of supernatural danger and to prepare potent medicines that
protect someone from their enemies, both mystical and mundane. The laibon is a sorcerer as well as a healer, one who can manipulate supernatural
forces to effect personal ends (Fratkin 1991). The laibon is not like the Samburu herbalist who treats various illnesses such as stomachaches or fever
with a large variety of plant preparations. The majority of these are potent and
toxic, as the goal of their application is rapid expurgation and "cleansing" of
the body (Fratkin 1996). The power of the laibon's treatments are not based
on a plant's physical properties; rather, they are effective because the laibon
and his patient share the same belief in the underlying cause of the illness or
misfortune—that of sorcery poisons directed by someone who means them
harm.

The laibon's ntasim is perceived to work through a similar mechanism as sorcery, through the action of mystically powerful substances capable of acting on the health and welfare of living people. This shared cosmology between the laibon and his community is the basis of his healing powers. Samburu say if a person is suffering from sorcery, no medical hospital in the world can save them; only the laibon's medicines will work.

Laibons are controversial among Samburu and Maasai because of their ability to make sorcery poisons as well as curative ntasim medicines. As one Matapato Maasai remarked, "If we did not have Lo'onkidong'i (the lineage of laibons), we would not need Loonkidong'i" (Spencer 1988:221). Consequently, the laibon is an outsider to the normative community and its moral order and occupies an ambivalent social position in Samburu society. Laibons do not behave like other elders; they like to drink and are not afraid to abuse others in public, particularly other laibons. Their position as outsiders is noted in their appearance and behavior, such as wearing green or blue cloths (rather than white or red, as other elders wear), using odd rather than even numbers in their ntasim medicine, or wearing strange and frightening items such as crocodile's teeth on their necklaces. The laibon stands outside the moral community, an intermediary between the human community and the forces of the universe. He is a dangerous person, someone whose divination and medicines can protect against as well as manipulate the dangers of sorcery.

In spite of their unsavory reputation, laibons who have proven their powers in prediction through divination and healing are accepted by many Samburu communities, particularly in isolated regions where the hazards of disease, predation, drought, and enemy raids must be faced without police, clinics, or rapid transportation. As long as these conditions exist, it is unlikely that the Samburu will give up their beliefs in the power of the laibon for some time to come.

Notes

1. Maa belongs to the eastern Nilotic group of Sudanic languages in the Nilo-Saharan family of African languages (Greenberg 1955), and is spoken by approximately one million people, including the Maasai (350,000), Samburu (100,000), Chamus (15,000), El Molo (5,000), and Ariaal (12,000) of Kenya and the Maasai (150,000), Arusha (100,000) and Paraguyu (30,000) of Tanzania. All these societies have lai-

bons, with the exception of the Arusha, who are settled farmers, and the El Molo, a small fishing community living on Lake Turkana, Kenya. Related Nilotic groups, including the Turkana of Kenya and the Nuer of Sudan, also have diviners and, in the recent past, "prophets" who have assumed political leadership during periods of political conflict (Anderson and Johnson 1995; Evans-Pritchard 1956; Lamphear 1998).

2. For detailed histories of the Maasai and their laibons, see Berntsen 1979; Sobania 1993; Spencer 1988, 1991; Spear and Waller 1993; and Waller 1995.

3. I have previously argued (Fratkin 1979) that Samburu laibons never obtained the same level of political leadership as they did among the Maasai in the nineteenth century, due to the differences in the warrior age-set organization and residence patterns between the two societies. Among Maasai, warriors *(il-murran)* live in *many-attas* (large interclan warrior villages), free from the direct control of their lineage elders but subject to ritual leadership and guidance by strong laibons, as in the case of Mbatiany. Samburu warriors, on the other hand, do not live in warrior villages but stay close to their lineage-based settlements or in small livestock camps based on lineage identity. Consequently, the Samburu elders play a more direct role in supervising the warrior age sets and laibons play less of a politically significant role. Spencer (1998:173) suggests that the Maasai developed their elaborate warrior age-set organization and manyatta system after pushing south from the Samburu, which allowed the Maasai greater military flexibility for "predatory expansion" during the nineteenth century. Similarly, Lamphear (1998:87, cf. 97) argues that laibons assumed a greater political role among Maasai warriors with development of many-atta villages and wars during the nineteenth century.

4. Quoted from Evans-Pritchard (1956:304), who described prophets as "the mouthpieces of God" for the Nuer of Sudan. See Anderson and Johnson (1995) for distinction of prophets from diviners in East Africa.

5. My appreciation to my wife, Marty Nathan, M.D., for her insights into the therapeutic efficacy of the laibon's treatments, and to T. O. Lambo's (1964) contributions on the therapeutic milieu.

6. I am grateful to Dr. James Copeland, Department of Linguistics, Rice University, who helped me understand the grammar of the nkidong divination.

10

The Ngawbe All-Night Home-Based Vigil

Diviner-Mediated Intrafamilial Healing

KEITH BLETZER

The Ngawbe of western Panama are known for a replenished population estimated at 150,000 (1990s) and a continuing occupation of homelands after a demise of indigenous peoples on the Isthmus of Panama. Few populations survived the Discovery of Terra Firma; many were relocated after a reduction in numbers: Teribe of eastern Costa Rica and western Panama; Bugle of north-central Panama; and Kuna, Embera, and Waunana of eastern Panama. Known as *Guaymí* in Spanish chronicles and *Ngawbeba* in their own origin narratives, the Ngawbe maintained an isolation that enabled their survival. In 1954 and 1956, lands extending across portions of the three western provinces of Panama were designated an Indigenous Reserve *(Reserva Indígena)*. After four decades of negotiation, this territory was designated Ngobe-Bugle Homelands in 1997.

This chapter considers the contribution of the diviner-sanctioned home-based vigil in sustaining Ngawbe cultural integrity and assuring cultural survival. As I propose, this rite of healing articulates the importance of household and family through the diviner's supervision of its performance rather than his attendance at the rite. Data that follow were collected along the northwestern coast of Panamá.

The Ngawbe Medico-Ritual System within an Acephalous Society

A diviner *(dawngin)* and herbalist *(kroko dianko)* provide ethnomedical services among the Ngawbe. The diviner is revered as the principal medico-politi-
cal guide in an acephalous society, wherein medicine is a device to "cure" social
and individual misfortune (Bletzer 1985, 1991, 1996). Diviners derive
authority from a conceptual system based on the interrelatedness of things
of the forest, streams, sea, and the sky above, and their close interconnected-
ness to a society that coexists with other living creatures. Ngawbe diviners
train for the role of healership before they reach puberty, wherein they
acquire rudiments of the empirical knowledge the medical system comprises.
Like diviners elsewhere (Zeitlyn 2001), diviners continue to learn through
observation and experimentation over adolescence and adulthood by hearing
illness complaints and making treatment recommendations in their homestead of residence and during travel within the Indigenous Reserve.

Classes of Ritual

There are two classes of Ngawbe ritual: "diviner-mediated" rites, which
require a diviner's sanction; and "sanction-free" rites, which are organized and
held without diviner acknowledgment (see table 10.1). The diviner-mediated class requires that a family member petition a diviner's permission before
holding a rite. Rites in this class include the following: "thunder festival" as a
response to a lightning bolt that strikes someone or damages a planted field
(ñüi dûi); "rite of harvest abundance" for a first planting *(mötaw);* and the "all-
night vigil" *(gütaw).* The consumption of fermented drink is prohibited in
mötaw and gütaw. The thunder festival includes consumption of food and
fermented drink; mixing several elements of Ngawbe rites, it manifests ritualized dancing and singing that appear only in this rite (Bletzer 1988).

Organized between families or within a family, the second class of rituals
does not require diviner sanction. Rites in this subclass include a ritual-sibling
pole-throwing festival *(krun kite),* known in Spanish as *La Balsería* and prohibited by the nativistic movement Mama Chi (Young 1971), and a festive labor
project *(huntaire)* held for large tasks such as clearing a tract of land. Many
people attend these rituals; hence, they require more care with food and

Table 10.1

Classes of Ngawbe Rituals,
Emphasis on Eight Types of All-Night Vigils

I. Diviner-mediated: sanction by diviner, diviner performance is selective.

   A. *Ñüi dûi* (rain-belongs to, the people's provider-belongs to): The Thunder Festival. May include participation and/or performance by the diviner.

   B. *Mötaw* (abundance-filled): Rite for First Planting. May include diviner.

   C. *Gütaw* (focused repair-filled): All-Night Vigil. Diviner sanctions ritual performance (1:a–c); diviner sanctions rite, performs ritual actions (2:a–e).

   1. Intrafamilial. Prescribed for four nights, enacted four times.

      a. *Gütaw húboto:* home-based rite, prototype for intrafamilial vigil.

      b. *Ni gütawi ni neantéboto:* preparation of members of a household for return of someone who has disappeared. Exception: prescribed for eight continuous nights, once only.

      c. *Gütaw icháboto:* purification of household where a snake entered, appeared, or was believed to have been present.

   2. Intrafamilial, intrahomestead. Prescribed four nights, enacted four times.

      a. *Gütaw ni bren chakoréboto:* exorcism of malignant spirit afflicting a woman for premarriage or early marriage; origin of spirit may be stream-based or forest-based and one that specifically has "taken on" a woman.

      b. *Gütaw ñóbiti:* exorcism of malignant spirit in or near a stream, owing to a concern for a force at the stream used by a family for bathing.

(continued)

c. *Gütaw mrúboto:* purification of the seeds of diseased plants, for replanting and rejuvenating of domestic crops.

d. *Gütaw nirúboto:* exorcism of malignant forces that afflict domestic animals.

e. *Gütaw meritreríboto:* prevention of birthing problems that may appear after an earthquake. Exception: prescribed for four nights, once only.

II. Interfamilial: diviner may participate, performance is optional.

A. *Krun kite* (balsa-pole toss): *La Balsería/* Ritual-Sibling Festival.

B. *Huntaire* (gonad-centered—obligated to repeat—belongs to): Cooperative Labor Festival. Suffix *-taire* refers to something done repeatedly, hence a custom or practice.

III. Intrafamilial: diviner may participate, performance is optional.

A. *Bromon* (come forth—state of plenty): Childbirth Rite performed postbirth.

B. *Ka kuota* (male-centered song-fest): Special-Occasion Song-Rite.

beverage than intrafamilial rites organized within a single family. Two rites of the intrafamilial subclass include a rite organized by women following childbirth *(bromon)* and a special-occasion song rite that features kinsmen as participants *(ka kuota).* Consumption of fermented drink is permitted in all but the childbirth rite; for this rite, a ritual meal is prepared and consumed after a same-day fast. During field research, I attended one or more rites from each type within the ritual classes and subclasses. There no longer is a puberty rite *(ngawro mike).* Similar to other peoples, this rite of passage was prohibited under missionary influence of Catholic priests and Protestant ministers in the early 1900s.

The All-Night Vigil

There are eight kinds of all-night vigils (gütaw) (see table 10.1). The core setting serving as a therapeutic arena is the family, which can range from a two-generation nuclear family (parents and children) to a multigenerational family (senior parents with children, grown children with or without spouses and/or children, plus temporary accommodations of other kin).

Ideally, each type of all-night gütaw takes place over four consecutive nights (one exception), and each is held as a series of four rituals over a cumulative sixteen nights (one more exception). I attended at least one type for six of the eight; for a seventh, I accompanied a diviner (Tayoz) to visit a family to sanction an eight-night vigil for their son who disappeared snorkeling at sea. The eighth type, the all-night vigil for injured or sick animals, was not held during the period of fieldwork. By far, the most common is the all-night home-based vigil *(gütaw húboto)* that is the all-purpose rite held for a variety of problems ranging from general illness to resolution of conflicts within a household related to cooperation in work on family lands. Anything problematic (for example, kinswoman with difficult menstruation; adolescent son who has difficulty in sleeping; wife with chore malaise) is a potential basis for the home-based vigil. Participation is centered on the household, since this unit assumes responsibility for subsistence on family lands, as well as distribution and consumption of food. Hence, it is the minimal social unit in Ngawbe society.

Five of the eight types of gütaw, on the other hand, are concerned with things affecting the widest social unit, namely, the homestead. Sick animals (domesticated) and diseased plants are examples of these adverse events. The vigil at one time was predominantly home based; given increased aggregation of residence within Ngawbe territory, the home-based setting of the household as the basic social unit shifted to permit the performance of some types of vigil across households. Hence, most all-night vigils currently are intrahomestead rather than intrahousehold; this may require constructing a site outside a single household in a "communal shelter" where the vigil is held.

Over two years of fieldwork in northwestern Panama, one home-based vigil took place in a full series of four. Most of the others were held as back-to-back vigils, one after the other in a manner that the Ngawbe call *bobu kore-ta,* meaning "twice repeated" (hence, eight nights per household rather than sixteen). Final vigil pairs for initial pairs were never held. Some were held as a single vigil that comprised four nights, without the remaining three rites.

Petitioning and Conducting the All-Night Home-Based Vigil

After visiting the diviner, two days pass before the household conducts a four-day home-based vigil; two more days pass before the next four-night vigil takes place. Requesting permission for the vigil, the petitioner delivers four cacao seeds in a small fist-sized medicinal bag *(kri)*. The purpose of the vigil today is provided in Spanish: *Más respeto entre familia* (More respect among family members). Code-switching to Spanish emphasizes the importance of the household as the basic unit of Ngawbe society, even while living within a Spanish-speaking, nonindigenous nation-state. Otherwise, all instructions to the petitioner are given in the native language (Ngawbere). The final instruction is *Mo kwain ti konti krobuko* (Come to my place four times): the petitioner is asked to return after each of the four vigils (five total times, counting the initial visit).

Each return visit to the diviner, after each vigil is finished, provides an opportunity for case review by the diviner. It is by this means that the diviner counsels the petitioner and, if necessary, alters therapy. Difficult problems require a five-night vigil. Less common is the diviner's recommendation for ritual enclosure of someone facing a serious problem. Over the course of five nights, that person remains enclosed in a small shelter constructed in a corner of the sleeping quarters, the one room encircled by walls and the one area of the household that is off-limits during the vigil.

Despite an expanded format to five days, this variation retains defining elements of the home-based vigil. As an example, one cluster of five vigils that were held on overlapping nights included three families that used a ritual enclosure: one for the second-born precourting daughter of a single mother, one for the second-born courting daughter of a couple who were the married heads of household, and one by a man for his spouse (married, with children). The basic rationale for enclosures emphasized the needs of women for privacy (these particular women) with respect to their preparation and adjustment in romantic relationships.

Medicinal elements of the vigil include construction of wild cane archways *(ibiako)* integrated with wooden crosses and a loop tied with a ritual vine *(nonküi)* at the house entrance (eight possible types of wood) and incense *(mukata)* from a tree resin *(ngunataw konsen)* placed atop a smoldering termite nest *(kebe)*. The main ritual actions during the vigil include a cleansing of the interior and exterior of the house by medicinal waters *(kroko ñüi),* placement of herbal medicine in the eyes of participants to prevent bad dreams *(mukata ütute okwote,* also *mürüoto),* and the distribution of a chocolate drink and/or food four times during the night (coincident to ritual cleansing of the house and placement of eye medicine). The eye medicine is made from a pair of seven possible plants; placement in the eyes by a young boy (for women) and young girl (for men) contraindicates the capacity of a dream to reverse waking reality. The medicine stings mildly once placed in the eyes, as I learned at the vigils I attended, which impedes falling asleep. Ceremonial actions and ritual elements incorporate cultural symbols of "belongingness" to a forest whose materials provide medicinal remedies, apart from food for daily sustenance. Reinforcement of belongingness is an integrative force for the family, and it is a component that articulates the principles of Westernized family therapy (Minuchin 1974:46–66).

Participants in the vigil convene in the cooking area or in an adjacent open shelter, where they converse in small groups or one-on-one. They stay awake for most if not the entire night. Except for vigils with a ritual enclosure, sleeping quarters are off-limits. Arrangements for sleeping are assigned by nuclear family, outside the sleeping quarters. If space is minimal, the rule is adjusted. For example, five sleeping clusters at Minún's vigil were based on actual or potential nuclear families. I stayed with Minún, his wife, their two children, and one neighbor child in the sleeping quarters; fifteen other kin, including the wife's mother, formed four more clusters. Separation by nuclear family is a reminder of the household as the basic Ngawbe social unit.

The wall dividers that create boundaries for sleeping quarters mark the inner limits of where participants cannot go at gütaw húboto, and exterior house walls mark the outer limits where participants should not wander after dark. The exception is when the men exit at night to urinate at the side of the house. When women exit to urinate, they remain close to the house. As the night continues, those in attendance move and talk with other participants. For vigils I attended, topics of conversation varied: subsistence work in the forest (many vigils); plans to return to the plantations (several vigils); dream reports (several vigils); mishaps such as a family member who fell and was injured (Calín's vigil); and house repairs (Maché's vigil, Ale's vigil). If desired by household coheads, vigil attendees assist with food preparation, as when a visiting youth at Halón's vigil tended the fire to heat water for the chocolate drink and grated the coconut for flavoring the fruit mash.

Holding gütaw húboto follows the degree of intensity that family members bring to household chores. The organization of overlapping home-based vigils often occurs across families by sharing materials recommended by the diviner, especially among families whose lands lack a full complement of prescribed materials. Field notes from a series of five overlapping vigils indicated variation: incomplete ritual archways at pathways; some use of the ritual vine; and some use of the recommended knot. Four of five households conducted a ritual cleansing with medicinal waters, two of five used eye medicine, and two of five kept a termite nest burning all night. All five served a drink of chocolate *(ñoba)*. Differences reflect an availability of resources on family lands and the time available to a family to prepare and perform the tasks of the vigil, as well as the attention that a family pays to small details.

All the vigils I attended were havens of talking and eating, similar to what occurs daily in a household. Adults typically sat with each other, or they joined younger participants in conversation. Separation by sex is not a feature of the vigil except, as indicated, in the placement of eye medicine. Selected male or female household members are assigned to tend the incense by the arch to keep it burning at the entrance to the house. On the surface, vigil activities appear similar to those that occur daily within a household, except that derision is prohibited. Adult attendees, kin and non-kin alike, encourage and instruct the young on communication and personal development, such as recognition of emotional states in reaction to another's behavior.

When the heads of household talked about vigils, they were concerned about correct performance of ritual actions and expenditure of sufficient amounts of ritual elements. When persons in the community reported on a home-based vigil as it unfolded, they took delight in detailing what food was served. Communication at a vigil and the corresponding accompaniment of ritual actions are meant to encourage growth of the household as a unit, hence the concern of the family that they benefit from the vigil. Community members on the other hand are not bound by vigil rules; through a review of food availability, they were describing foundational resources a family has available in the forest (that is, naturally) and that which they can accrue with reciprocated requests (that is, socially). I never heard anyone comment on improprieties at someone else's vigil, only their own. Family response to diviner directions tells how well a family can learn to accept who they are and what they can do to accrue diviner-recommended resources, from an ideal of what a family would like to do, if they had greater resources and more time to comply.

Psychosocial Aspects of the All-Night Home-Based Vigil

Home-based vigils are performed to correct or alleviate problems that affect subsistence production. These problems emanate from *inside* a household, such as a malaise that co-occurs with illness. Or problems emanate from *outside* the family, such as an earthquake that affects wild and domesticated fruits of the forest (Bletzer 1992) or problems such as ill crops and sick animals. Sometimes the reason may be something that under other circumstances may not cause concern. On a visit where I accompanied a diviner (Tayoz) to a family in another homestead, I was told by Ate that her sister, Oly, petitioned to hold a vigil at her house because she found a snake in clothes she washed at the stream. Ate had held a vigil a few days earlier: "I had a large jar. It got lost. Later it was found outside the house, empty. That's why I asked [the diviner] for the vigil." Removing the jar and emptying it had violated the respect of the (single-parent) head of household. The diviner sanctioned each rite. During our visit, he reviewed each case, after the vigil was completed.

Entrances to the house where arches are constructed define the boundaries between the inner world of the nuclear family and the outer world comprising the rest of Ngawbe society. By extension, boundaries of the nuclear family reinforce the boundaries of the individual self in matters of subsistence-related social relations, psychosocial support, and information sharing. Thus, the home-based vigil acts as a reminder of one's personal obligations to the nuclear family, wherein a member works and eats, and the larger family, of which the nuclear family is a crucial and necessary component. The procedure of enclosure in particular is one that encourages reflection on individuality and reinforces the need for social boundedness by the enclosed person, as well as family members who attend the vigil. Enclosure secondarily provides the opportunity for a restful respite (albeit only five days) from the daily pressures of household responsibilities.

Participants at the vigil are family: Ngawbe-defined as consanguineous kin ascending two generations from one's parents and descending two generations from oneself. Called *ha mroko* (kin with whom one eats), family members are those with whom one works assigned lands to produce food, as well as shares in its distribution and consumption. Family structure is a set of demands to organize the ways in which the members of a family interact. A family system operates through transactions that establish patterns of how, when, and with whom to interact that underpin the system of interpersonal communication. It is this communication, as well as person-based social-cultural identity as a contributing member of Ngawbe society, that is reinforced through the vigil. Home-based vigils are structured as a solution-oriented forum (Washburn 1994) for the personal growth of household members that replicates the principles of intrapersonal maturation and dyad-distinct intrafamilial communication that form the basis of Western family therapy (Minuchin and Fishman 1981).

Communication skills are a fundamental part of the formation as well as maintenance of Ngawbe identity. An inversion of what Hanks (1996:259–66) calls "hurled speech" among the Maya appears as one of several genres of Ngawbe speech, among others, that occur during vigil interactions. For example, one evening at Kau's vigil in the house shared with her mother (not at home), Kau employed the Ngawbe convention of "invitation to disclosure." I was the only nonfamily individual in attendance at her vigil. She employed a pair of couplets to indicate that what gave impetus to her vigil was a sense of alienation from her social support system. I in turn sought to guide talk to social relations that provided her support. In the end, I specified the location of her spouse, who has a second wife, bringing the talk back to her concern and paying attention to that matter that she had said troubled her the most.

> Kau: I'm alone-sad, Kitis. Meat-protein's lacking. Food's lacking. My spouse's not around. He's at his other woman's house. I'm poor and alone-sad. [Ti ülire, Kitis; meden ñaka; mru ñaka; ti muko ñaka; taw merire mdá konti; ti bobre ülire.]
>
> KVB: Your brothers? [?Mo ngwae *(refers to cross-sex sibling; she has no sisters).*]
>
> Kau: Not home. [Ñaka gwi.]

KVB: How many brothers? [?Ngwae krobe.]

Kau: Three brothers, all on the plantations. [Nimo, lineámiti.]

KVB: Your mother? [?Mamá.]

Kau: She's visiting. [Taw basare.]

Cholu [Kau's brother]: She's at Treasure-Cove-Inlet. [Gwianímiti.]

KVB: *[soft-speech]* Your spouse is on the beach at the household of his second woman? [?Muko taw mötrita.]

Kaku: *[pause]* He alone would find that out. [Gare ye-ah *(serves secondarily as a complement)*.] *[Translation by author]*

Kaku appreciated the effort I made to remember when someone told me a little about her (where her spouse's second woman lived) and that I took the time to listen when she told me what bothered her. She complimented me for my effort. This kind of talk on my part became possible only after attending a number of vigils and witnessing the way in which the diviner (or seniors) constructed a frame of support in which they would return to someone's primary burden. As an inversion of hurled speech (an initiator and a pivot speak collusively to criticize, within hearing distance, a third-party target), the genre of concentric concern among the Ngawbe turns the speech of initiator and pivot inward to the needs of the initiator, based on information already provided to the pivot by an absent third party. It was this form of talk, among several, that formed a basis for communication at all-night vigils.

The home-based vigil differs in marked ways from therapies that rely on client-therapist interaction as the core of the healing process, and these differences place the vigil close to the principles of family therapy. Since the diviner as therapist does not attend the vigil—he is "present" before and after a vigil—this rite becomes a case of therapist-absent therapy that occurs within this country—for example, for families within migrant head-start programs, visited by outreach workers (Snyder and McCollum 1999). Three factors that improve the outcome in Westernized family therapy also occur with the vigil: the social unit as an open system for communication; clarification of psychosocial boundaries; and the development of individuality in relation to family integration. Similar to family therapy where membership is targeted for growth (Minuchin 1974), the diviner encourages all family members to attend the vigil. Nothing is more important than a family's participation; however, those on the plantations are exempt and not obligated to return home to attend.

Implementation of ritual behaviors central to the home-based vigil alters the context of how family members function. By participating, each person's experience is accentuated within age-related and sex-based dyads across the extended family, focused within a single household. Individuals of the same age gather for conversation, but sameness of age also may include persons of different ages. Through the vigil, boundaries of the family are clarified and redefined. Family members are encouraged to disregard similarity of age or sameness of gender as the principal basis for familial interaction (Madanes 1981; Minuchin 1974). Interpersonal resourcefulness and individuality are reinforced. For example, a malarial-eradication worker spent part of the night at his mother-in-law's vigil compiling a report that was due when he returned to the provincial capital the following day; he was illustrating for young kin the importance of honoring Ngawbe practices (by attendance) and the retention of membership as a Ngawbe male who contributes to the household (by working). As another example, students at several vigils completed homework assignments for the local elementary school, encouraged by their parents.

For vigils I attended, there was a general absence of the directives that characterize interactions outside a ritual context: "Fetch kindling" *(Ngi den),* "Carry those yams" *(Tami gwen),* "Bring me fishhooks" *(Kutu gwen ti kroke),* "Let's go to the forest" *(Bron konsenta),* "Watch your step" *(Oise).* Whereas directives represent subordination of one person directed by another in action taking, the home-based vigil emphasizes shared interaction. Talk I observed at vigils occurred within and across age-related dyads for exchange of information at a pace encouraging retention. For example, while the woman who organized a vigil was talking to a firstborn child from a nearby household (on ritual loan), she discussed poisonous snakes and distinguished between a fer-de-lance and boa constrictor by head shape and coloration. Why this was significant was the non-kin status of the youth, who might never get a chance to talk with this woman knowledgeable on local snakes. As another example, Macón attended the vigil of a neighbor with whom he was unrelated; over the course of conversation one evening, he noted dissimilarities in what Minún was suffering (for whom the vigil was given) with an illness that the Ngawbe associate with poor dreaming (Bletzer 1991). By participation, rather than gossip outside the vigil, he was recommending a shift in their approach to therapy for the cohead of household (Minún). One exception to nonuse of directives was a reminder that laughter is not permitted at the vigil; the common directive I heard from old to young was "No giggling" *(Ña kûta).*

The diviner who sanctions each vigil acts as its supervisor, similar to an act of therapeutic supervision that occurs when a head therapist monitors a colleague's case outside the presence of the individual client or family of clients (Hodas 1985; Madanes 1981). Rather than a therapist colleague, the family member who petitions the vigil "becomes" a situational therapist in consultation with the diviner. He or she returns to the household for the vigil and later reports back to the diviner after each vigil. Rather than observe a live session through a one-way mirror or videotaped performance of family interaction, as occurs in Westernized therapy (Hodas 1985), the diviner serves as a "therapy animator" and uses knowledge of interpersonal interactions in families to recommend treatment. Owing to residence among proximal kin-based homesteads, the diviner has access to knowledge of family interactions. This information is supplemented with the details of symptom complaints, dream reports, and behavior descriptions from the petitioner. Occasionally the diviner visits a family at home to increase familiarity with circumstances that facilitate a recommendation. Such visits improve his ability to interpret the nuances of Ngawbe interactions reported during a presentation of complaints by those who petition a vigil. By nonattendance, the diviner as an absent supervisor of a family therapy rite avoids turf issues that occur in Western approaches to therapy (Thomas, McCollum, and Snyder 1999). He excludes himself from potential pressure to align himself with individual family members (Howe 2000).

Comparison to Other People's Therapy

The basic difference between the home-based vigil and the therapies of other peoples is nonattendance of the vigil by the diviner who sanctions it. The vigil begins with a request that the diviner permit household members to hold the vigil and consultation with a family member after each vigil is concluded (up to four). The Ngawbe home-based vigil does not seek to reorder social relations by performance of singing and ritual actions (Faris 1990; Laderman 1991), song and dance (Atkinson 1989), the movement of objects with medicinal properties (Sharon 1978), or dramaturgical methods that promote a catharsis (Feshbach 1984). Many of these elements appear in vigils other

than the home-based vigil and in other types of Ngawbe rituals. Hence, the
home-based vigil is one rite that differs considerably. It is integrity of family as
the main unit of subsistence production that is reinforced in the home-based
vigil. Unlike other rites, there is no effort to communicate with spirit-entities
(Atkinson 1989; Laderman 1991) that may become manifest in social conflicts. Ngawbe acknowledge their existence and accept their power, but the
externalization of spirit forces places the potential for danger and contagion
at a distance. Household members grow and evolve, but they use the momentum of communication among nuclear and extended kin relations, not the
momentum that could be set into motion through orchestration of a ritual
by an aural tradition healer (Atkinson 1989) or a literate tradition therapist
(Tyler and Tyler 1986).

   Gütaw húboto is neither performance-centered (Schiefflin 1998) nor
liturgy-based (Zeitlyn 2001). Based on principles of communication among
kin whom one should know best, and reconstruction of one's present rather
than one's past, vigils are structured as solution-oriented and setting-mediat-
ed. Ngawbe have a saying that when one diviner dies, another will take his
place "from the same lineage." The saying's basis is the idea that no one healer
will gain supremacy over another healer or manipulate a family for gain, a risk
that accompanies power entrusted to a counselor by a family in Westernized
therapy (Haley 1989). By parallel fashion, no one family among the Ngawbe is
assured of survival above others. Through the vigil, each family is encouraged to do its own healing in mediation with the diviner. Ngawbe society has
assured that its core social units, the household and the family, maintain
strength and continue, despite a loss that may occur to other, similar units
within Ngawbe society.

Divination: Placing the Special within Reach

The home-based vigil is a vehicle whereby Ngawbe permit family members to
actualize tenets of the ethnomedical system and incorporate ritual symbols
and actions for vigil-specific use. Rather than rely on the diviner to plan and
direct ritualized actions (for example, manipulation of objects that he performs in all-night intrahomestead vigils) or to communicate his insights that
will establish principles to live by (an aspect of some interfamilial rites where

the diviner may voluntarily participate), the vigil makes the specialness of
the Ngawbe medico-ritual system both accessible and dependent on family-
based performance without the diviner's presence. The home-based vigil
merges a sense of ordinariness with an atmosphere of specialness created by
diviner-prescribed medicinal items. Family members become self-healers in
matters of recognizing a need (petitioning), organizing the ritual tasks (collecting forest materials), and making the best of intrafamilial participation
during the vigil. The reverence with which the Ngawbe hold diviners in
esteem is a key factor. By giving a small bag with four cacao seeds, a family
establishes a temporary connection to the diviner as the vigil's "therapy animator," and, in turn, they receive a "blessing" to go forth and hold the vigil.
The extent to which a household can actualize principles of Ngawbe culture
in a home-based environment to promote personal growth of household
members is based on generating a comfortable atmosphere for the vigil's
success, which starts with a diviner's sanction (blessing) and ends with a family's participation.

All kin who attend the vigil share in ritual responsibility to communicate
and inculcate important values of Ngawbe culture, as well as instruct others
who are younger than themselves in communication skills and the enactment
of healthy lifestyles. Social interaction in the home-based vigil combines an
integrative communication style used in Westernized forms of asymmetrical
conflict resolution—high concern for self, high concern for others—with ritual symbols and actions. At the same time, the home-based vigil utilizes the
diviner as a third-party "therapy animator" rather than the co-present arbi-
trator or negotiator in asymmetrical conflict resolution or the omniscient
counselor. Reverence toward the diviner as a healer who can demonstrate
the interactive skills of responsive communication permeates the atmosphere
of a family vigil and encourages family members to perform at the home-
based vigil for the benefit of the household.

Conclusion

Genocide on the isthmus of Panama removed several indigenous peoples.
Those who remained include the diminished Bugle, Teribe, Embera, Waunana,
Kuna, and the expanded Ngawbe, the only indigenous people of lower Cen-

tral America who reside on what were native homelands before European col-
onization. The Ngawbe maintained a claim to territorial and cultural integrity because outsiders were not permitted to establish interpersonal linkages or
to work and settle indigenous lands (Jimenez Miranda 1984). In addition to
a will to maintain a position of historic isolation, inclusion of the home-based
vigil in a larger medico-ritual system made an integral contribution to survival
as a people. As such, the home-based vigil can be added to the inventory of
nonactions, counteractions, and subversive transcripts that constitute
"weapons of the weak" (Scott 1985, 1990). Similar to other surviving peoples,
the Ngawbe rely on the autonomy and strength of the household and make
this their source of power and basis for survival. They put into action the common axiom that the power to heal the individual starts with the family.
Despite a sink-or-swim strategy that has the household assume full responsibility for its success, as they follow the diviner's instructions the home-based
vigil is an indigenous form of family therapy that bases its efficacy on the
family's capacity to work together through emphasis on communication skills
that are learned through, and recommended by, the Ngawbe diviner. He
shares a little of the knowledge that forms the basis of his authority and
empowers family and household as the core units of subsistence production
and distribution.

11

Yaka Divination

Acting Out the Memory of Society's Life-Spring

RENÉ DEVISCH

N goombu is one of the major possession and healing cults currently practiced among the Yaka in southwestern Congo (formerly Zaire) and the capital city of Kinshasa.[1] While the diviner's oracle determines which cult one is to consult for various afflictions (De Boeck and Devisch 1994; Devisch 1993; and Dumon and Devisch 1991), mediumistic divination, *ngoombu* or *ngoombwa weefwa*, itself originates with this particular cult.[2] It has been estimated that there is approximately one mediumistic diviner, whether male or female, per 3,000 persons among the rural Yaka, estimated at some 350,000. While that proportion is more difficult to determine for the perhaps half a million Yaka people now inhabiting the capital city, Kinshasa, Yaka diviners there enjoy nearly the same level of authority as in the rural areas. Circumstances usually leading to consultation of a Yaka diviner may be a death, the abnormal duration of an illness, or the onset or aggravation of some state of affliction. Moreover, diviners in the urban areas are more likely to be consulted by isolated individuals rather than family groups, as well as for problems such as those related to employment, business initiatives, or amorous relations. Despite ready access in the city to biomedicine and the overwhelming presence of (Christian) religions of salvation, the scene of the etiology of misfortune and healing is dominated by less cosmopolitan idioms. Also, many people here do consult diviners at one time or another.

The practice of mediumistic divination refers to society's and the indi-

Mediumistic diviner Lusuungu; Yibeengala village (photograph by René Devisch, 1974)

vidual's most profound life-spring, considered in the Yaka worldview as the egglike womb of the world *(ngoongu)*. Beating out a rhythm on his or her small slit drum with a light drumstick, the diviner performs the oracle. In approaching the oracle, the diviner melodiously recollects the scenes of his or her initiation. While entering into an altered state of consciousness (ASC), the diviner emits a *"coh coh coh"*-like sound, evoking the rooster's crow or the clucking of a hen laying an egg. These inchoate incoherent sounds gradually give way to an esoteric yet melodious speech and eventually those present for the consultants take up the refrain. These initial statements are meant to be genuinely clairvoyant by pointing accurately to the social network and context of the subject of consultation. The diviner meanwhile crouches on his or her slit drum and may refer to visions experienced since the arrival of the clients. The oracle thereby serves to engender in the diviner a libidinal sensing out of the problem through passionately associating his or her body in ASC to the slit drum's sexual symbolism. This is evoked by the metaphors in the diviner's initial esoteric pronouncements and the chorus of participants. I postulate that what occurs here is an acting out of some form of corporal reminiscence of the beginnings of life and of society. The entire oracular drama enacts the life-giving symbolism, especially that of the slit drum (with a long wide slit and surmounted by a head) symbolically figuring both the phallus and the uterus while bearing the characteristics of a sonorous envelope. Clairvoyance and the divinatory pronouncements represent for the Yaka a yearning to return to the uterus of the world and the origination of all life. While drawing on the aptitudes of the energetic, affective, and passional orders, divination orientates them, binding them together with an ontogenesis—that is, a matrixlike space-time order of reorigination. This pristine space-time order is figured by the white kaolin clay found in the marshes, associated with the well-spring of the earth and the site where the moon sets early in the morning, or in the ravines leading to a large river.

From Possession to Mediumistic Clairvoyance

The initiation into the art of diviner-medium may be instigated by an illness inflicted by the ngoombu spirit soon after the death of the former diviner-custodian of that spirit. Divinatory mediumship is considered a matrilineally transmitted hereditary *(yibutukulu)* talent whose paroxysmal manifestation is the ASC or clairvoyance. A few months following the death of a diviner, a consensus is sought on a matrilineal descendant to succeed the deceased. The diviner-to-be will experience some form of affliction that undermines his or her vitality, a symptom indicating that the ngoombu spirit is seeking to take possession of him or her. Other symptoms include what are said to be states of "eruption or dispersion" *(n-luta):* individuals afflicted in this way tend to meddle in other people's affairs, experience persecution complexes, or even suffer hysterical or epileptic fits. Some candidate-diviners suffer "a state of contraction" *(yibiinda):* they experience chronic cervical pains, insomnia, anxieties, suffocation, asthma, or other respiratory problems or even show signs of melancholic withdrawal. Further symptoms may include skin disease (mange, inflammatory infections, eczema, scabies), gastric troubles, nausea, amenorrhea, or stiffness. Candidates sometimes complain of harassment by a spirit, likely that of a recently deceased diviner belonging to the extended family. Anxious, irritable, and incommunicative at times, candidate-diviners may undergo periods of manic-depressive frenzy accompanied by acute fever and auditory, visual, or even tactile hallucinations.

According to diviners themselves, the sight of fire or a reference to sorcery induces in the candidate-diviner an irrepressible need to break out of oneself or causes some force to surge within oneself. At this point, candidates tend to become agitated, often attempting to mutilate or throw themselves into a fire or to flee the village. In ASC, the medium or candidate-diviner climbs to the top of a palm tree or jumps *(-puumbuka,* take flight) onto the roof of a nearby house, where he or she stands astride the ridgepole and begins to tear away the thatch. From this perch the medium then reveals, in the esoteric speech of diviners, the name of the uterine diviner forebear whose divinatory spirit has taken possession of him or her. Such behaviors are designated by the terms *-kaluka,* to release or deliver oneself, and *-vuula,* to slip away. If, following the crisis, the candidate-diviner is able to demonstrate an ability for authoritatively divining, the individual is considered ready for initiation in seclusion.

Some of the capacities pointing to a worthy aspirant, in distinction from the average person, are an uncommonly vivacious spirit and an unbridled imagination. Once they have gotten over their introverted and mute state, they show an ability to speak in a precise and incisive way. Most candidates nonetheless go on to appear insecure, edgy, and even timid, avoiding boisterous company. Male aspirants do not behave in a particularly virile manner; such behavior would even seem to belie their talent for clairvoyance. This is in part due to the understandable fear of the threat of death should their pronouncements be proved false; for this reason, diviners often appear irritable and withdrawn when consulting an oracle. The very appearance and mannerisms of the diviner change during the oracle: his or her voice becomes shrill and the eyes appear exorbitant, as if their gaze is turned inward and focuses on the clairvoyant's inner visions.

After the apprentice's vocation has been endorsed by the family elders' inviting a master-diviner for the initiation, the aspirant's first typical ASC then signals the beginning of the initiation process. It begins with up to nine months' seclusion supervised by the master-diviner, called the "mother-demiurge" *(ngula ngaanga)*. The latter is always an experienced diviner of the ngoombu cult who now takes on the roles of master and mother (preferably, of maternal uncle) to the candidate. A small seclusion hut is constructed on the outskirts of the village in which the major furnishing is a bed made of the wood of the parasol tree *(n-seenga: Musanga cecroioides,* Moraceae) and river plants. In the Yaka region the parasol tree is the first large plant to flourish on fallow ground. Fast-growing, it reaches its full height of three to five meters in three years, while its foliage develops only at the top of the smooth trunk. The seclusion hut also contains symbolic items (forklike sculptures, eroded river stones) denoting cult spirits and preancestral beings *(bisiimbi)* living in the water and the forest.

On the first day of seclusion the master-diviner or initiator, chanting all the while, leads the novice to the initiatory house when the village usually retires for the night. There the initiate is instructed to "sleep on the bed" in order to undergo the initiatory mutation. She or he will lie secluded on this bed for the greater part of the entire period. Seclusion is understood as a healing, as a time when the aspirant consolidates his or her sensory abilities in order to be able to perceive and scrutinize the invisible. All the various prescriptions regarding the behavior of the novice, the chants and the paraphernalia, as well as the approbation of the group, are all directed to this single purpose. While in seclusion, the initiate is susceptible to entering an ASC every time he or she hears the village members allude to sorcery—for example, when they join in the evening singing.

The presence of the initiator throughout the seclusion is unobtrusive but reassuring to the initiate. Each day the master brings the initiate bouquets of fresh odoriferous plants from the savanna and woodland. These are used in the preparation of decoctions, which the novice will take in the form of enemas. In this context, enemas are intended to transform the initiate's lower torso into a channel of communication between the physical and sensory body and life-milieu or cosmos. This treatment therefore signifies and promotes the mastery of life-giving forces and their intertwinement with the physical and cosmic bodies. There are very precise prescriptions for collecting the vegetal substances making up this bouquet. The master-diviner must enter the savanna and woodland at sunrise and proceed in a downstream direction. Once an appropriate tree has been located, the master-diviner begins collecting at the base then works his or her way gradually up through various levels, each providing habitats to different species of animals or birds, all the way to the top. Ultimately the prescribed method aims to create a transitional space for the initiate, at this point withdrawn into him- or herself, and to establish a link between the novice and the various dimensions of the life-world. As the forest denotes a male space in Yaka cosmology, an equivalent number of plant essences must be harvested from the savanna that represent a female space. The latter group of plant substances evoke the transformation of affliction into a source of healing (Devisch 1993:218).

At the heart of the metamorphosis undergone by the initiate lies a profound metaphorical dynamic insofar as the ritual house and the prescribed initiatory practices promote the interaction of various animal, cosmic, or extra-human transformational processes, transcribing them in the physical and sensory body of the initiate (compare with Majumdar's contribution in this volume). The ritual drama enacted here connects these fields of forces and signs or values with the social and cultural body through the performative capacity of metaphor. Six different levels of interaction may be discovered in this tapestry of interwoven metaphors, as I explain in the following.

On the first level, the ritual house provides a metaphor for the womb. The state of seclusion evokes a fetal condition comparable to nesting; this dimension is supported by the regulations governing seclusion as well as the construction and various furnishings of the ritual house. The entrance to the hut, for example, carries genital connotations: the doorway is hidden by a curtain of raffia palm called *luleembi* or *masasa,* a word that in Koongo (a language very close to Yaka) means "pubic hair," a connotation clearly given to the raffia loincloth worn by the novice. By entering the seclusion hut backward through the curtain, the initiate evokes a birth in reverse. This metaphorical scheme is evident in the gradual process of coming out of seclusion as well. First, the aspirant is ordered to spend three nights sleeping on a raffia mat on the floor. The three days' seclusion is terminated when the master leads the novice at sunrise to a pond or backwater in a nearby river where the initiate is for the first time permitted to bathe since going into seclusion. In the course of the bath, initiates rub oil and kaolin over the body for fear that the ngoombu leaves (literally, "aborts") the initiate. The head is shaven upon returning to the village. Once the initiate has left the seclusion hut for the last time and is reborn, he or she may return to the conjugal home, a moment confirmed by the gift of a slit drum.

The seclusion period is brought to an end with the initiate performing a rite in which he or she exhibits carnivorous behavior. Early on the morning of the inauguration as a fully fledged diviner, the apprentice withdraws to the edge of the forest and, going into an ASC, tears off a cock's head with his or her teeth. In this way the aggression of the divining spirits to which the novice had fallen victim is turned onto the cock.

At yet another level, the ritual house may be likened to a hen and its brood. The novice's gestures and walk (called -*kebukila;* literally, turn and look around in all directions) and the noises the individual makes evoke the behavior of the chicken, especially its squawking. The popular imagination is struck not only by the conduct and warning cries of the chicken but also by its habit of waking early in the morning, before any other animals, and jumping or flying away when threatened. Further, the hen that lays or broods evokes a corporal disposition, a dimension of the habitus, similar to the initiate's repose. All of these aspects link the chicken to the gift of clairvoyance that is believed to "hatch" within the diviner, "like an egg in the brood." The generating capacity of hen and egg is thus metaphorically "bred" within the mediumistic diviner, who, in an ASC, jumps onto the thatch roof and walks around it on his or her tiptoes in imitation of a hen or cock. A clucking "coh coh coh" sound is interspersed throughout the speech of the initiate, who during initiation announces sunrise and sunset with the cries of a rooster.

Thus the diviner-initiate reappears in the village on the dawn of the day marking the end of the seclusion holding a chicken head in his or her mouth.

While the novice's eye, head, and body movements imitate a hen or cock, the sounds and gestures he or she makes in response to the drumming of the great phallic dance drum and the small slit drum clearly denote the act of copulation. At this point the head of the family (called n-twa phoongu; literally, head of the cult/spirit) picks up the initiate and carries him or her back to the ritual house, whose construction and role evokes both the egglike womb of the world and the image of the initiate as a brooding hen. There, a chicken head has been hung on a branch of the parasol tree that was planted at the beginning of the seclusion: the head comes from a fowl that the maternal uncle had given as a sacrifice to the candidate and was eaten by the family at its last meal before the seclusion. Closing the seclusion period, the master-diviner helps the initiate exit the ritual hut through a hole pierced in the wall behind the bed; in doing so, the novice imitates a chick breaking out of its egg. For the Yaka, the chicken signifies intermediacy and mediation: it walks on two legs like a human and displays transgressive mobility—particularly in relation to conventional opposites such as up-down, in-out, forest-village, or day-night; it can leap from the ground to the roof, moves from house to house, eats both wild and prepared foods, forages between the forest and the village; and the cock's crow marks the transition between night and day. Similarly, the egg can be seen as an intermediary between that which transmits and that which receives life.

Once the initiate has definitively left the house of seclusion, he or she proceeds to imitate, in an ASC, yet another amphibious animal, the otter shrew. Both the initiate and the diviner-initiator wear pieces of otter shrew skin on their heads during this phase of the initiation. Considered to be a mediator between the earth and water, the world of day and the world of night, this amphibious mammal comes out of the water at night to eat insects and fish. Its lair has a double entrance, one under water and one on the surface. At this stage the initiate's face is painted white, the color of the deceased (and of the moon, as shown below), an aspect that implies the diviner is also an apparition from the world of the deceased. The novice, imitating an otter shrew, digs a body-length tunnel in the sandy soil with his or her bare hands, sometimes assisted by the initiator, and crawls through it. During the underground passage, the apprentice comes in contact with the world of the tutelary spirits, who inhabit him or her from this point on, and is reborn.

Demonstrating invulnerability in the face of sorcery or evil, the apprentice emerges from this lair brandishing a knife—here denoting the order of evil—with which he or she lashes out at potatoes or other tubercles. The latter are substitutes for the evil, prototypically considered a theft, that was at the origin of the affliction and brought on the persecution by the ngoombu spirit. The novice is now able to recover health and become the master of his or her personal destiny; the curse has been lifted and the initiate now possesses the spirit of divination in its most auspicious form. The co-villagers acknowledge this by making food offerings to the initiate. Due to the initiation, any discord, curses, or afflictions previously affecting the family have been transformed into healing.

In the Yaka understanding of the ngoombu cult, the diviner becomes something of a demiurge in that the recluse is made to personify the Yaka founding ancestors, Kamwaadi and Kakuungu, who are represented in the ritual hut by a barely sculpted forked stick. By metaphorically integrating both the transformational capacities of the hen brooding and of her egg before hatching, the initiate effects a radical transgression—and thus an unequivocal restitution—of the prescribed divisions and categories upon which the Yaka cosmology reposes.

The Divinatory Oracle: Consulting a Diviner

In order to validate the divinatory message and assure the credibility of its paranormal status, representatives of both the maternal and paternal lineages of the severely afflicted or the deceased, as well as any other representatives of the in-laws, are called to join in the consultation and witness the oracle. All present are careful to maintain their anonymity, and diviners residing far from the locality in question are usually sought out, as their likely ignorance of the case and the group in question will better demonstrate the veracity of the divination. Consultants refrain from speaking during their journey, and upon arrival at the diviner's home they refuse to shake hands or sit down until the first diagnosis has been pronounced. When they arrive, they silently hand the diviner a piece of cloth or some kaolin that has been in contact with the client's or the deceased's body; this object mediates the presence for the afflicted person, who is never actually present, just as the body of the deceased is not brought to the divination.

The diviner sets about revealing the fundamentals of the case, without any help from those present, during the first phase of the consultation. Diviners themselves state that their principal source of information resides in their powers of clairvoyance. From time to time, the diviner may sniff at the cloth or kaolin or hold it in front of a small mirror and, when ready to initiate the consultation, the diviner goes into an ASC. Chanting an esoteric language, the diviner poses a series of structured questions to which the answers are either yes or no (De Beir 1975 provides typical examples); this ritual interrogation develops an etiological inventory based on the most common categories of affliction and misfortune resulting from acts such as theft, sorcery, or a violation of matrimonial and uterine rights. The questions allow the diviner to bring the problem at hand into focus before initiating the oracle proper. The consultants are drawn into the process and are even forced to do some introspection through their responses in a typical fixed wording. Ideally, their answers should not offer any particularly significant or specific information, to make sure that the diviner's success is ultimately due only to skill in clairvoyance. The diviner should alone identify the basic facts of the consultation, learn the client's identity, and map out the relationships among the individuals concerned, describe the site where the events occurred, and accurately ascertain the nature of the case, indicating whether it is an issue of death, illness, loss of resources, sorcery, or some other misfortune. Following this initial pronouncement, the consultants may provide further details about the case and make a first payment if they are satisfied with the diviner.

The second and strictly etiological phase of the consultation can only take place a day later, in the morning, allowing the diviner the opportunity to draw on any dreams he or she may have during the night to corroborate the clairvoyance. The diviner may, for example, envision any number of typical images related to the case at hand: sorcery, ritual treatments performed on the patient, initiations, a curse, the behavior of the uncle, and so on. In short, the diviner's dreams may allude to specific events in the evolution of the individual's affliction and family history inasmuch as these events witness to the fields of forces having a bearing on the occurrence of the misfortune in the life of the individual and his or her family. Applying an etiologic grid to the case, the diviner can then determine the role and responsibility of various members of the family in the illness or death and indicate the appropriate means of therapeutic intervention based on the facts he or she has gleaned through clairvoyance.

The Divinatory Etiology

The following reviews some of the fundamental and recurring aspects of etiology (a more extended analysis can be found in Devisch 1993:169–78). The etiology is founded on the principle that anything which inhibits or obstructs life may ultimately be attributed to one or another instance of transgression, including some envious or abusive conduct or a sorcerer's spell cast by a uterine ascendant of the suffering individual. Illness or affliction is essentially interpreted as a knot or a binding that impedes the vital flow in both the patient's body and the family network insofar as it obstructs the life-giving exchange between the body, family group, and the world. Contrastingly, illness or afflictions are also conceived as an irregular cooling off or torsion that encloses or introverts the individual; the image evoked here is of "the heart closed in on itself like a stiff ball of manioc." A wide range of symptoms such as fever, intemperance, dissolution or "effusion," such as sexual intrusion and bulimia, may indicate this sort of ailment; alternatively, it may manifest itself as an inversion of conventional behavior, particularly those involving bodily orifices (vomiting, ejaculation outside of coitus, or breaking wind during a meal). Still other abnormal gestures and behaviors reflect an intrusion of sexual or anal things into the alimentary sphere: sexual allusions during the preparation or consumption of a familial meal, preparing food while one is menstruating. In this light, adultery committed within the conjugal home, excretion at the entrance to a dwelling (a maternal space), or an obscene act (such as baring the buttocks) in the same context connotes an eruption of the antisocial. The consequences of such behavior are serious: the body of either the victim or the aggressor will be "loosened" or "emptied" through chronic and possibly fatal bleeding or diarrhea. To restore life, fertility, and collective well-being, therapies inspired by numerous metaphors relating to knotting, tying, intertwining, or weaving are prescribed.

Relations of exchange among uterine kin, those determining one's health and the ability to transmit life, make up the first etiological register. The occurrence of any serious or chronic illness will have consequences for the uterine descendants who are then obliged to submit to the divinatory oracle. One of the first tasks of the oracle is to identify the extent of the maternal *uncle's* mediating role in linking the mother and her forebears to the uterine source of life. A series of major prohibitions, also handed down along uterine lines, serve to consolidate the uterine network and facilitate the transmission of life. Of all the male forebears, it is the afflicted individual's uncles, the great-grand-uncle, who embodies the uterine origins of life and therefore represents the origin of whatever prohibitions, curses, or sanctions pertain to the victim or patient in question. In this light, divinatory etiology attributes the responsibility for any conduct hindering the flow of life to the uterine ascendants: this may be an act of sorcery, adultery or any other comportment depriving descendants of their rightful access to the source of life. The ultimate cause of the affliction, according to the oracle, therefore comprises theft or a similarly serious infraction committed by a uterine ascendant. An oracle is less precise, however, when it comes to piecing together the historical context of the deed and usually is successful only in identifying a particular generation of one or another group as culpable. Should the oracle name a particular individual, the wrongdoer will be identified only in his or her titular capacity, such as uncle or family head. In this etiological perspective, the victim of a distant transgression will be found to have pronounced a curse on the offender such that his or her descendants should suffer the punishment. However, the very pronouncement of the curse binds the lineages of both the wrongdoer and the victim to suffering the punishment for any equivalent transgressions committed by any of the uterine descendants. It thus becomes evident that curses constitute the perspective valence of the prohibition which, when transgressed, imposes an appropriate sanction.

A second etiological register comprises the linking of the particular affliction to a prohibition or curse pronounced in favor of cult spirits, since the cults determine, along maternal lines, both the curses and the acts they seek to avenge as well as the unfortunate consequences they bring about. A number of elements in the context of affliction and therapy are provided by the cults: the ritual structure of the curse pronounced; the group's horizon of values, which founds the primacy of the rule of exchange; an etiological framework interpreting affliction as sanction; and a context providing for and determining the organization of therapy. It can then be understood that the healing of afflictions caused by such curses and sanctions in effect involves initiation of the suffering person into the cult of the spirits who have persecuted him or her; this initiation is the only means of rupturing the cycle of retaliation. Healing, in such cases, is at the same time a form of group or family therapy, for every translineage cult is composed of a group of individuals who have all undergone a cure within the context of that same cult. It then follows that as many translineage colleges or sodalities may be created as there are forms of affliction and corresponding therapy.

The inevitable question as to why an illness or misfortune has afflicted this particular individual rather than another points to a third register of divinatory etiology. An oracle reconstructs a case history essentially according to dimensions of kinship, and it never attributes an affliction to one sole factor such as sorcery. A gynecological ailment, for example, could be a consequence of some illicit sexuality or some breakdown in relations with the maternal uncle. In all cases the underlying issue is perceived to be that of a perversion of corporal boundaries: when the body is no longer able simultaneously to be both a confined space and a site of exchange, it drifts toward one of two symptomatic extremes, becoming either extremely closed or completely incontinent. It is believed that the victim suffers an impairment *(yibiinda),* originating outside her, which impedes or prevents *(-biindama)* her from fulfilling her reproductive functions.

Diagnostic divination establishes in general terms an etiological logic based on a recurrent pattern of history in the uterine line. When presented with a serious illness, the diviner initially attributes the problem to a recent infraction of the rights and obligations defining the position and relations of the members of the uterine, matrimonial, or conjugal network to which the victim belongs. This event is portrayed by the oracle in terms of a transgression of a prohibition whose sanction has already been mobilized by a curse attached to some previous violation of a similar nature. When a uterine ancestor pronounces a curse, it places the whole of the uterine descent in jeopardy. In sum, divinatory logic is founded upon a structural redundancy juxtaposing notions of communal law, the principle of exchange, prohibition, transgression, and sanction. Affliction comes about when the rights and interests of parties sharing in a process of exchange have been infringed upon, as it causes an obstruction of the flow of life; this transgression constitutes a violation of a prohibition. Pronounced by the victim or his or her protector (a parent or uncle), the curse following an offense instigates the affliction as a sanction for the wrongdoing.

Divination and the Ethical Order of Communal Law

Yaka divinatory etiology is governed by a structural causality; it mobilizes a system of values, rather than a system of law, founded on the sort of ethical order one finds inherent to the performances of the councils of elders and the chief's court. Divinatory oracles reflect the same form of logic as curses, one based on certain axioms establishing the link between previous afflictions and the present ailment. This link confers a performative and metaphorical form on the primary signification of the disorder or illness. The oracle's basic function is to postulate a curse event that adequately interconnects the notions of exchange, prohibition, transgression, and sanction in relation to one another. In doing so, the oracle is capable only of providing an inescapably recurrent historical narrative: a narrative of evil meeting its punishment, it is not intending to indicate a direct, instrumental, and historically demonstrable "cause" lying at the source of the affliction. The oracle superimposes a structural paradigm (exchange—prohibition—malediction—sanction) on the problem at hand and provides a hermeneutic for determining the meaning of the circumstances and constituent elements of the misfortune. Ultimately, the oracle also creates an opportunity for therapeutic intervention, in which both the victim's patrilineage and generations of the uterine line participate, establishing a correspondence between the past and the present and making the reason for the misfortune intelligible. The oracle is, therefore, a story of the restoration of the familial, social, and symbolic orders.

Divination, however, neither derives from nor implies an ethical order of communal law. The elements of rule or prohibition, in divinatory etiological perspective, enter into the question only when an individual suffers a wrong that is recognized as damaging to the interests of the group and the violation has been judged illicit through palaver or oracle. Divinatory etiology consists of re-inscribing the story of the wrongdoing and the misfortune in the familial saga of the emergence of the normative order.

A combined verdict and prescription bring the divinatory séance to an end. The verdict consists of the accusation of one of the parties of sorcery or of some infraction that has reactivated the past curse. As a prescription, the oracle will indicate a sacrifice or a compensation to be made or the renewal of relations with a particular uncle or the preparation of a cult.

If the treatment prescribed by the oracle in the case of illness should fail, the value of the divinatory process is nonetheless preserved due to the multiple antecedents and the variety of levels in terms of the etiological sanctions it can deploy. Similarly, a network of factors (such as the identification of a curse or a succession of matrimonial alliances in the uterine line) might rescue the therapeutic process when the first steps prescribed by the oracle appear to be ineffective (for example, the alleviating intervention of the uncle initially appears unsuccessful). Ultimately, the efficacy of the treatment prescribed cannot invalidate the etiological model of the divinatory process. If it fails, it simply demonstrates that the initial diagnosis was, for whatever reason, inadequate, perhaps because it was incomplete, because dishonest consultants had derailed it, or because participants had knowingly disregarded the prescribed rules.

Making Use of the Divinatory Assertions

It is critical to distinguish between the oracle proper and the social use of it, namely the strategies guiding the consultants and the subsequent reinterpretation, in a family council, of the divinatory assertions. Diviners are expected not only to justify their claims to their audience by offering criteria substantiating both their skills and the source of their knowledge, but also to demonstrate their impartiality. Divination entails the basic assumption that human relations may be the cause of affliction. Divinatory etiologies subject disorder and misfortune to basic social rules of exchange in the uterine and matrimonial circuits of social reciprocity and reintroduce clients into an order of discourse. The oracle achieves its aims through the symbolic function and foundational public discourse of diviner and clients following the fashion laid down by tradition. The divinatory oracle relativizes its own etiology, leaving room for individual freedom and genuine initiative. Insofar as it establishes multiple links between the misfortune and various social and axiological (cosmological) registers of meaning (the social organization, the rule of exchange, offenses, curses, persecutions, spirits), the oracle domesticates the doom of destiny.

Divination in the margins of the public order is more of a birthing process than an arbitrage, and a hermeneutics of disorder more than a discourse of truth or a causal or ethical inquiry into them (Devisch 1993:chap. 5). Unlike the judicial council, divination is not an exercise of redressive power or domination. Divinatory revelation stands to the jural council of elders as dreamwork to representational and discursive argument, as "speaking from the heart"—or "from the womb"—stands to men's rhetorical reassertion of power relations in the masculine order of seniority. Mediumistic divining is concerned with the source rather than the cause of events; thus, it deals with the consensual moral order and with the interplay between the health of the group members and the forces in the group and its life-world. Divinatory etiology may treat the patient as a weave in the social fabric or variously as a hunting ground: the diviner traces back the sets of knots that are untied or loosened between the client, his or her family, and the life-world, or he or she tracks down evil spirits and their sorceries. Where it uncovers deviancy in exchange and reciprocity, the oracle does not so much ask for redress as it instigates growth, healing, or "making whole."

The Slit Drum and the Oracular Message

It is striking that the diviner pronouncing the oracle declares him- or herself not to be its author. Nor, by definition, could the diviner be the subject who discloses and informs all in etiological discourse. Nor does the diviner speak in his or her own name, unlike the diviner-prophet who utters "inspired" messages on his or her own personal authority (Devisch 1996:169). However, I would argue that the diviner is the agent of the corporal and sensory drama, with its self-generating meaning, and in this sense the oracle does not efface the psychic- and metaphor-bearing subject. It would appear then that a problematic situation is first expressed, nonverbally, through the diviner's body or corporal drama, as it were, before it is translated, ostensibly in response to the questions posed by the consultants but more formally in function of the etiological registers offered by the axiological tradition. The author of the oracular enunciation can then be seen to be constituted by the intertwinement of anomaly and norm, of the deficient and the normal, or of the social, cosmological, and bodily domains, all of which are actualized through the diviner's corporeity or more precisely through the intercorporeity of diviner, client, and consultants. The agents of this intertwining and the place in which it takes place are the initiatory ASC and heightened perception (the keen sense of smell, clairvoyance, and capacity to listen) experienced by the diviner.

The diviner's drum (documented by Bourgeois 1983, 1984) is oblong, with a long, particularly wide slit. A head bearing an amalgamation of human and chicken features surmounts it. It is exclusive to the ngoombu cult and its usage is monopolized by fully initiated medium-diviners. Only the master-diviner may initiate the slit drum, transforming it into a place of contact or mediation with the ancestor. The master-diviner takes the drum to the cemetery of the defunct diviner who conferred his or her clairvoyance on the novice in question. There, the master-diviner then lets it "sleep three nights" (*-niimba yitatu).*

The drum thus incorporates the spirit of the predecessor who will serve as the oracle's voice. This ancestral voice articulates the uterine resonances emitted from the drum's slit, or mouth-vagina. The master-diviner

Slit drum, nkookwa ngoombu, *of diviner Tseembu; Nkoongu village (photograph by René Devisch, 1974)*

coats the slit of the drum with kaolin mixed with white nut, tonic *(toondi),* salt, and pepper; this is the principal offering inviting the elder, ancestor, or spirit to proffer life-giving speech.

As described above, the first phase of the oracle commences when the diviner enters into an ASC accompanied by the rhythmic beating of his or her slit drum. At this point, the diviner is bent over the drum, whose slit opening is turned to face the consultants, or he or she squats on it. A powerful object of collective fantasy, the slit drum is a representation of a dimension of the unconscious where energies and images charged with corporal effects or sensations coalesce with signs. Everything that the drum and the art of divination evoke in the Yaka mind relates to a realm of untamed forces or energies: night, spirits, the brooding hen, shared orgasm (and the fusion of the sexes), gestation (fermentation or couvade), birth and its travail, and ASC. All these forms of energy constitute the Yaka idiom employed by divination to put into speech the various fields of the imaginary-symbolic material comprising the collective unconscious and subjective fantasy. One thus understands how the oracle itself is necessarily removed from the diurnal life of the community: it takes place on the fringes of the social order and especially at moments of transition (dusk and dawn) in order to revitalize the resources of body, sensation, fantasy, and the collective imagination.

In this context, then, the slit drum functions not as a simple prop but as a mirror and an utterance: it is a resonating envelope, voice and ear expressing a person's status as a subject. Insofar as it is impossible to root out the evil (which, ultimately, is none other than the persecuting dimension of *ngoombu*) from the possessed individual, the secluded individual responds to this state of affairs by turning his or her body inside out. Now the ritual house, kaolin, and drum constitute the initiate's new skin. In other words, the body of the afflicted person possessed or of the initiate successively undergoes what we may call a sort of "exvagination" and "invagination." The genital connotations of the slit drum and its beating, the cry of "coh coh coh" emitted by the diviner as he or she is swaying to the rhythm, bring about a process of engendering, a generation of meaning. The cock's crow is a reenactment of a memory of the dawn of all life, for it evokes a profound bodily reminiscence concerned with life's beginnings.

As the seclusion ends, the novice exits the ritual house in the manner of a chick hatching from its egg, burrowing under the ground with a hatching movement, renews links with all origins. In burying oneself in the ground, one operates a sort of corporal reversal (exvagination/invagination) in which the exterior of the initiate is transformed into the interior; simultaneously, the messages of the slit drum and the contact with the underground realm impart to the initiate a new skin and a new identity.

The oracle of the slit drum expresses itself in a uterine language. Adding its utterances to the rhythm of the slit drum, the oracle develops this language symbolically, emitting the message of the matrix, or vaginal mouth, in the context of an apparently maternal relationship with the client. This element is made explicit in the divinatory chant: "*Yeebeetaka n-kooku maama, kangwaana phenya mbuta*" (Oh, Mama, I beat my slit drum so that he will confide in my big vagina). Evoking ngoongu, the primordial uterine space, the slit drum is carried like a child on the left arm. Grounded in the senses, the body, and the passions, the oracle incarnates a movement toward the symbolic: the more the oracle evokes the social and ancestral order, the more its utterances emanate, so to speak, from the upper body, the diurnal and virile order. The function of the drum is to create a bond between ngoongu, the primordial uterine space, and *ndaka phoongu* (literally, the tongue/uvula), the mouth or voice of the cult. That the oracle issues from the vaginal mouth and, correspondingly, the most basic and physical of rhythms, that which accompanies the transmission of life in conjugal union and birth, is symbolically denoted by several elements: the expressiveness of the ASC, the slit drum, and the three slit cowry shells, called "ngoombu's eye," that are fastened to the skin of an otter shrew the diviner wears on his or her head. The regenerating capacity of the oracle may also be compared to the sap gathered from the male flower of the palm tree that is transformed into wine. The Yaka believe palm sap emerges from the uterine life-spring in the earth, from there flowing through the arteries of the palm tree to the inflorescence. This natural liquid is collected in a calabash (an object bearing many maternal connotations) and is transformed through fermentation into a precious cultural product. During the seclusion, it is said, the initiate drinks only palm wine as nourishment; while divining, the diviner drinks the palm wine from the (vaginal) slit of his or her drum. Drinking palm wine places the initiatory seclusion, like the divinatory oracle, in a time of fermentation and maturation—that is, of endogenous processes of transformation. In these rituals one is struck by the fact that it takes some time before the diviner or elder can bring him- or herself to speak. By prescribing the diviner nothing but palm wine during the initiatory period, the consultants cultivate and elicit the diviner's utterance. This leads one to conclude that, within the Yaka context of affliction and divination, the oracular pronouncement and its reference to the preeminence of ancestor and the normative order can exercise their emancipatory function only to the extent they nourish themselves in the bodily effects and in a maternal and chthonic origin.

Conclusion

Acting as mediators between worlds, diviners assist clients in transmitting messages and channeling life-bearing forces between spirits and themselves. The diviner disavows authorship of vision and judgment and pretends that whatever message he or she may be voicing stems from the divinatory forces at work in him or her or in the divinatory media. Divination brings about intermediacy or mediation, twinning head and heart, heart and womb, and male and female concerns.

Notes

1. From January 1972 to October 1974, I was privileged to live in the Taanda village settlements in the north of Kwaango along the Angolese border, about 450 kilometers southeast of Kinshasa. It was as a participant in everyday life there that I was able to witness two ngoombu initiation rites, take note of some two hundred divinatory oracles, work closely with some five diviners, and maintain intimate contact with eighteen therapists. During my two short stays in 1991 in the north of Kwaango, as well as during my annual three- to six-week sojourns in the poverty-stricken Yaka milieu in Kinshasa (since 1986), I was able to interview at length a dozen Yaka diviners practicing in Kwaango and/or Kinshasa.

The research among rural and urban Yaka has been financed by the Belgian National Fund for Scientific Research, the Fund for Scientific Research-Flanders, the European Commission Directorate-General XII (B4 Sector Health—STD2 0202-B and STD-TS3 CT94-0326), and the Harry-Frank Guggenheim Foundation, New York. The research was carried out in collaboration with the IMNC (Institute of the National Museums of Congo), as well as CERDAS (Centre for the Co-ordination of Research and Documentation in Social Science for Africa South of the Sahara), based at the University of Kinshasa. I thank Peter Crossman for his editorial help.

2. Cults among the Yaka have much in common with those of the Ndembu in north-western Zambia, who have become so well known through the carefully detailed and insightful analyses by Victor and Edith Turner (see also this volume). Both the Ndembu in Zambia, southwestern Congo, and northeastern Angola and the Yaka in southwestern Congo have for more than three centuries been exposed to the Luun-da sphere of influence.

References

Abbink, J. 1993. Reading the entrails: Analysis of an African divination discourse. *Man* 28:705–26.

Abimbola, W. 1997. *Ifa: An exposition of Ifa literary corpus.* New York: Athelia Henrietta Press.

Adelowo, E. D. 1989. A comparative look at the phenomenon of divination as an aspect of healing processes in the major religions in Nigeria. *Asia Journal of Theology* 3(1):206–26.

———. 1990. Yoruba traditional religion, magic, and medicine: Divination and sacrifice in relation to the health of society. *Asia Journal of Theology* 4(2):456–71.

Adeoye, C. L. 1985. *Igbagbo Ati Esin Yoruba.* Ibadan: Evans Brothers.

Anderson, D. M., and D. H. Johnson, eds. 1995. *Revealing prophets: Prophecy in East African history.* London: James Currey.

Atkinson, J. M. 1989. *The art and politics of Wana shamanship.* Berkeley: University of California Press.

Bahr, D. M., J. Gregorio, D. I. Lopez, and A. Alvarez. 1974. *Piman shamanism and staying sickness (Ká:cim Múmkidag).* Tucson: University of Arizona Press.

Barbeau, M. 1958. *Medicine men on the North Pacific Coast.* Ottawa: National Museum of Canada.

Barnett, H. G. 1957. *Indian Shakers: A messianic cult of the Pacific Northwest.* Carbondale: Southern Illinois University Press.

Bartlett, H. H. 1930. The labors of the *Datoe.* Part I: An annotated list of religious, magical, and medical practices of the Batak of Asahan. *Papers of the Michigan Academy of Sciences, Arts, and Letters* 12:1–74.

———. 1931. The labors of the *Datoe.* Part II: Directions for the ceremonies. *Papers of the Michigan Academy of Sciences, Arts, and Letters* 14:1–34.

265

Bascom, W. 1969. *Ifa divination: Communication between gods and men in West Africa.* Bloomington: Indiana University Press.

Beattie, J.H.M., and J. Middleton. 1969. *Spirit mediumship and society in Africa.* London: Routledge and Kegan Paul.

Bergson, H. 1934. *La Pensée et le muvant.* Paris: Alcan.

Berntsen, J. L. 1979. Maasai age-sets and prophetic leadership, 1850–1910. *Africa* 49(2):134–46.

Bier, U. 1980. *Yoruba myths.* Cambridge: Cambridge University Press.

Bletzer, K. V. 1985. Fleeing hysteria *(chakore)* among the Ngawbere of northwestern Panama. *Medical Anthropology* 9:297–318.

———. 1988. La chichería among Ngawbere of the northern Valiente Peninsula: Some notes and comments. *Anthropos* 83(1–3):135–51.

———. 1991. Biobehavioral characteristics of a culture-bound syndrome perceived as life-threatening illness. *Qualitative Health Research* 1:200–233.

———. 1992. Un análisis del rito de vigilia de las mujeres embarazadas entre los indígenas Ngawbere, Panamá. *Vínculos* (Costa Rica) 17:53–74.

———. 1996. Changing illness images. In *Jahrbuch für Transkulturelle Medizin und Psychotherapie,* ed. W. Andritzky, 301–17. Berlin: Verlag.

Blier, S. P. 1990. "King" Glele of Danhomey: Divination portraits of a lion king and man of iron. *African Arts* 23 (October):42–53, 93–94.

———. 1995. *African Vodun art, psychology, and power.* Chicago: University of Chicago Press.

Boas, F. 1907. The Eskimo of Baffin Land and Hudson Bay. *Bulletin of the American Museum of Natural History* 15:1–570.

Boddy, J. 1988. Spirits and selves in northern Sudan: The cultural therapeutics of possession and trance. *American Ethnologist* 15(1):4–27.

———. 1989. *Wombs and alien spirits: Women, men, and the Zar Cult in northern Sudan.* Madison: University of Wisconsin Press.

———. 1994. Spirit possession revisited. *Annual Review of Anthropology* 23:417–34.

Bornstein, R. F., and T. S. Pittman, eds. 1992. *Perception without awareness: Cognitive, clinical, and social perspectives.* New York: Guilford Press.

Boscana, G. 1969. Chinigchinich. In *Life in California,* ed. A. Robinson, 225–341. New York: Da Capo Press.

Bourgeois A. 1983. Mukoko Ngoombu: Yaka divination paraphernalia. *African Arts* 16(3):56–59, 80.

———. 1984. *Art of the Yaka and Suku.* Paris: A. and F. Chaffin.

Bunzel, R. L. 1932. Introduction to Zuñi ceremonialism. *Annual Report of the Bureau of American Ethnology* 47:467–544. Washington: Smithsonian Institution.

Burton, J. W. 1991. Nilotic cosmology and the divination of Atuot philosophy. In *African divination systems: Ways of knowing,* ed. P. M. Peek, 41–52. Bloomington: Indiana University Press.

Caquot, A., and M. Leibovici. 1968. *La Divination.* 2 vols. Paris: Presses Universitaires de France.

Child, A. B., and I. L. Child. 1993. *Religion and magic in the life of traditional peoples.* Englewood Cliffs, N.J.: Prentice Hall.

Cohen, J. D., and J. W. Schooler, eds. 1997. *Scientific approaches to consciousness.* Mahwah, N.J.: L. Erlbaum Associates.

Cohen, K. 1998. Native American medicine. *Alternative Therapies in Health and Medicine* 4(6):45–57.

Colby, B. N., and L. M. Colby. 1981. *The daykeeper: The life and thought of an Ixil diviner.* Cambridge, Mass.: Harvard University Press.

Coon, C. S. 1971. *The hunting peoples.* Boston: Little Brown.

Csordas, T. J. 1983. The rhetoric of transformation in ritual healing. *Culture, Medicine, and Psychiatry* 7:333–75.

———. 1987. Health and the holy in African and Afro-American spirit possession. *Social Science and Medicine* 24(1):1–11.

———. 1988. Elements of charismatic persuasion and healing. *Medical Anthropology Quarterly* 2(2):121–42.

———. 1990. Embodiment as a paradigm for anthropology. *Ethos* 18:5–47.

Curtin, J. 1898. *Creation myths of primitive America.* Boston: Little, Brown.

D'Aquili, E. G., and C. Laughlin. 1975. The biopsychological determinants of religious ritual behavior. *Zygon* 10(1):33–58.

D'Aquili, E. G., C. D. Laughlin, and J. McManus. 1979. *The spectrum of ritual : A biogenetic structural analysis.* New York: Columbia University Press.

De Beir, L. 1975. *Religion et magie des Bayaka.* St. Augustin, Bonn: Anthropos.

De Boeck, F., and R. Devisch. 1994. Ndembu, Luunda, and Yaka divination compared: From representation and social engineering to embodiment and world-making. *Journal of Religion in Africa* 24(2):98–133.

Deikman, A. J. 1975. Deautomization and the mystic experience. In *The psychology of consciousness,* ed. R. Ornstein, 200–220. New York: Penguin Books.

Densmore, F. 1918. Teton Sioux music. *Bureau of American Ethnography, Bulletin 61.* Washington: Smithsonian Institution.

———. 1929. Chippewa customs. *Bureau of American Ethnology, Bulletin 86.* Washington: Smithsonian Institution.

Desjarlais, R. 1991. Dreams, divination, and Yolmo ways of knowing. *Dreaming* 1:211–24.

Devisch, R. 1985. Perspectives on divination in contemporary Sub-Saharan Africa. In *Theoretical explorations in African religion,* ed. W. van Binsbergen and M. Schoffeleers, 50–83. London: KPI/Routledge and Kegan Paul.

———. 1993. *Weaving the threads of life: The Khita gyn-eco-logical healing cult among the Yaka.* Chicago: University of Chicago Press.

———. 1996. "Pillaging Jesus": Healing churches and the villagisation of Kinshasa. *Africa* 66:555–86.

Devisch R., and C. Brodeur. 1999. *The law of the lifegivers: The domestication of desire.* New York: Harwood Academic Publishers.

Douglas, M. 1970. Witchcraft confessions and accusations. *Association for Social Anthropology Monograph 9.* London: Tavistock.

———. 1979. "If the Dogon . . . ." In *Implicit meanings: Essays in anthropology,* ed. M. Douglas, 124–41. London: Routledge and Kegan Paul.

Dow, J. 1986. Universal aspects of symbolic healing: A theoretical synthesis. *American Anthropologist* 88:56–69.

Drucker, P. 1937. The Tolowa and their southwest Oregon kin. *University of California Publications in American Archaeology and Ethnology* 36(4):221–300.

———. 1939. Contributions to Alsea Ethnography. *University of California Publications in American Archaeology and Ethnology* 35(7):81–102.

DuBois, J. 1994. Meaning without intention: Lessons from divination. In *Responsibility and evidence in oral discourse,* ed. J. H. Hall and J. Irvine. Cambridge: Cambridge University Press.

Duder, C. J., and G. L. Simpson. 1997. Land and murder in colonial Kenya: The Leroghi land dispute and the Powys "murder" case. *Journal of Imperial and Commonwealth History* 25:440–65.

Dumon, D., and R. Devisch. 1991. *The oracle of Maama Tseembu: Divination and healing amongst the Yaka of south-eastern Zaire.* 50 min. film in Dutch, English, French, and German versions. Belgian radio-television, Section Science.

Edgerton, R. B. 1966. Conceptions of psychosis in four East African societies. *American Anthropologist* 68:408–25.

———. 1974. Pastoral-farming comparison. In *Culture and personality,* ed. R. A. Levine, 345–68. Chicago: Aldine Press.

Eglash, R. 1997. Bamana sand divination: Recursion in ethnomathematics. *American Anthropology* 99(1):112–22.

Eliade, M. 1974. *Shamanism, archaic techniques of ecstasy, translation.* Vol. 76. Bollingen Series, ed. W. R. Trask. Princeton: Princeton University Press.

Elmendorf, W. W. 1993. *Twana narratives*. Seattle: University of Washington Press.

Evans-Pritchard, E. E. 1956. *Nuer religion*. New York and Oxford: Oxford University Press.

———. 1968. *Witchcraft, oracles, and magic among the Azande*. Oxford: Clarendon Press.

Faris, J. C. 1990. *The Nightway: A history and documentation of a Navajo ceremonial*. Albuquerque: University of New Mexico Press.

Fernandez, J. 1991. Afterword. In *African divination systems: Ways of knowing*, ed. P. M. Peek, 213–21. Bloomington: Indiana University Press.

Feshbach, S. 1984. The catharsis hypothesis, aggressive drive, and the reduction of aggression. *Aggressive Behavior* 10:91–101.

Fogelson, R. D. 1977. Cherokee Notions of Power. In *The anthropology of power*, ed. R. D. Fogelson and R. N. Adams, 185–94. New York: Academic Press.

———. 1980. The conjuror in eastern Cherokee society. *Journal of Cherokee Studies* 5(2):60–87.

Foster, G. M., Jr. 1941. String-figure divination. *American Anthropologist* 43:126–27.

Frankfurter, D. 1998. *Religion in Roman Egypt*. Princeton, N.J.: Princeton University Press.

Fratkin, E. 1979. A comparison of the role of prophets in Samburu and Maasai Warfare. In *Warfare among East African herders*, ed. K. Fukui and D. Turton, 54–65. Osaka: Senri Museum of Ethnology.

———. 1991. The Loibon as sorcerer: A Samburu Loibon among the Ariaal Rendille, 1973–1987. *Africa* 61(3):318–33.

———. 1996. Herbal medicine and traditional healing among Samburu pastoralists of Kenya. *Journal of Ethnobiology* 16:63–97.

———. 2004. *Ariaal pastoralists of northern Kenya*. 2d ed. Needham Heights, Mass.: Allyn and Bacon.

Freeland, L. S. 1923. Pomo doctors and poisoners. *University of California Publications in American Archaeology and Ethnology* 20:57–73.

Fridman, E. J. N. 2004. *Sacred geography: Shamanism among the Buddhist peoples of Russia*. Budapest: Akadémiai Kiadó, Bibliotheca Shamanistica.

Gifford, E. W. n.d. Central Miwok Shamanism. Unpublished manuscript, Museum and Department of Anthropology Archives, Ethnological Document no. 179 (Archives no. CU–23.1), Bancroft Library, University of California, Berkeley.

———. 1933. The Cocopa. *University of California Publications in American Archaeology and Ethnology* 31(5):257–334.

270

References

─────. 1936. Northeastern and Western Yavapai. *University of California Publications in American Archaeology and Ethnology* 34(4):247–354.

Gleitman, L. R., and E. L. Newport. 1995. The invention of language by children: Environmental and biological influences on the acquisition of language. In *Language: An invitation to cognitive science,* ed. L. R. Gleitman and M. Liberman, 1–24. Cambridge, Mass.: MIT Press.

Good, B. J. 1994. *Medicine, rationality, and experience: An anthropological perspective.* New York: Cambridge University Press.

Goodman, F. D. 1988. *Ecstasy, ritual, and alternate reality: Religion in a pluralistic world.* Bloomington: Indiana University Press.

─────. 2000. Trance, posture, and ritual. In *The nature and function of rituals: Fire from heaven,* ed. R. Heinze. Westport, Conn.: Greenwood Publishing.

Grant, R. E. 1982. Tuuhikya: The Hopi healer. *American Indian Quarterly* 6:291–304.

Greenberg, J. H. 1955. *Studies in African linguistic classification.* New Haven: Compass Press.

Gufler, H. 1995. Yamba spider divination. *Journal of the Anthropological Society of Oxford* 26:43–67.

Haley, J. 1989. *Problem-solving therapy.* San Francisco: Jossey-Bass.

Handelman, D. 1967. The development of a Washo Shaman. *Ethnology* 6:444–64.

Hanks, W. F. 1996. *Language and communicative practices.* Chicago: University of Chicago Press.

Harner, M. 1980. *The way of the shaman: A guide to power and healing.* San Francisco: Harper and Row.

Heinze, R. 1982. *Tham khwan: How to contain the essence of life: A socio-psychological comparison of a Thai custom.* Singapore: Singapore University Press.

─────. 1988/1997. *Trance and healing in Southeast Asia today.* Bangkok/Berkeley: White Lotus/Independent Scholars of Asia.

─────. 2000. The nature and function of rituals. In *The nature and function of rituals: Fire from heaven,* ed. R. Heinze. Westport, Conn.: Greenwood Publishing.

Hodas, G. R. 1985. A systems perspective on family therapy supervision. In *Adjunctive techniques in family therapy,* ed. R. L. Ziffer, 209–45. Orlando, Fla.: Grune and Stratton.

Hoffman, W. J. 1896. The Menomini Indians. *Annual Report of the Bureau of Ethnology* 14:3–328. Washington: Smithsonian Institution.

Hookway, C., and D. Peterson, eds. 1993. *Philosophy and cognitive science.* New York: Cambridge University Press.

Howe, L. 2000. Risk, ritual, and performance. *Journal of the Royal Anthropological Institute* 6:63–79.

Hultkrantz, Å. 1992. *Shamanic healing and ritual drama.* New York: Crossroad.

Hunt, H. 1995. *On the nature of consciousness.* New Haven: Yale University Press.

Jackson, M. 1978. An approach to Kuranko divination. *Human Relations* 31:117–38.

Jacobs, M. 1939. Coos narrative and ethnologic texts. *University of Washington Publications in Anthropology* 8:126.

Jacobsen, F. F. 1998. *Theories of sickness and misfortune among the Hadandowa Beja of the Sudan.* New York: Kegan Paul.

Jakobson, R., C.G.M. Fant, and M. Halle. 1952. *Preliminaries to speech analysis.* Cambridge, Mass.: MIT Acoustics Laboratory.

Janzen, J. M. 1991. *Ngoma: Discourses of healing in central and southern Africa.* Berkeley: University of California Press.

Jenness, D. 1922. The life of the Copper Eskimos. *Report of the Canadian Arctic expedition, 1913–18.* Vol. 12. Ottawa: F. A. Acland.

Jimenez Miranda, G. 1984. *Ngobe: La comarca Guaymi.* Panama City: Universidad Santa María la Antigua.

Junod, H. A. 1927. *The life of a South African tribe.* New Hyde Park, N.Y.: University Books.

Kelly, I. T. 1932. Ethnography of the Surprise Valley Paiute. *University of California Publications in American Archaeology and Ethnology* 31(3):67–210.

Kenin-Lopsan, M. B. 1993a. *Magiya Tuvinskikh Shamanov.* Kyzyl, Tuva: Novosti Tuvi.

———. 1993b. Ritual practice and folklore of Tuvinian Shamanism. *Anthropology and Archaeology of Eurasia* 31(3):44–81.

———. 1994. Whereabouts of the soul among the Tuvans. In *Shamanism in Tuva,* ed. T. Budegechi, 17–37. Kyzyl, Tuva: Scientific Center for the Study of Shamanism.

———. 1997. *Shamanic songs and myths of Tuva.* Budapest: Akadémiai Kiadó.

Kilpatrick, J. F., and A. G. Kilpatrick. 1967. *Run toward the nightland.* Dallas: Southern Methodist University Press.

Kirby, J. 1993. The Islamic dialogue with African traditional religion: Divination and health care. *Social Science Medicine* 36(3):237–47.

Kirmayer, L. 1993. Healing and the intervention of metaphor: The effectiveness of symbols revisited. *Culture, Medicine, and Psychiatry* 17:161–95.

Knudtson, P. H. 1975. Flora, shaman of the Wintu. *Natural History* 84(5):6–17.

Koppert, V. A. 1930. *Contributions to Clayoquot Ethnology.* Anthropological Series No. 1. Washington: Catholic University of America.

Kroeber, A. L. 1925. *Handbook of the Indians of California. Bureau of American Ethnography, Bulletin 78.* Washington: Smithsonian Institution.

————. 1935. Walapai ethnography. *Memoirs of the American Anthropological Society* 42:1–293.

Kyrgys, Z. 1993. *Ritmi Shamanskovo Bubna (Rhythms of the shaman's drum).* Kyzyl, Tuva: Medjdunarodni Nauchnii Tsentr Khoomei.

Lacan, J. 1977. *The seminar. Book XI. The four fundamental concepts of psycho-analysis.* London: Hogarth Press and Institute of Psycho-Analysis.

Laderman, C. C. 1991. *Taming the wind of desire. Psychology, medicine, and aesthetics in Malay shamanistic performance.* Berkeley: University of California Press.

Lambo, T. A. 1964. Patterns of psychiatric care in developing African countries. In *Magic, faith, and healing,* ed. A. Kiev, 443–53. New York: Free Press.

Lamphear, J. 1998. Brothers in arms: Military aspects of East African age-class systems in historical perspectives. In *Conflict, age, and power in North East Africa,* ed. E. Kurimoto and S. Simonse, 79–97. London: James Currey.

Langer, A., and A. Lutz. 1999. *Orakel.* Zurich: Museum Rietberg.

Laughlin, C. D. 1997. Body, brain, and behavior: The neuroanthropology of the body image. *Anthropology of Consciousness* 8(2–3):69–87.

Laughlin, C. D., J. McManus, and E. G. D'Aquili. 1992. *Brain, symbol and experience: Toward a neurophenomenology of human consciousness.* New York: Columbia University Press.

Leighton, A., and D. Leighton. 1941. Elements of psychotherapy in Navajo religion. *Psychiatry* 4:515–23.

————. 1965. Magic, witchcraft, and divination: Introduction. In *Reader in comparative religion: An anthropological approach,* ed. W. A. Lessa and E. Z. Vogt, 413–65. 3d ed. New York: Harper & Row.

Lévi-Strauss, C. 1972. *Structural anthropology.* London: Penguin.

Levy, J. E., R. Neutra, and D. Parker. 1987. *Hand trembling, frenzy witchcraft, and moth madness.* Tucson: University of Arizona Press.

Livingston, J. 1993. *Anatomy of the sacred: An introduction to religion.* New York: Macmillan.

Loeb, E. M. 1932. The Western Kuksu cult. *University of California Publications in American Archaeology and Ethnology* 33(1):1–137.

————. 1933. The Eastern Kuksu cult. *University of California Publications in American Archaeology and Ethnology* 33(2):139–232.

Loewe, M., and C. Blacker, eds. 1981. *Oracles and divination.* Boulder, Co.: Shambhala.

Luhmann, N. 1986. The autopoiesis of social systems. In *Sociocybernetic paradoxes: Observation, control, and evolution of self-steering systems,* ed. G. F. and J. van der Zouwen, 172–92. London: Sage.

MacLean, P. 1990. *The Triune Brain in Evolution.* New York: Plenum.

Madanes, C. 1981. *Strategic family therapy.* San Francisco: Jossey-Bass.

Mails, T. E. 1991. *Fools Crow: Wisdom and power.* Tulsa: Council Oak Books.

Malinowski, B. 1954. *Magic, science, and religion.* New York: Doubleday Anchor.

Malmström, V. H. 1997. *Cycles of the sun, mysteries of the moon; the calendar in Mesoamerican civilization.* Austin: University of Texas Press.

Mandell, A. 1980. Toward a psychobiology of transcendence: God in the brain. In *The psychobiology of consciousness,* ed. D. Davidson and R. Davidson, 379–464. New York: Plenum.

Marriott, M. 1976. Hindu Transactions: Diversity without Dualism. In *Transaction and meaning: Directions in the anthropology of exchange and symbolic behavior,* ed. B. Kapferer, 109–42. Philadelphia: Institute for the Study of Human Issues.

————. 1980. The open Hindu person and interpersonal fluidity. Unpublished article, University of Chicago.

————. 1989. Constructing an Indian ethnosociology. *Contributions to Indian Sociology,* n.s., 23(1):1–39.

Marshall, L. 1962. !Kung Bushmen religious beliefs. *Africa* 32(3):221–52.

Maslow, A. 1964. *Religions, values, and peak-experiences.* Columbus: Ohio State University Press.

Meyerson, E. 1925. *La déduction relativiste.* Paris: Payot.

Miller, G. A. 1956. The magical number seven, plus or minus two: Some limits on our capacity for processing information. *Psychological Review* 63:81–97.

Minuchin, S. 1974. *Families and family therapy.* Cambridge: Harvard University Press.

Minuchin, S., and C. C. Fishman. 1981. *Family therapy techniques.* Cambridge: Harvard University Press.

Monod, J. 1970. *Le hasard et la nécessité: Essai sur la philosophie naturelle de la biologie moderne.* Paris: Seuil.

Montilus, M. G. 1972. *La naissance dans la pensee traditionelle fon.* Mimeograph. Contonou, Benin.

Mooney, J. 1932. The swimmer manuscript: Cherokee sacred formulas and medicinal prescriptions. Ed. Frans M. Olbrechts. *Bureau of American Ethnology, Bulletin 99.* Washington: Smithsonian Institution.

Morgan, W. 1931. Navaho treatment of sickness: Diagnosticians. *American Anthropologist* 33:390–402.

Murdock, G. P. 1965. Tenino shamanism. *Ethnology* 4(2):165–71.

Nelson, E. W. 1899. The Eskimo about the Bering Strait. *Annual Report of the Bureau of American Ethnology* 18:3–518. Washington: Smithsonian Institution.

Newton, N. 1996. *Foundations of understanding.* Philadelphia: John Benjamin's Publishing Co.

Nomland, G. A. 1938. Bear River ethnography. *University of California Publications in Anthropological Records* 2(2):1–26.

Nuckolls, C. 1991. Deciding how to decide: Possession-mediumship in Jalari divination. *Medical Anthropology* 13(1–2):57–82.

Ohnuki-Tierney, E. 1981. *Illness and healing among the Akhalin Ainu: A symbolic interpretation.* London: Cambridge University Press.

Opler, M. K. 1959. Dream analysis in Ute Indian therapy. In *Culture and mental health,* ed. M. K. Opler, 97–117. New York: Macmillan.

Ortiz De Montellano, B. 1990. *Aztec medicine, health, and nutrition.* New Brunswick, N.J.: Rutgers University Press.

Park, G. 1963. Divination and its social contexts. *Journal of the Royal Anthropological Institute* 93(2):195–209.

Park, W. Z. 1938. Shamanism in western North America: A study in cultural relationships. *Northwestern University Studies in the Social Sciences, No. 2.*

Parkin, D. 1991. Simultaneity and sequencing in the oracular speech of Kenyan diviners. In *African divination systems: Ways of knowing,* ed. P. M. Peek, 173–89. Bloomington: Indiana University Press.

Parsons, E. C. 1939. *Pueblo Indian religion.* Chicago: University of Chicago Press.

Pedaya, H. 1998. Divinity as place and time and the holy place in Jewish mysticism. In *Sacred space: Shrine, city, land,* ed. B. Kedar and R. J. Zwi Werblowsky, 84–111. Jerusalem: Israel Academy of Sciences and Humanities.

Peek, P. M. 1981. The power of words in African verbal arts. *Journal of American Folklore* 94(371):19–43.

———, ed. 1991. *African divination systems: Ways of knowing.* Bloomington: Indiana University Press.

———. 1998. Never Alone—African Diviners and their others. Paper presented at the African Studies Seminar series, Indiana University, Bloomington, October 21.

———. 2000. Recasting divination research. In *Insight and artistry in African divination,* ed. J. Pemberton, 25–33. Washington: Smithsonian Institution Press.

Pelissero, A. 1993. Divinatory Techniques in Sivapurana V 25: A Common Ground to Medicine, Divination and Speculative Thought. *East and West* 43(1–4):141–54.

Pemberton, J., ed. 2000. *Insight and artistry in African divination.* Washington: Smithsonian Institution Press.

Pennebaker, J. W. 1997. *Opening up: The healing power of confiding in others.* New York: Guilford Press.

Pennebaker, J. W., S. D. Barger, and J. Tiebout. 1989. Disclosure of traumas and health among holocaust survivors. *Psychosomatic Medicine* 51:577–89.

Propp, V. 1988. *Morphology of the folktale.* Trans. L. Scott. Austin: University of Texas Press.

Radin, P. 1914. An Introductive Enquiry in the Study of Ojibwa Religion. *Papers and Records of the Ontario Historical Society* 12:210–20.

Reichard, G. A. 1944. Prayer: The compulsive word. *Monographs of the American Ethnological Society No. 7.* New York: J. J. Augustin Publisher.

Ritzenthaler, R. E. 1953. Chippewa preoccupation with health. *Bulletin of the Public Museum of the City of Milwaukee* 19(4):175–258.

Rogers, S. L., and L. Evernham. 1983. Shamanistic healing among the Diegueño Indians of southern California. In *From culture to method: The anthropology of medicine,* ed. L. Romanucci-Ross, D. E. Moerman, and L. R. Tancredi, 103–18. New York: Praeger Publishers.

Rohner, R. P. 1975. *They love me, they love me not: A worldwide study of the effects of parental acceptance and rejection.* New Haven: HRAF Press.

———. 1986. *The warmth dimension: Foundations of parental acceptance-rejection theory.* Beverly Hills: SAGE.

Rorty, R. 1989. *Contingency, irony, and solidarity.* Cambridge: Cambridge University Press.

Russell, F. 1908. The Pima Indians. *Annual Report of the Bureau of American Ethnology* 26:3–389. Washington: Smithsonian Institution.

Scheper-Hughes, N., and M. Lock. 1987. The mindful body: A prolegomenon to future work in medical anthropology. *Medical Anthropology Quarterly,* n.s., 1:6–41.

———. 1990. A critical-interpretive approach in medical anthropology: Ritual and routines of discipline and dissent. In *Medical anthropology: Contemporary theory and method,* ed. T. M. Johnson and C. F. Sargent, 47–72. New York: Praeger.

Schiefflin, E. L. 1998. *Problematizing performance in ritual, performance, media.* London: Routledge.

Scott, J. C. 1985. *Weapons of the weak: Everyday forms of peasant resistance.* New Haven: Yale University Press.

———. 1990. *Domination and the arts of resistance: Hidden transcripts.* New Haven: Yale University Press.

Seguin, M., ed. 1984. *The Tsimshian.* Vancouver: University of British Columbia Press.

Seligman, K. 1971. *Magic, supernaturalism, and religion.* New York: Pantheon Books.

Sharon, D. 1978. *Wizard of the four winds: A Shaman's story.* New York: Free Press.

Shaw, R. 1992. Dreaming as accomplishment: Power, the individual, and Temne divination. In *dreaming, religion, and society in Africa,* ed. M. Jedrej and R. Shaw. Leiden, The Netherlands: Brill.

Skinner, A. 1915. Associations and ceremonies of the Menomini Indians. *Anthropological Papers of the American Museum of Natural History* 13(2):167–215.

————. 1920. Medicine ceremony of the Menomini, Iowa, and Wahpeton Dakota, with notes on the ceremony among the Ponca, Bungi, Ojibwa, and Potawatomi. *Indian Notes and Monographs* 4:189–261.

Smith, M. W. 1940. *The Puyallup-Nisqually.* New York: Columbia University Press.

Snyder, W., and E. E. McCollum. 1999. Their home is their castle: Learning to do in-home family therapy. *Family Process* 38:229–42.

Sobania, N. W. 1993. Defeat and dispersal: The Laikipiak and their neighbors in the nineteenth century. In *Being Maasai: Ethnicity and identity in East Africa,* ed. T. Spear and R. Waller, 105–19. London: James Currey.

Spear, T., and R. Waller. 1993. *Being Maasai: Ethnicity and identity in East Africa.* London: James Currey.

Speck, F. G. 1909. Ethnology of the Yuchi Indians. *Anthropological Publications of the University Museum* 1:1–154. Philadelphia: University of Pennsylvania.

————. 1935. *Naskapi: The savage hunters of the Labrador Peninsula.* Norman: University of Oklahoma Press.

————. 1949. *Midwinter rites of the Cayuga long house.* Philadelphia: University of Pennsylvania Press.

Spencer, P. 1988. *The Maasai of Matapato.* Bloomington: Indiana University Press.

————. 1991. The *Loonkidongi* prophets and the Maasai: Protection racket or incipient state? *Africa* 61(3):334–42.

————. 1998. Age systems and modes of predatory expansion. In *Conflict, age, and power in North East Africa,* ed. E. Kurimoto and S. Simonse, 168–85. London: James Currey.

Spiro, M. E., and R. D'Andrade. 1958. A cross-cultural study of some supernatural beliefs. *American Anthropologist* 60:456–66.

Staewen, C. 1996. *Ifa African gods speak.* Hamburg: Lit Verlag.

Stephen, A. M. 1936. Hopi Journals of Alexander M. Stephen. Ed. Elsie Clews Parsons, 1–1417. *Columbia University Contributions to Anthropology 23.* 2 vols.

Stewart, K. M. 1970. Mojave Indian shamanism. *Masterkey* (1):15–24.

Sullivan, L. 1988. *Ichanchu's drum: An orientation to meaning in South American religions.* New York: Macmillan Press.

Swanton, J. R. 1928. Religious Beliefs and Medical Practices of the Creek Indians. *Annual Report of the Bureau of American Ethnology* 42:473–672. Washington: Smithsonian Institution.

Tambiah, S. J. 1968. The magical power of words. *Man* 3(2):175–208.

———. 1970. *Buddhism and the spirit cults in North-East Thailand.* Cambridge: Cambridge University Press.

Teit, J. A. 1900. The Thompson Indians of British Columbia. *Memoirs of the American Museum of Natural History* 2(4):163–390.

Thomas, V., E. E. McCollum, and W. Snyder. 1999. Beyond the clinic: In-home therapy with Head Start. *Journal of Marital and Family Therapy* 25:177–89.

Turner, E. 1986. Encounter with neurobiology: The response of ritual studies. *Zygon* 21(2):219–32.

———. 1992a. *Experiencing ritual: A new interpretation of African healing.* Philadelphia: University of Pennsylvania Press.

———. 1992b. The reality of spirits: A tabooed or permitted field of study? *Anthropology of Consciousness* 3(3):9–12.

Turner, V. 1961. Ndembu divination: Its symbolism and its techniques. *Rhodes-Livingstone Papers, No. 31.* Manchester: Manchester University Press.

———. 1964. An Ndembu doctor in practice. In *Magic, faith, and healing,* ed. A. Kiev, 230–63. New York: Free Press.

———. 1967. *The forest of symbols: Aspects of Ndembu ritual.* Ithaca: Cornell University Press.

———. 1968. *The drums of affliction: A study of religious processes among the Ndembu of Zambia.* Oxford: Clarendon.

———. 1973. The center out there: The pilgrim's goal. *History and Religions* 12:211–15.

———. 1975. *Revelation and divination in Ndembu ritual.* Ithaca: Cornell University Press.

Tyler, M. G., and S. A. Tyler. 1986. The sorcerer's apprentice: The discourse of training in family therapy. *Cultural Anthropology* 1:238–56.

Underhill, R. 1946. *Papago Indian religion.* New York: Columbia University Press.

Verger, P. 1976. The use of plants in Yoruba traditional medicine and its linguistic approach. In *Department of African Languages and Literatures, University of Ife Seminar Series,* ed. O. Oyelaran, 243–95. Ile-Ife: University Publication.

————. 1977. Awon Ewe Osanyin (Yoruba Medicinal Leaves) Ile-Ife. *Institute of African Studies Publication 45.*

Voegelin, E. W. 1938. Tübatulabal ethnography. *University of California Publications in Anthropological Records* 2(1):1–90.

Voeks, R. A. 1997. *Sacred leaves of Candomblé: African magic, medicine, and religion in Brazil.* Austin: University of Texas Press.

Vogt, E. Z. 1969. *Zinacantan: A Maya community in the highlands of Chiapas.* Cambridge, Mass.: Harvard University Press.

Wagner, R. 1983. Visible ideas: Toward an anthropology of perceptive values. *South Asian Anthropologist* (Essays in Honor of Victor Turner) 4(1):1–8.

————. 1986. *Symbols that stand for themselves.* Chicago: University of Chicago Press.

Wales, H.G.Q. 1983. *Divination in Thailand.* London: Curzon Press Ltd.

Walker, E. H. 2000. *Physics of consciousness: The quantum mind and the meaning of life.* Cambridge: Perseus Publishing.

Waller, R. 1995. Kidongoi's kin: Prophesy and power in Maasailand. In *Revealing Prophets,* ed. D. M. Anderson and D. H. Johnson, 28–64. London: James Currey.

Washburn, P. 1994. Advantages for brief solution-oriented focus in home-based family preservation services. *Journal of Systematic Therapies* 13:42–58.

Werbner, R. 1989. *Ritual passage, sacred journey: The process and organization of religious movement.* Washington: Smithsonian Institution Press.

————. 1999. "Truth-or-balance": Knowing the opaque other in wisdom divination. Paper presented at the African Research Centre Seminar, Leuven, January 1999.

Whyte, S. Reynolds. 1997. *Questioning misfortune: The pragmatics of uncertainty in eastern Uganda.* Cambridge: Cambridge University Press.

Wildschut, W. 1975. Crow Indian medicine bundles. *Contributions from the Museum of the American Indian, Heye Foundation* 17:1–178.

Winkelman, M. 1982. Magic: A theoretical reassessment. *Current Anthropology* 23:37–44, 59–66.

————. 1990. Shamans and other "magico-religious" healers: A cross-cultural study of their origins, nature, and social transformations. *Ethos* 18(3):308–52.

————. 1992. Shamans, priests and witches: A cross-cultural study of magico-religious practitioners. *Anthropological Research Papers #44.* Tempe: Arizona State University.

————. 1996. Psychointegrator plants: Their roles in human culture and health. In *Sacred plants, consciousness, and healing: An interdisciplinary perspective.* 1995 Yearbook of Cross-Cultural Medicine and Psychotherapy Series, ed. M. Winkelman and W. Andritzky, 9–53. Berlin: VWB—Verlag fur Wissenschaft und Bildung.

————. 1997. Altered states of consciousness and religious behavior. In *Anthropology of religion: A handbook of method and theory,* ed. S Glazier, 393–428. Westport, Conn.: Greenwood.

————. 2000. *Shamanism: The neural ecology of consciousness and healing.* Westport, Conn.: Bergin and Garvey.

Winkelman, M., and C. Winkelman. 1991. *Shamanistic healers and their therapies: A cross-cultural study.* 1990 Yearbook of Cross-Cultural Medicine and Psychotherapy Series, ed. W. Andritzky, 163–82. Berlin: VWB—Verlag fur Wissenschaft und Bildung.

Young, D., and J. Goulet, eds. 1994. *Being changed by cross-cultural encounters: The anthropology of extraordinary experience.* Ontario: Broadview Press.

Young, P. D. 1971. *Ngawbe: Tradition and change among the Western Guaymi of Panama.* Urbana: University of Illinois Press.

Zeitlyn, D. 2001. Finding meaning in the text. *Journal of the Royal Anthropological Institute* 7:225–40.

Zeusse, E. 1987. Divination. In *The encyclopedia of religion,* ed. M. Eliade, 375–82. New York: Macmillan.

Index

About the Contributors

KEITH BLETZER was trained in medical anthropology at Michigan State University. He studied health-seeking behavior for more than two years among the Ngawbe of western Panama, where he conducted ethnomedical fieldwork. He worked with a local diviner, accompanying him on visits to the ill among local families along the coast, and secured a sample of more than two hundred short-term and long-term "illness cases" that he observed over the course of his fieldwork. He attended nearly all of the several types of ritual that make up the Ngawbe ritual system. Bletzer's research interests include folk syndromes and their symptoms, indigenous ritual systems, and local practitioners of medicine. Recently, he has been conducting research on the social and cultural dimensions of HIV/AIDS, having worked for more than ten years with migrant and seasonal farmworkers in labor camps and high-risk settings of the midwestern and southeastern United States. He holds a doctorate in anthropology from Michigan State University, a master's in anthropology from New York University, and a master's in public health from University of Arizona.

BENJAMIN N. COLBY holds a B.A. with high honors from Princeton University and a Ph.D. in Social Relations from Harvard University. He was an instructor at Harvard and later became a curator at the Laboratory of Anthropology in Santa Fe. Currently, he is an emeritus professor at the University of California, Irvine. He has conducted field studies in Chiapas, Mexico, among the Zinacantecos, and in New Mexico, among the Zuni and Tesuque Pueblos and the Navajo. He also conducted a brief ethnographic study in Japan. His major fieldwork to date has been with the Ixil Maya of Guatemala. Publications include studies of ethnic relations in Mexico and Guatemala, Ixil Mayan narrative traditions, and the Japanese tea ceremony. Since the violence that took place in Guatemala, he has shifted his attention away from ethnography to the study of cultural pathology and the development of culture theory. He has developed a scale of adaptive potential that predicts health, the use of psychological defense mechanisms, anxiety, and other measures. His research grants include those from the National Institute of Mental Health, the National Science Foundation, and the National Institute on Aging. He is a member of the new Interdisciplinary Program in Anthropological Sciences in the School of Social Sciences, University of California, Irvine.

RENÉ DEVISCH is a senior professor in the Department of Anthropology, Catholic University of Leuven, and has been affiliated with the Belgian School of Psychoanalysis for ten years. He is also a member of the Belgian Royal Academy of Overseas Sciences. Over the past twenty-five years, he has applied, successively or in combination, the paradigms of Lévi-Straussian structuralism, French phenomenology (in line with Merleau-Ponty), Bourdieu's poststructuralist praxiology, and, more recently, Deleuze's rhizomatic thinking. His work has at the same time displayed a number of consistent concerns in relation mainly to the Yaka population of Congo, but also Moroccan, Turkish, and Flemish epigastric patients in family medicine in Brussels and Antwerp, mental patients in Tunisia, and incest victims in Flanders. Throughout the years, Devisch's research has involved problematizing the relation between culture, body symbolism, and experience of misfortune and suffering, psychic symbolism, and symptom formation; study of culture-specific forms of etiology, healing, and management of misfortune and violence; philosophical and anthropological reflection on, and concern with, the limitations and possibilities of intersubjectivity between actors and the researcher in cultural and health research, in a bid to reduce north-south inequities in the production of knowledge. His career has led him to carry out or supervise research, if more briefly, in several other African countries, including Tunisia (Tunis); Egypt (Cairo); southern Ethiopia; (Druze communities in) northern Israel; southwest Kenya; northwest Namibia; southern Nigeria; northern Ghana; and central and northwest Tanzania, southwest of South Africa.

ELLIOT FRATKIN is a professor in the Department of Anthropology at Smith College, Northampton, Massachusetts. Since 1974, he has conducted research on African pastoralist societies, particularly Samburu and Ariaal Rendille of Kenya, and he has written numerous articles and books on pastoralist ethnography, ecology, health, and development. Adopted into the Leaduma family of Samburu diviners, Fratkin has maintained his friendships and research and has authored several papers on Samburu traditional medicine. Fratkin received his Ph.D. at the Catholic University of America, M.Phil. degree from the London School of Economics and Political Science, and B.A. from the University of Pennsylvania, all in anthropology. He is the author of *Surviving Drought and Development in Kenya's Arid Lands* (Westview, 1991); *African Pastoralist Systems,* co-edited with Kathleen Galvin and Eric Abella Roth (Lynne

Rienner, 1994); *Ariaal Pastoralists of Kenya* (Allyn and Bacon, 2d ed., 2004); and the textbook *Cultural Anthropology,* with Daniel G. Bates (Allyn and Bacon, 3d ed., 2003). Fratkin has held academic positions at Duke University, University of Maryland, Pennsylvania State University, University of Nairobi, and University of Asmara. He has received research awards from the National Science Foundation, Social Science Research Council, National Geographic Society, and the Smithsonian Institution, and in 2002–3 he was a U.S. Fulbright Scholar to Eritrea. In 2002 and 2003, he served with the World Bank Inspection Panel Investigation of the Chad-Cameroon Oil Pipeline Project, investigating indigenous peoples' policy with regard to Mbororo pastoralists and Bakola hunter-gatherers. He is currently an associate editor of the journal *Human Ecology,* an editorial board member of the journals *African Studies Review* and *Nomadic Peoples,* and a founding member of the Association for Africanist Anthropology in the American Anthropological Association.

EVA JANE NEUMANN FRIDMAN received her B.A. cum laude from Radcliffe College, Harvard University, in the field of history and literature. After earning an M.S. from Simmons School of Social Work in psychiatric social work, she began to work as a psychotherapist in psychiatric hospitals and in mental health clinics. Since 1964 she has had a continuing private practice in psychotherapy, treating adults and adolescents for a variety of disorders. She received her M.A. from Harvard University in the field of anthropology and archaeology. Her Ph.D. (1997) at Brown University, Department of Anthropology, focused on the ethnography and archaeology of the Middle East, Eurasia, and Inner Asia with a special focus on nomadism and belief systems. Her fieldwork was conducted in Mongolia and in the former USSR, in Siberia and Kalmykia, on the regeneration of shamanism in the post-Soviet period. She has published a number of papers on various topics of shamanism, religious syncretism in the former USSR, ethnic identity, and current adaptations of Old Believers in Tuva. Her book *Sacred Geography: Shamanism among the Buddhist Peoples of Russia* will be published in 2004 by Akadémiai Kiadó, Bibliotheca Shamanistica Series. She is co-editor of *Encyclopedia of Shamanism* (ABC-CLIO, forthcoming). She has been actively teaching and lecturing in the field of anthropology and psychology. A former senior fellow in the Center for the Study of World Religions, Harvard Divinity School, Harvard University, she is a research fellow in the Department of Anthropology at Brown University.

RUTH-INGE HEINZE has been active in Asia, Europe, and the United States in the field of comparative religion and psychological anthropology for over sixty years. Trained in anthropology in Germany, she was awarded a B.A. in Anthropology (1969), an M.A. in Asian Studies (1971), and a Ph.D. in Asian Studies (1974) from the University of California, Berkeley. She speaks nine languages, three of them Asian, and holds licenses in acupuncture, Chinese herbal medicine, and Reiki I and II. In 1978, she received a Fulbright Research Grant for Thailand, Malaysia, and Singapore, where she studied and participated in the healing rituals of shamans and mediums. She also conducted extensive research in India, the Philippines, Indonesia, and Burma. Since 1979, she has been instrumental in organizing the Universal Dialogue Series in the San Francisco Bay Area and, since 1984, the Annual International Conference on the Study of Shamanism and Alternative Modes of Healing, San Rafael, California. In 1981, she also founded Independent Scholars of Asia, Inc., a professional, nonprofit organization that represents Asian experts. She has published six books: *The Role of the Sangha in Modern Thailand* (Oriental Cultural Services, 1974); *Tham Khwan: A Socio-Psychological Comparison of a Thai Custom* (Singapore University Press, 1982); *Trance and Healing in Southeast Asia Today* (White Lotus Company, 1988/1997); *Shamans of the Twentieth Century* (Irving Publishers, 1991); *The Search for Visions* (Independent Scholars of Asia, 1994/2000); and *Fire from Heaven: The Nature and Function of Rituals* (Bergin and Garvey, 2000). She has also edited nineteen books and contributed more than one hundred essays to professional journals and books. She is also a long-term meditator, working for the Spiritual Emergence Network.

WILLIAM S. LYON received his Ph.D. in anthropology from the University of Kansas in 1970. He is currently professor of anthropology and a member of the graduate faculty of the Center for Religious Studies at the University of Missouri at Kansas City, where he specializes in North American Indian religions. An expert on American Indian shamanism, he has conducted continuous field research for over two decades among the Lakota Sioux shamans from the Pine Ridge and Rosebud Sioux Reservations in South Dakota. In addition to his many professional publications on shamanism, Lyon is the editor of a rare, in-depth, first-person account of Lakota shamanism, given by Lakota shaman and elder Wallace Black Elk, entitled *Black Elk: The Sacred Ways of the Lakota,* which is currently translated into French and German. He has also recently published two volumes of scholarly encyclopedias giving a detailed account of Native American shamanism: *Encyclopedia of Native American Healing* (ABC-CLIO, 1996) and *Encyclopedia of Native American Shamanism* (ABC-CLIO, 1998.) Currently, Lyon is writing a scholarly overview on the extent and nature of American Indian shamanic powers, entitled *Spirit Talkers: Medicine Powers of the North American Indians* (forthcoming). He is a member of the American Anthropological Association, the Society for the Anthropology of Consciousness, and the editorial advisory board of *Shaman's Drum* magazine, and he is a field associate of the Foundation for Shamanic Studies.

KRISHNAKALI MAJUMDAR is currently an assistant professor of anthropology at Ferris State University in Michigan. She has a doctorate in medical anthropology from Michigan State University and a master's degree in social anthropology from University of Delhi, India. Her interests include embodiment, spirit possession, healing, gender relations, and reproductive health and sexuality. She has conducted ethnographic fieldwork among the Nagas, the Lodhas, and the Jaunsaris in India. Her areas of research interest are medical anthropology, psychological anthropology, anthropology of religion, gender studies, and South Asian culture and society. Her current work focuses on the considerations of reproductive health, health policy relating to women's health, and, specifically, how power differences between men and women influence reproductive decision making.

JACOB K. OLUPONA is professor of African and African American Studies at the University of California, Davis, where he served as the director of the Religious Studies Program. He studied at Boston University and taught at Obafemi Awolowo University Ile-Ife, Nigeria, from 1983 to 1990. He is the author of *Kingship, Religion, and Rituals in a Nigerian Community* (Almqvist and Wiksell, 1991) and the editor of a number of works, including *African Traditional Religions in Contemporary Society* (Paragon Press, 1991); *Religious Plurality in Africa: Essays in Honour of John S. Mbiti* (Mouton Press, 1993); *African Spirituality* (Crossroads Press, 2002); and *Beyond Primitivism: Indigenous Religious Traditions and Modernity* (Routledge Press, forthcoming). He was a John Simon Guggenheim Fellow and a Davidson Visiting Professor in the Humanities at Florida International University, Miami. Currently, he is doing research, sponsored by the Ford Foundation, on African immigrant religious communities in America. In 1995, he organized an international conference on indigenous religious traditions and modernity. He also convened another international conference in Miami in 1999 on the global Yoruba religion. He has served as a member of the executive council and board of trustees of the American Academy of Religion and is the current president of the African Association for the Study of Religion. He was awarded Honorary Doctor of Divinity of the University of Edinburgh, Scotland, in 2002.

PHILIP M. PEEK is professor of anthropology at Drew University. His interests in African Studies began with the Peace Corps in Nigeria (1964–66). Following graduate study at the University of California, Berkeley (M.A., Folklore, 1968), and Indiana University (Ph.D., Folklore, 1976), he conducted ethnohistorical research among the Isoko of the Niger Delta. In addition to contributing to numerous publications on African visual and verbal arts, he has recently completed two major projects: "Ways of the River: Arts and Environment of the Niger Delta" (2002), an exhibition and catalog co-curated and co-edited with Martha Anderson for the Fowler Museum of Cultural History, UCLA, and *African Folklore: An Encyclopedia*, co-edited with Kwesi Yankah (Routledge Press, 2004). Interests in African divination culminated in his edited volume, *African Divination Systems: Ways of Knowing* (Indiana University Press, 1991), and several articles. Currently, he is a visiting fellow at the Sainsbury Arts Centre, University of East Anglia, and is pursuing research projects on silence and on twins in African cultures.

KOEN STROEKEN is a postdoctoral research fellow for the Fund for Scientific Research in Flanders. He received his Ph.D. in social and cultural anthropology at the Catholic University of Leuven. Most of his fieldwork has been conducted in Sukuma villages (Tanzania), where he lived and worked in the company of healers and diviners from May 1995 until June 1997. His participation resulted respectively in membership in the medicinal society for village elders, apprenticeship in the art of haruspication, and, finally, initiation into the Swezi cult for mediumistic healing. Subsequent ritual participation in 2000 and 2002 helped to explore the concept of the human as cyberzone (in the co-edited volume *Ageing in Africa* [Ashgate, 2002]) and rituals as forms of synchrony (articles published in *Dialectical Anthropology* [2001] and *Anthropology Today* [2002]).

EDITH TURNER is a faculty member of the Department of Anthropology at the University of Virginia and has been awarded honorary doctorates by the College of Wooster and Kenyon College. She specializes in ritual, religion, healing, and aspects of consciousness including shamanism. She has done participatory fieldwork in Zambia (healing and divination); Uganda (ritual); rural Ireland (ritual, spiritual experience, and healing); Mexico, Europe, and Israel (pilgrimages); Brazil (Umbanda, carnival); eastern Siberia; and northern Russia (healing). In northern Alaska, among the Iñupiat, she studied and participated in Eskimo healing and its relationship to shamanism. Her publications include *The Spirit and the Drum* (University of Arizona Press, 1987); *Experiencing Ritual: A New Interpretation of African Healing* (University of Pennsylvania Press, 1992); and *The Hands Feel It: Healing and Spirit Presence among a Northern Alaskan People* (Northern Illinois University Press, 1996). She is the editor of the journal *Anthropology and Humanism*.

MICHAEL WINKELMAN holds a doctorate from the University of California, Irvine (1985), and a master's in public health from the University of Arizona (2002). He is the head of the Sociocultural Subdiscipline in the Department of Anthropology, Arizona State University. He is interested in shamanistic healing, particularly the roles of altered states of consciousness (ASC) in diagnosis and therapeutics. He examined the role of ASC and psi processes in divination in "Magic: A Theoretical Reassessment," published in *Current Anthropology* (1982). The universal bases of shamanistic ASC healing practices and the cross-cultural differences in magico-religious practitioners are examined in *Shamans, Priests, and Witches* (1992). In *Sacred Plants, Consciousness, and Healing*, co-edited with Walter Andritzky (Verlag für Wissenschaft und Bildung, 1996), he explored the roles of hallucinogenic plants as psychointegrators and their role in information integration across levels of the brain. *Shamanism: The Neural Ecology of Consciousness and Healing* (Bergin and Garvey, 2000) examines the basis of shamanistic practices in the psychobiological, psychosocial, and cognitive-emotional effects of ASC. This work focuses on the role of spirit beliefs as representations of neurognostic principles foundational to the structures of consciousness, and visionary experiences as a presentational symbolic capacity. He is currently examining the potentials of shamanistic healing practices for addressing the causes and consequences of drug abuse (see "Complementary Therapy for Addiction: 'Drumming Out Drugs,'" *American Journal of Public Health* 93, no. 4 [2003]: 647, 651, and "Alternative and Traditional Medicine Approaches for Substance Abuse Programs: A Shamanic Perspective," *International Journal of Drug Policy* 12 [2001]: 337–51). Winkelman practices divination through shamanic journeying and reading the tarot.